T-SHIRT

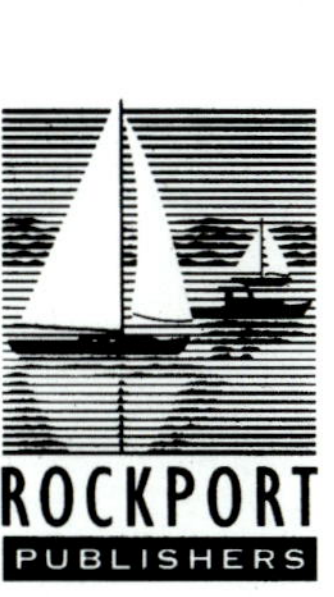

ROCKPORT
PUBLISHERS

ROCKPORT PUBLISHERS, INC.
ROCKPORT, MASSACHUSETTS

First published in the United States of America by:
Rockport Publishers, Inc.
146 Granite Street
Rockport, Massachusetts 01966-1299
Telephone: (508) 546-9590
Fax: (508) 546-7141

ISBN 1-56496-245-8

10 9 8 7 6 5 4 3 2 1

Layout: Sara Day
Cover Photographs appear on: (*clockwise from top left*)
     Page 15
     Page 37 *(far right and lower right)*
     Page 53

Manufactured in Hong Kong by
Regent Publishing Services Limited

Introduction

The popularity of the T-shirt has become so far reaching that the word needs no translation from language to language. Once just a piece of clothing, the T-shirt has become the world's first choice as a communication vehicle.

Whether for self-expression, self-promotion, advertising, or identity the T-Shirt has become the voice of the 21st century. Pretty much everything fit to print, (and many things not so fit) has been printed, painted, silk-screened, sewn or airbrushed onto a T-shirt.

The increasing popularity of T-shirts has obviously increased the interest in T-shirt design—what's being designed, who's designing it, and how it's done. This new volume in Rockport's Design Library *series presents the best designs for T-shirts from the Rockport design archives. Selected from hundreds, this volume presents T-shirt designs of all types, created for a wide range of purposes, including fine art, commercial, promotion, and advertising. This is the best of T-shirt Graphics presented in an affordable, beautifully designed format.*

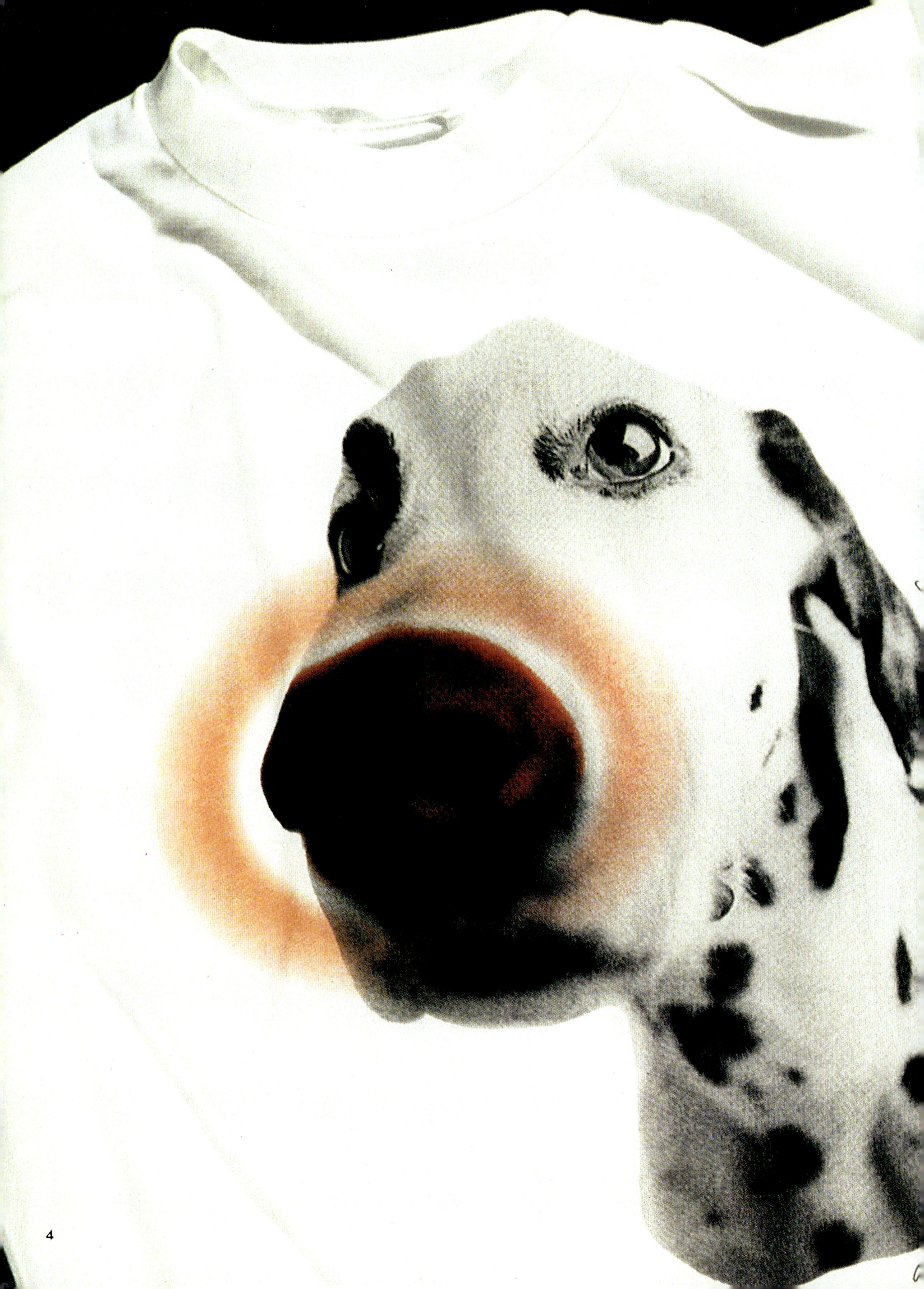

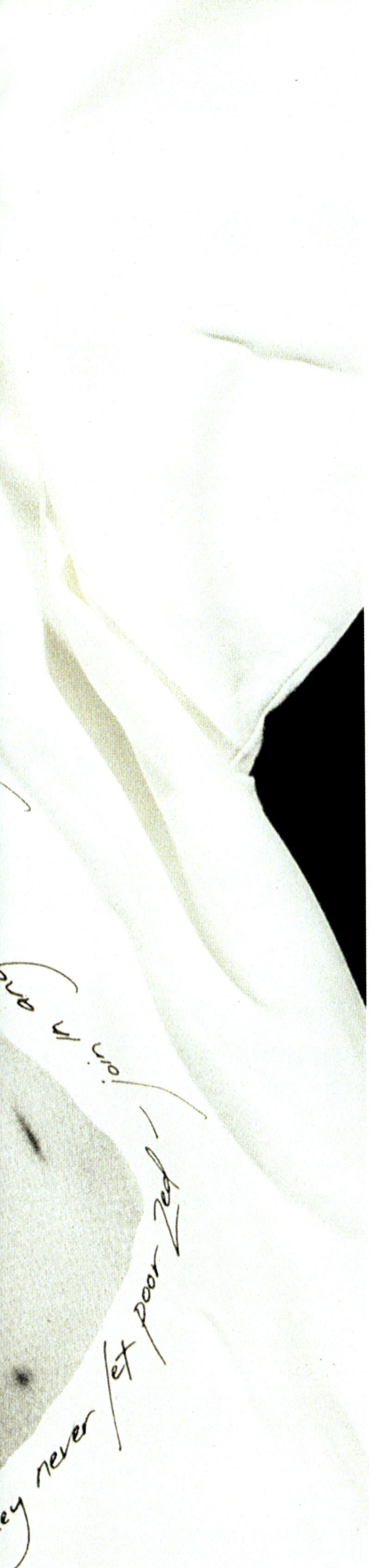

Design Firm: Zedwear
Art Director: John Klaja/George Mimnaugh
Designer: John Klaja/George Mimnaugh
Photographer: Stuart Diekmeyer
Client: Zedwear
Purpose or Occasion: Holiday Retail
Number of Colors: 2
Title: "Spotlight"

Design Firm: Zedwear
Art Director: John Klaja/George Mimnaugh
Designer: John Klaja/George Mimnaugh
Illustrator: John Klaja/George Mimnaugh
Client: Zedwear
Purpose or Occasion: Retail
Number of Colors: 5 front/4 back
Title: "Zillion Zeds"
One hundred "Zed" heads on front of the shirt and one on the back of the shirt.

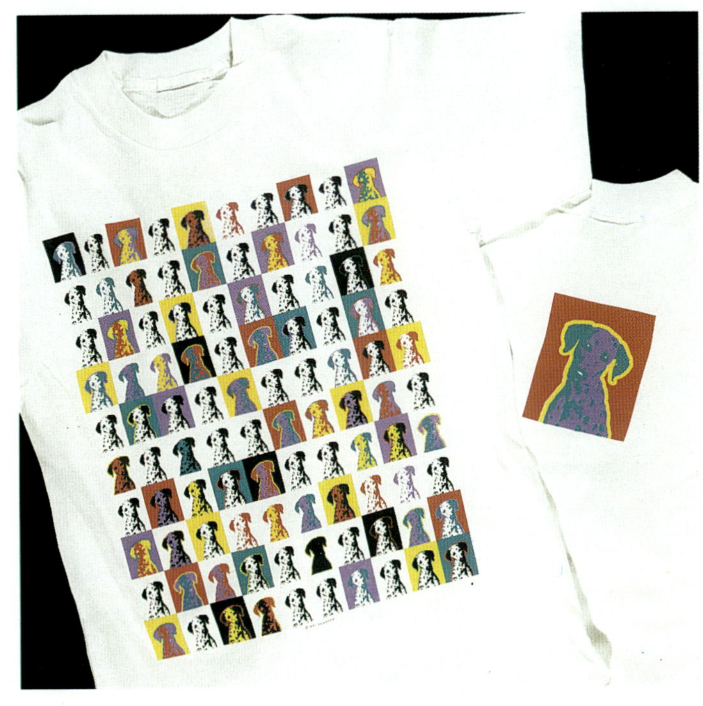

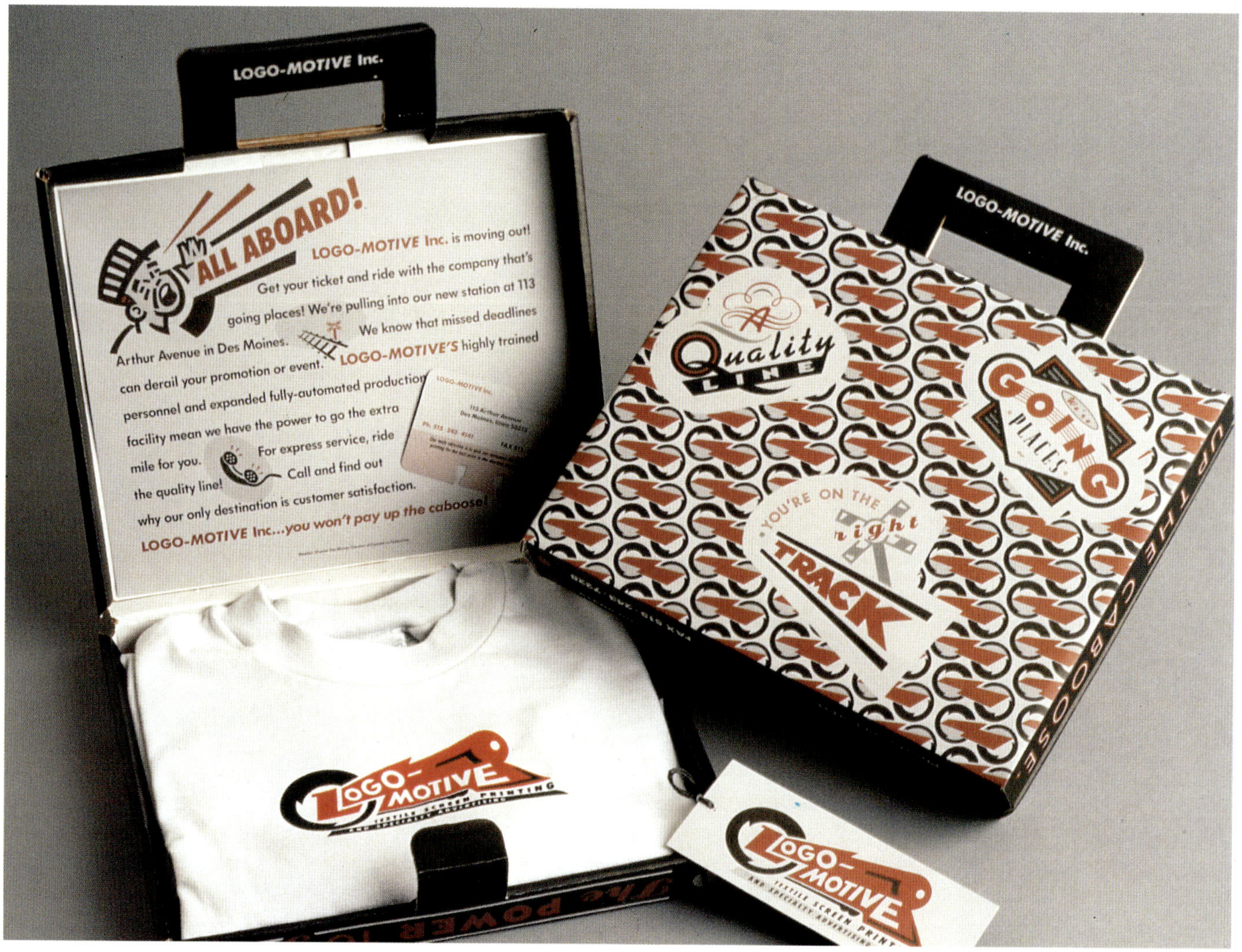

ALL ABOARD!
LOGO-MOTIVE Inc. is moving out! Get your ticket and ride with the company that's going places! We're pulling into our new station at 113 Arthur Avenue in Des Moines. We know that missed deadlines can derail your promotion or event. LOGO-MOTIVE'S highly trained personnel and expanded fully-automated production facility mean we have the power to go the extra mile for you. For express service, ride the quality line! Call and find out why our only destination is customer satisfaction.
LOGO-MOTIVE Inc...you won't pay up the caboose!
Quality LINE
GOING places
YOU'RE ON THE right TRACK
LOGO-MOTIVE

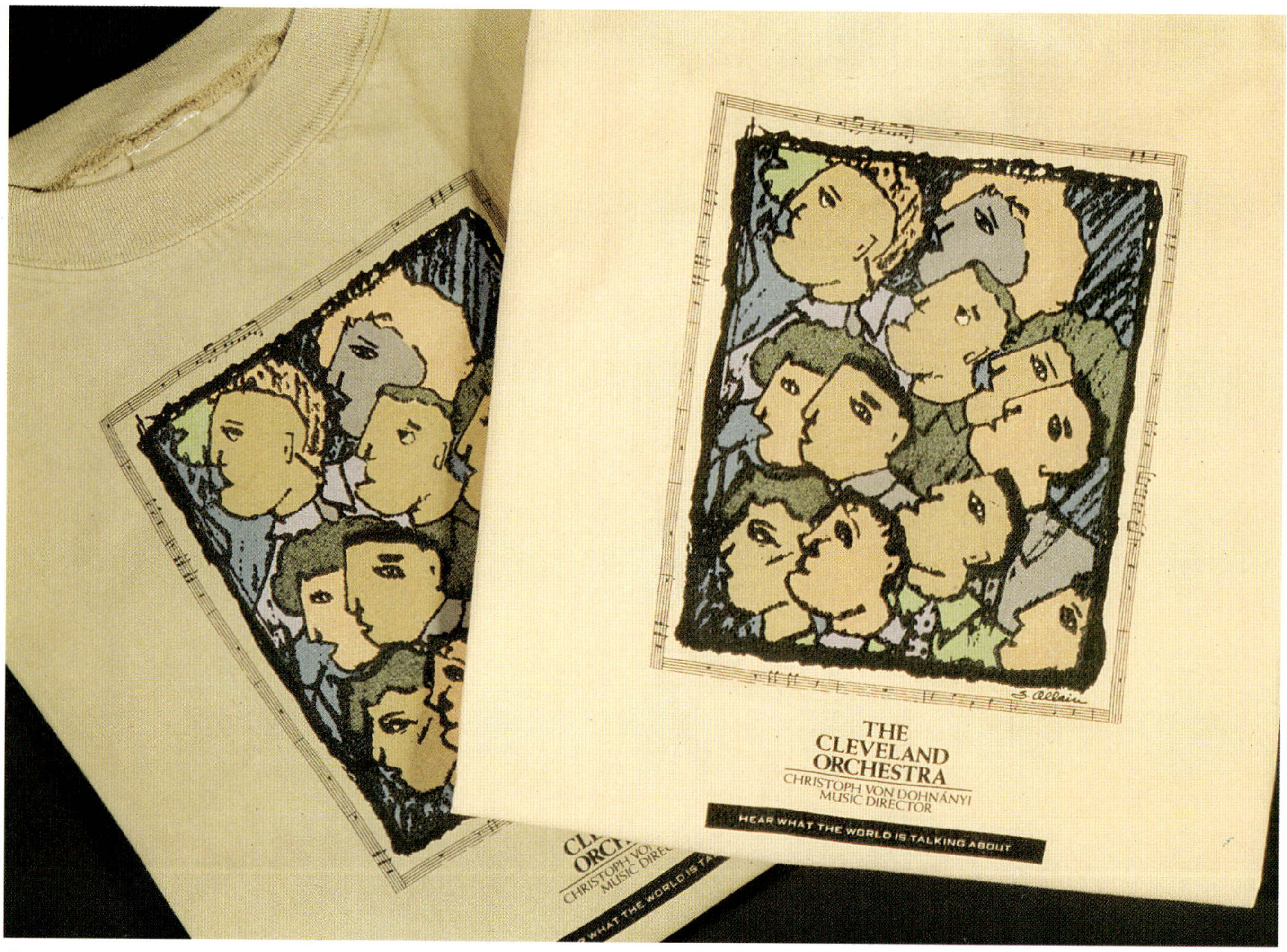

THE CLEVELAND ORCHESTRA
CHRISTOPH VON DOHNÁNYI
MUSIC DIRECTOR
HEAR WHAT THE WORLD IS TALKING ABOUT

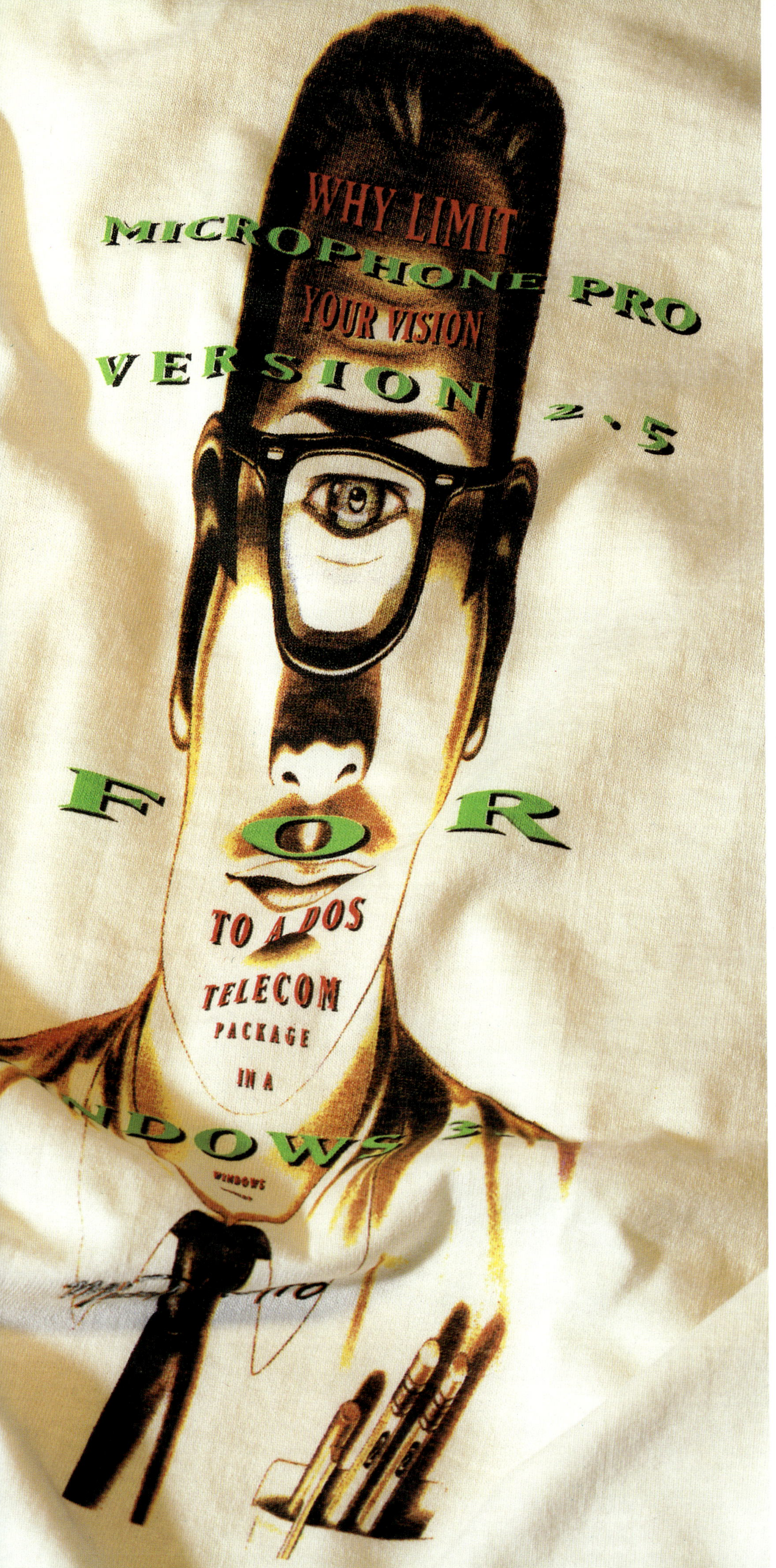

◄

Design Firm: Sayles Graphic Design
Art Director: John Sayles
Designer: John Sayles
Illustrator: John Sayles
Client: Logo-Motive
Purpose or Occasion:
Promotional
Number of Colors: 2

◄

Design Firm:
Epstein, Gutzwiller, Schultz & Partners
Art Director: Sylvie Hanna
Designer: Sylvie Hanna
Illustrator: Sylvie Hanna
Client: The Cleveland Orchestra
Purpose or Occasion:
Fundraising & Promotion
Number of Colors: 6

◄

Design Firm:
Mike Salisbury Communications
Art Director: Mike Salisbury
Designer: Mike Salisbury
Illustrator: Greg Huber
Client: Software Ventures
Purpose or Occasion:
Introduce new software
Number of Colors: 6

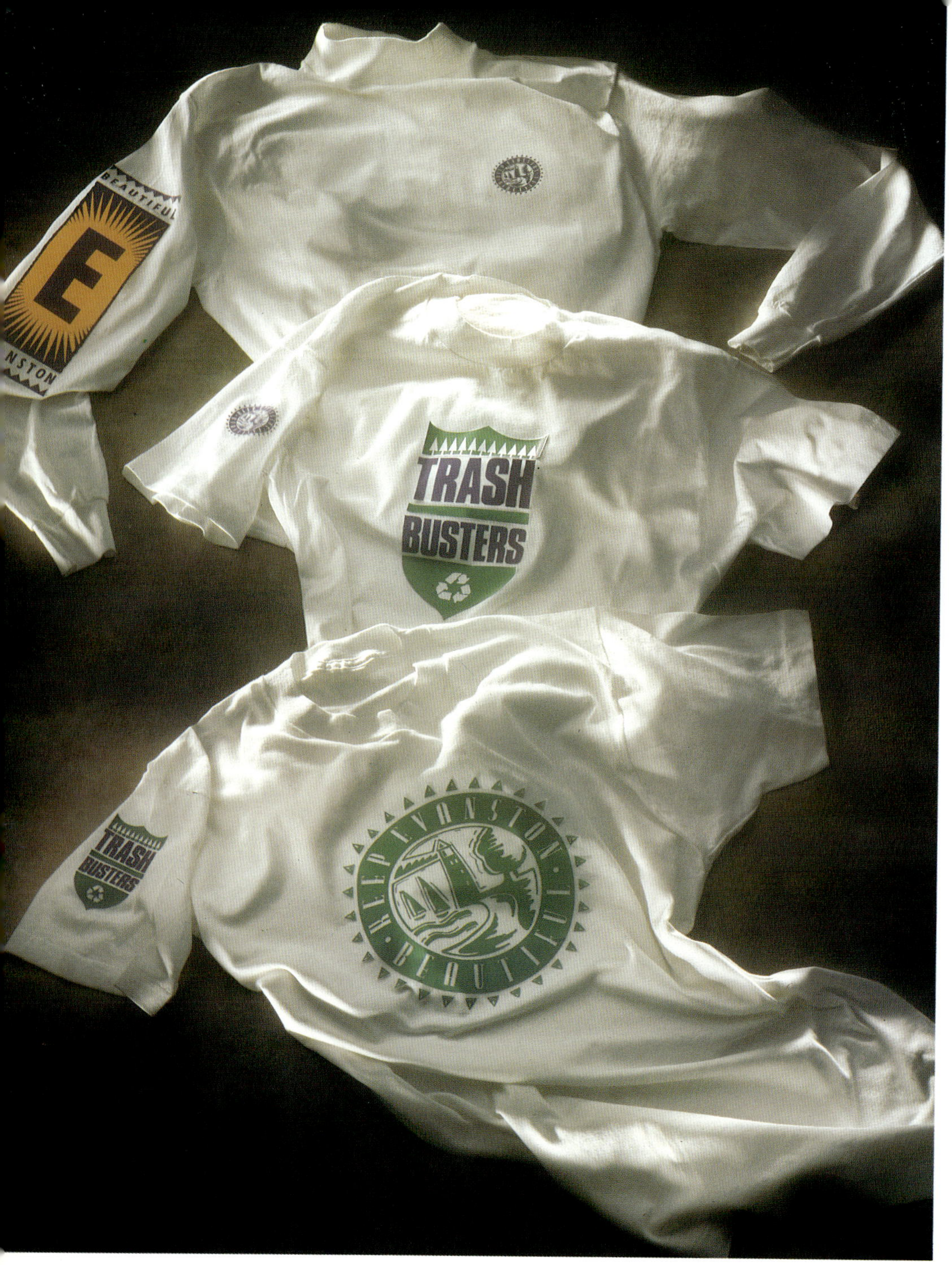

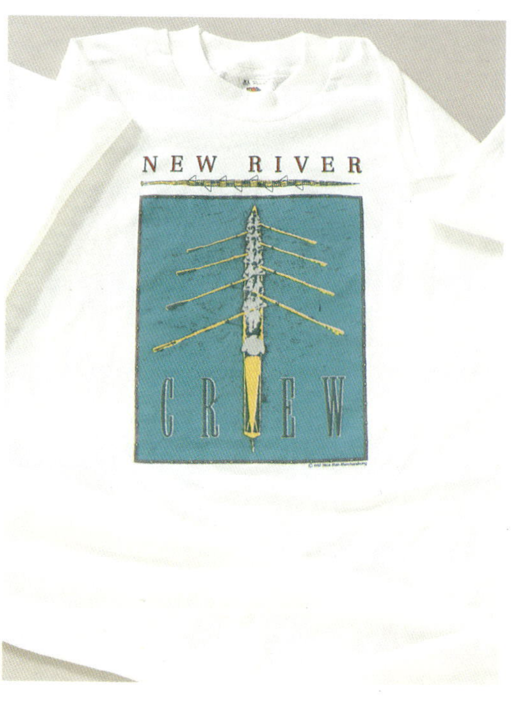
NEW RIVER
CREW

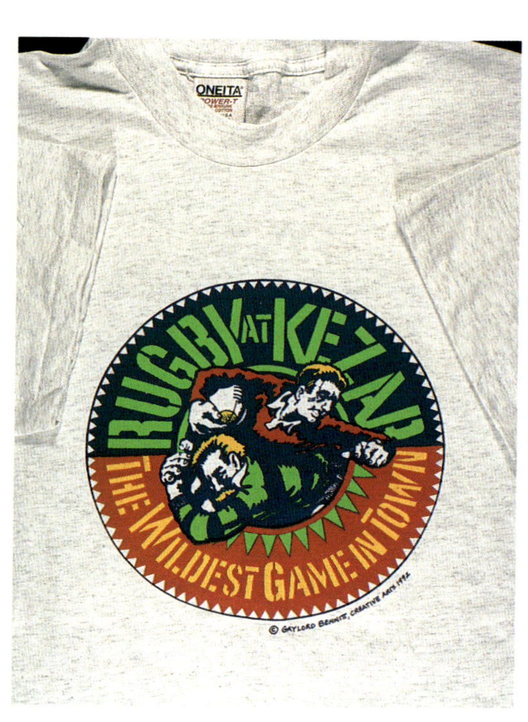
ONEITA
RUGBY AT KEZAR
THE WILDEST GAME IN TOWN

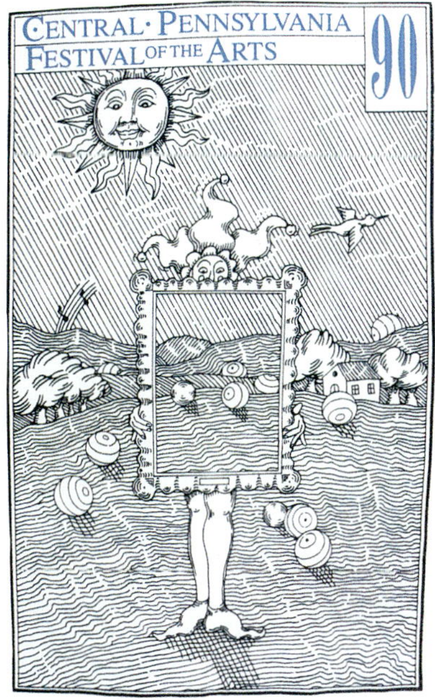
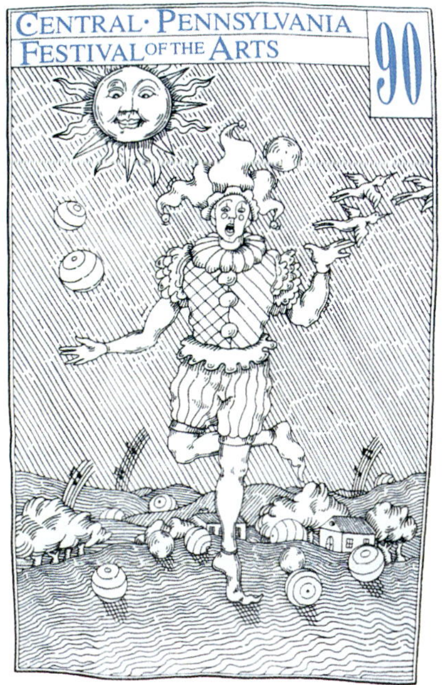

◄

Design Firm: Sommese Design
Art Director: Lanny Sommese
Designer: Lanny Sommese
Illustrator: Lanny Sommese
Client: Central Pennsylvania Festival of the Arts
Purpose or Occasion: Annual Summer Festival of the Visual and Performing Arts
Number of Colors: 2

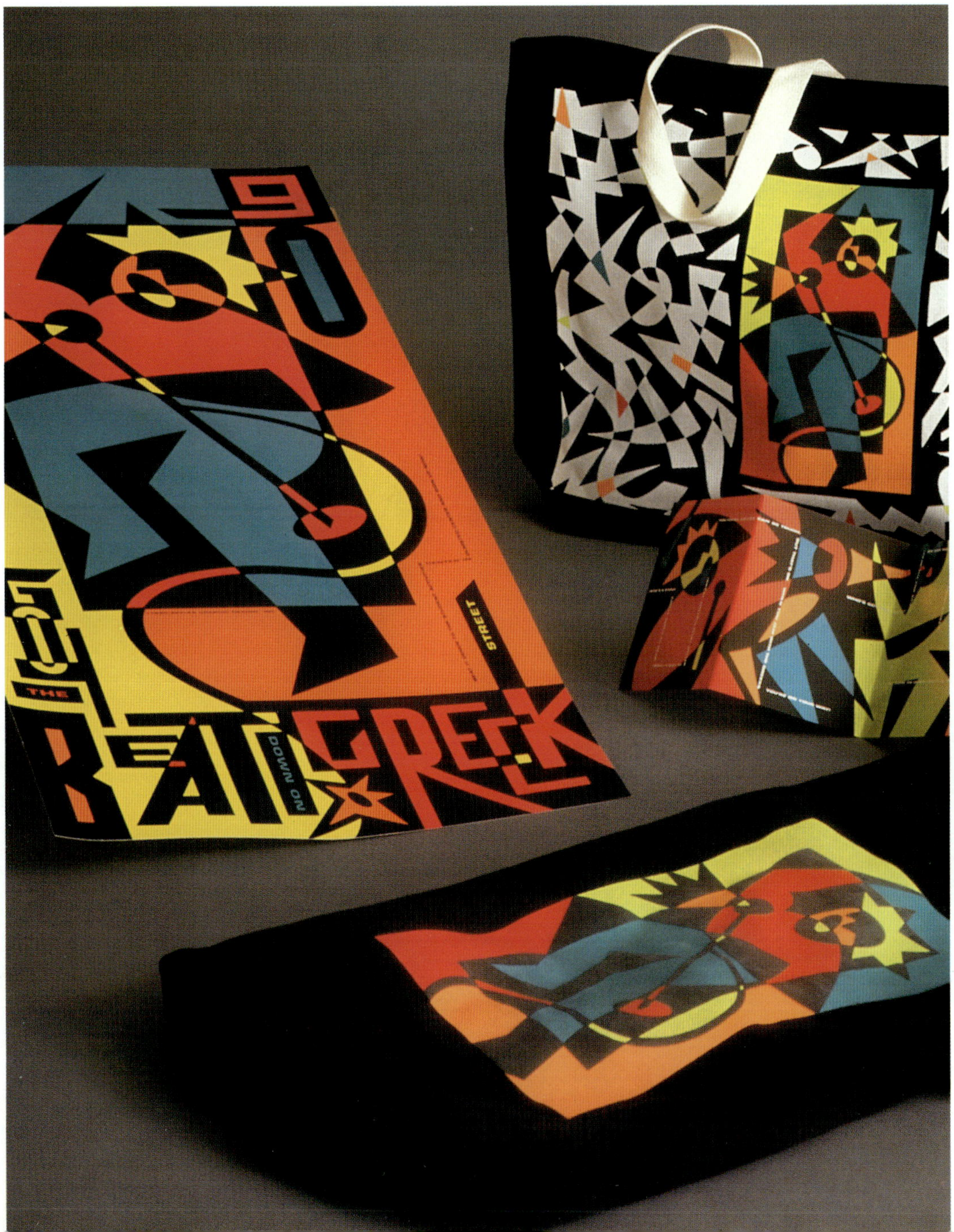

◄

Design Firm: Sayles Graphic Design
Art Director: John Sayles
Designer: John Sayles
Illustrator: John Syales
Client: Drake University
Purpose or Occasion: Promotional
Number of Colors: 5

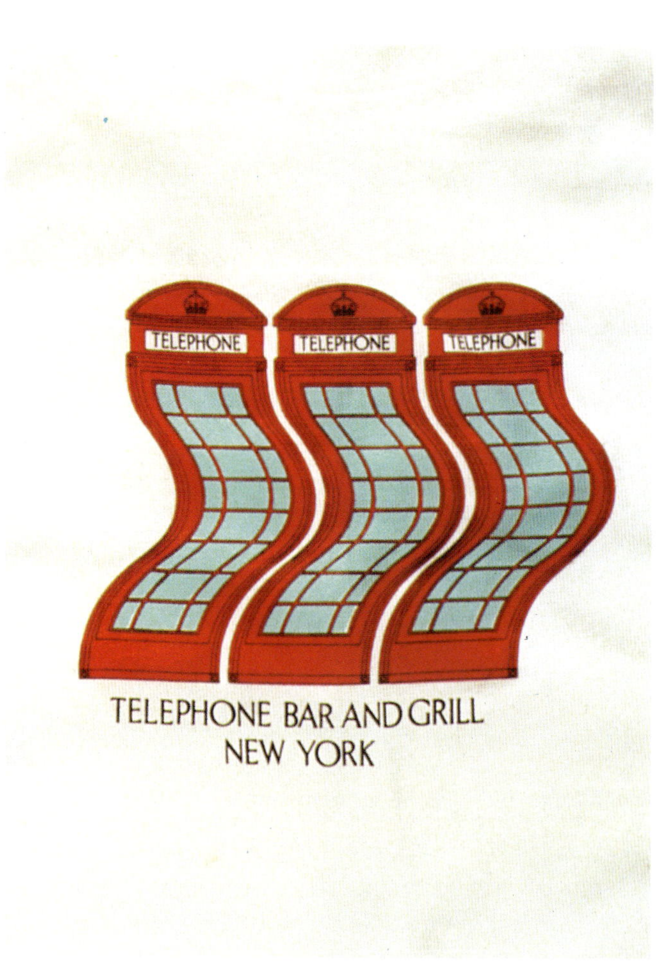

TELEPHONE
TELEPHONE
TELEPHONE
TELEPHONE BAR AND GRILL
NEW YORK

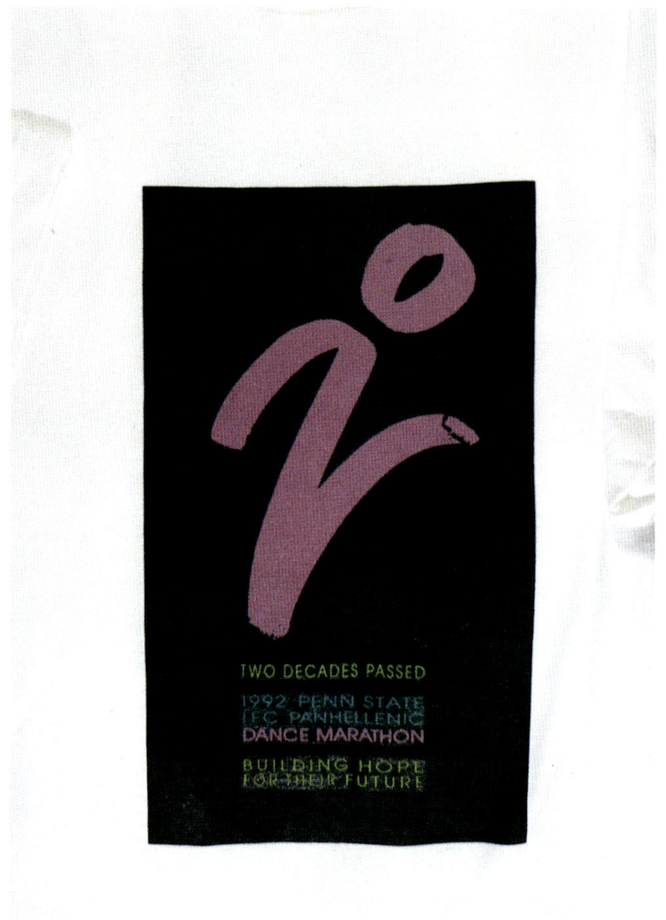

TWO DECADES PASSED
1992 PENN STATE
IFC PANHELLENIC
DANCE MARATHON
BUILDING HOPE
FOR THEIR FUTURE

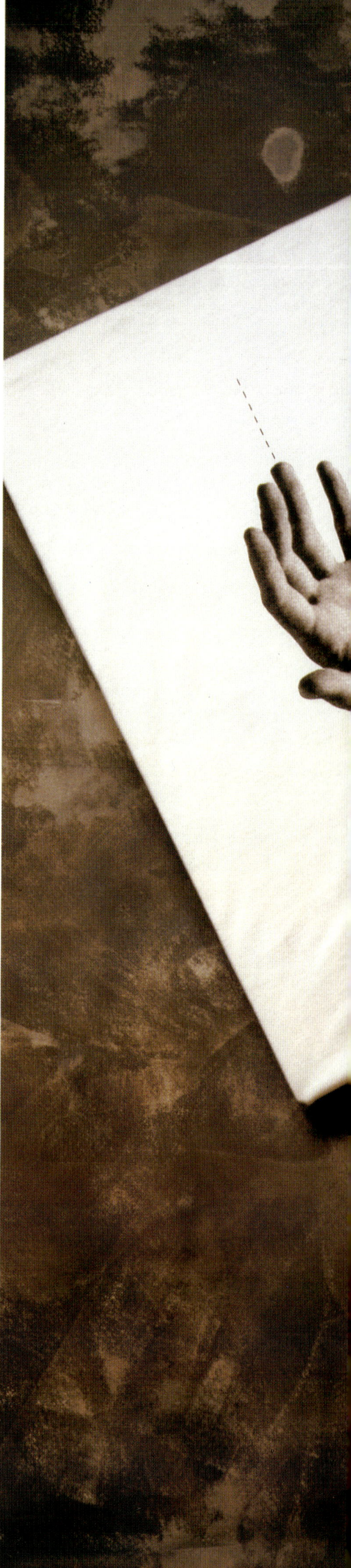

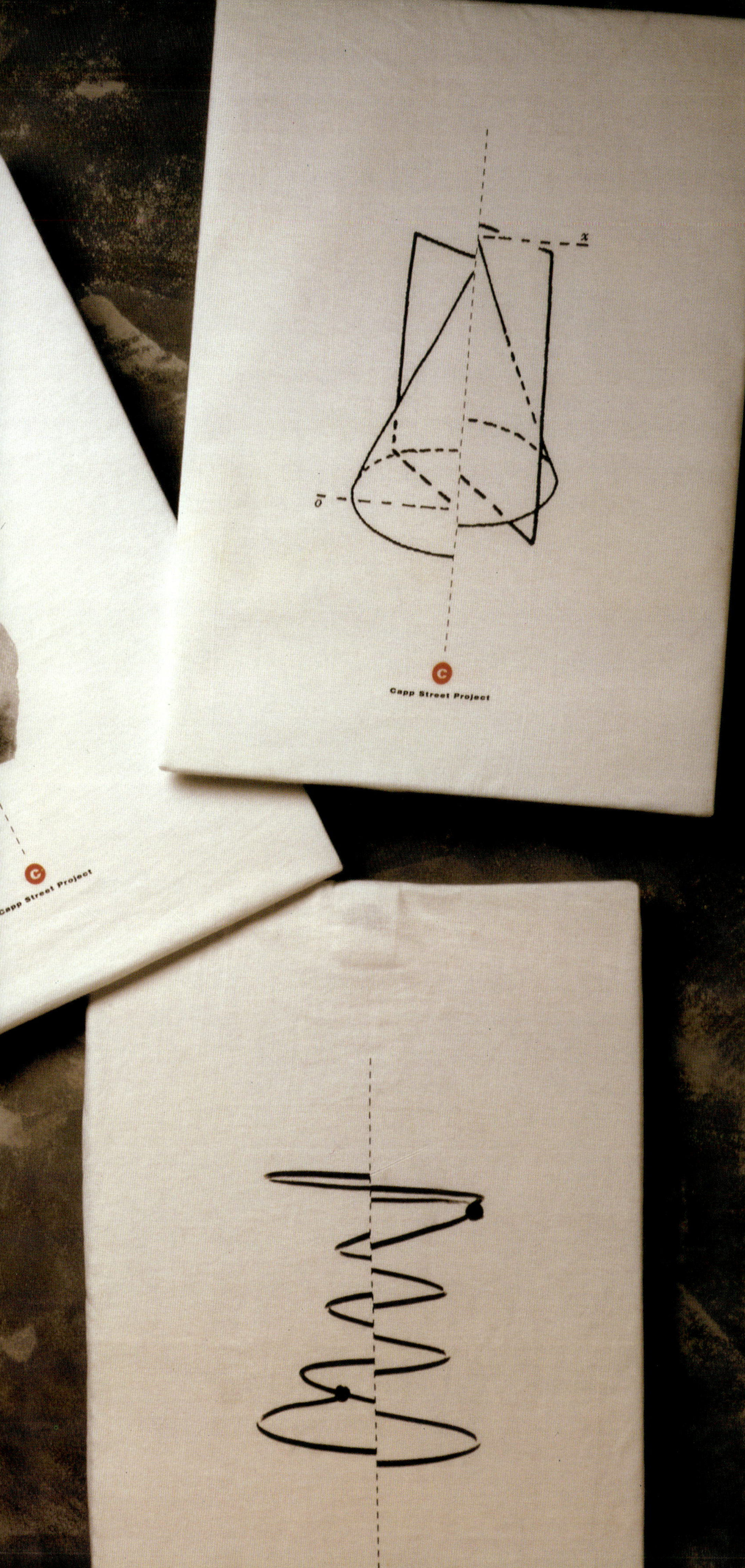

Capp Street Project
Capp Street Project

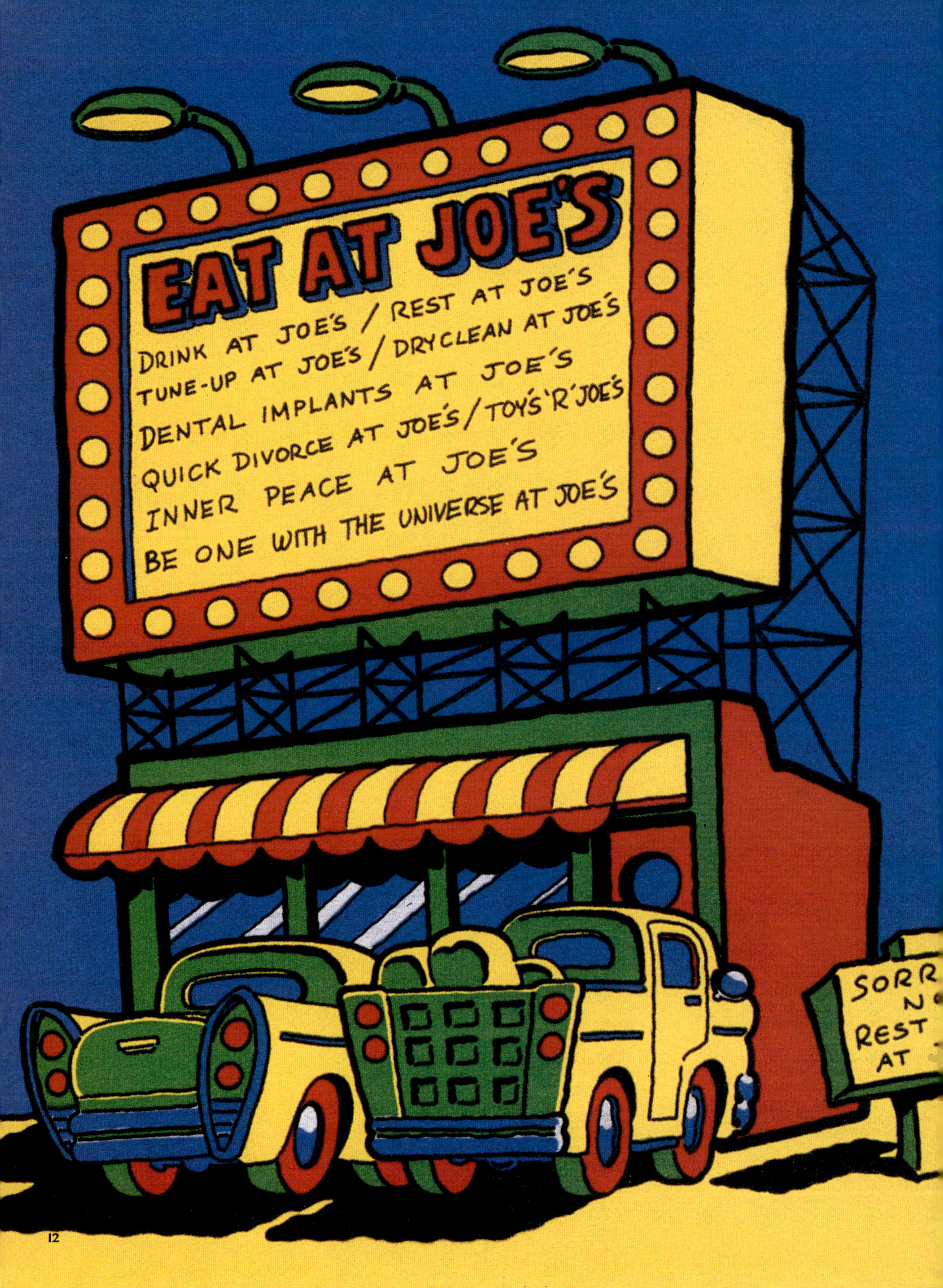

EAT AT JOE'S
DRINK AT JOE'S / REST AT JOE'S
TUNE-UP AT JOE'S / DRYCLEAN AT JOE'S
DENTAL IMPLANTS AT JOE'S
QUICK DIVORCE AT JOE'S / TOYS 'R' JOE'S
INNER PEACE AT JOE'S
BE ONE WITH THE UNIVERSE AT JOE'S
SORR
N
REST
AT

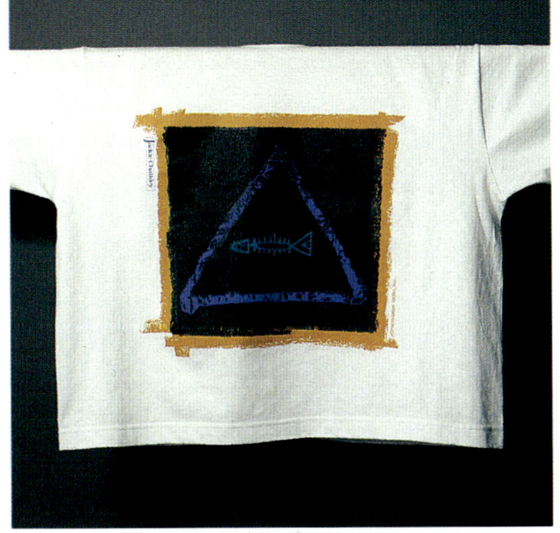

◀ facing page
Design Firm: Aardvark Studio
Illustrator: Andy Lackow
Client: Mega Designs
Purpose or Occasion: Retail

◀

Design Firm: Pictogram Studio
Art Director: Stephanie Hooton
Designer: Hien Nguyen/Stephanie Hooton
Illustrator: Stephanie Hooton
Client: Pictogram Studio

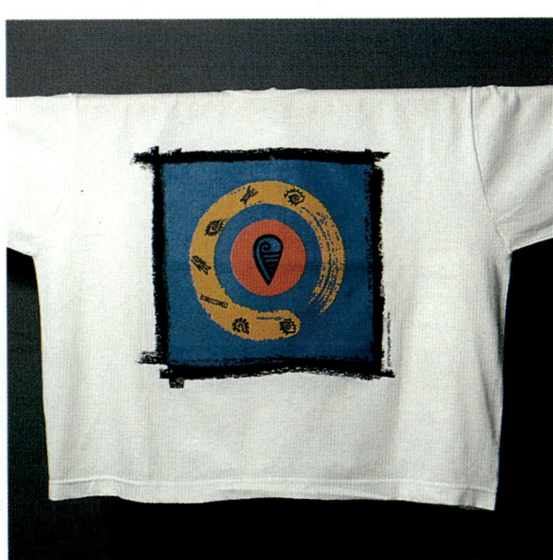

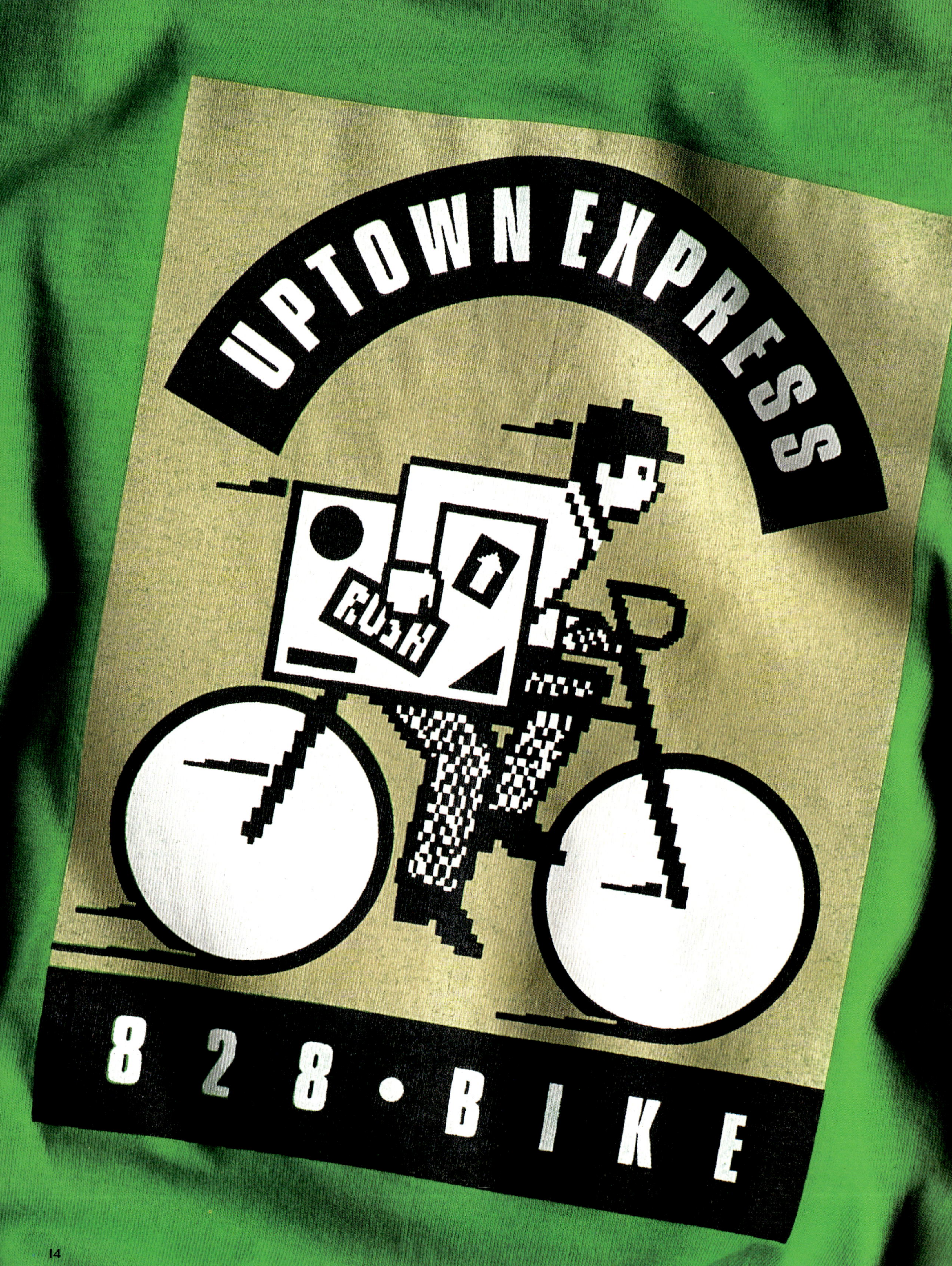
UPTOWN EXPRESS
RUSH
828 • BIKE

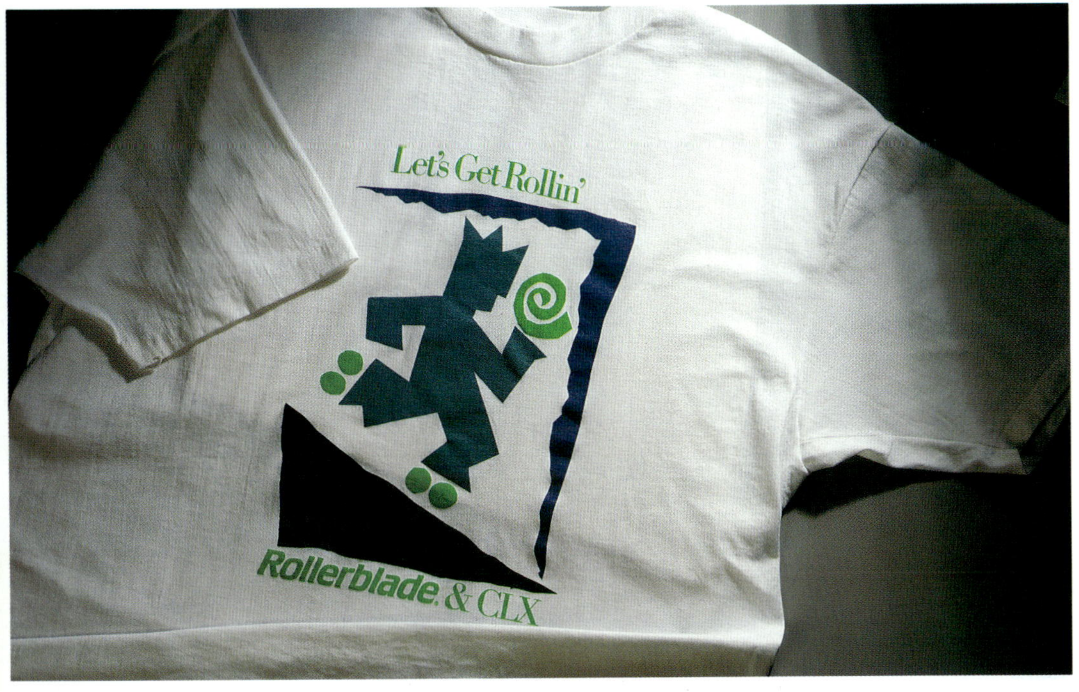

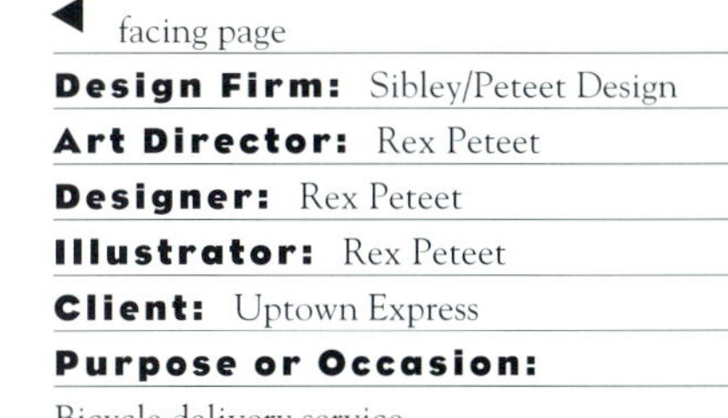

◄ facing page

Design Firm: Sibley/Peteet Design
Art Director: Rex Peteet
Designer: Rex Peteet
Illustrator: Rex Peteet
Client: Uptown Express
Purpose or Occasion:
Bicycle delivery service
Number of Colors: 3

◄

Design Firm: Carmichael-Lynch
Art Director: Peter Winecke
Designer: Peter Winecke
Illustrator: Peter Winecke
Client: CLX
Purpose or Occasion:
New business
Number of Colors: 4
Illustration created on the Mac.

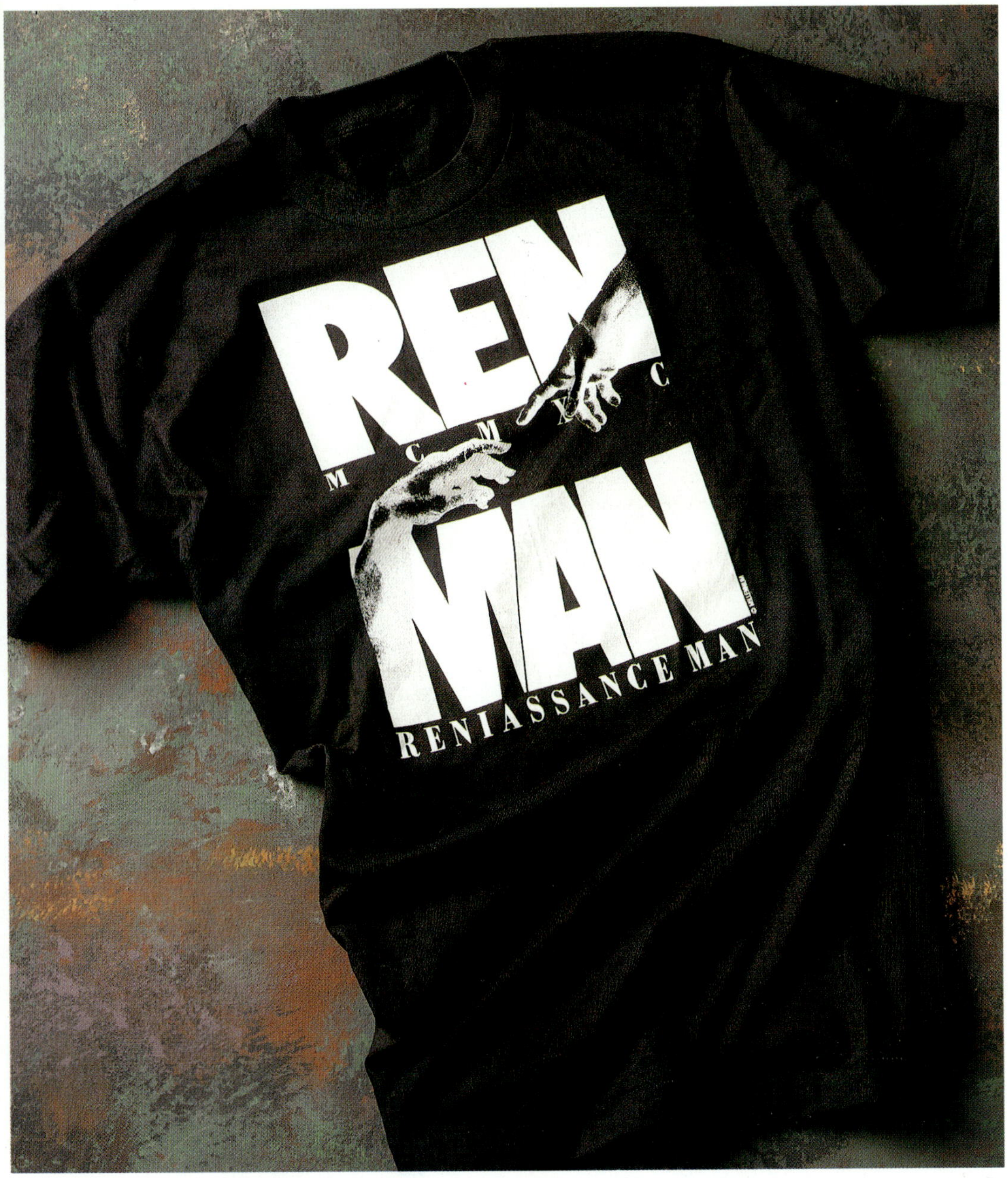

◄

Design Firm: Michael Stanard, Inc.
Art Director: Marcos Chavez
Designer: Mark Naden
Client: Millenium
Purpose or Occasion: Retail
Number of Colors: 1

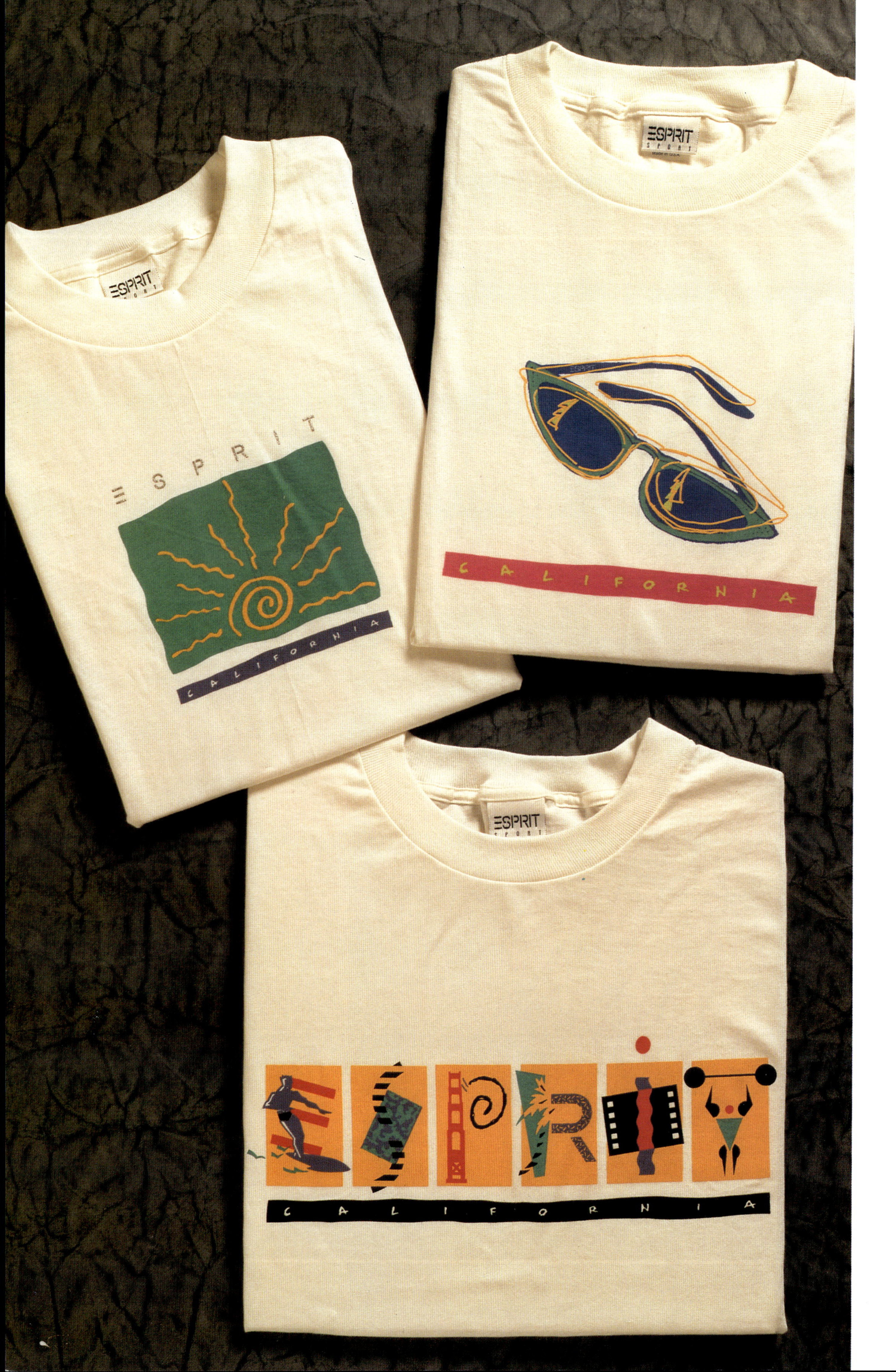

ESPRIT
sport
ESPRIT
CALIFORNIA
CALIFORNIA
ESPRIT
CALIFORNIA

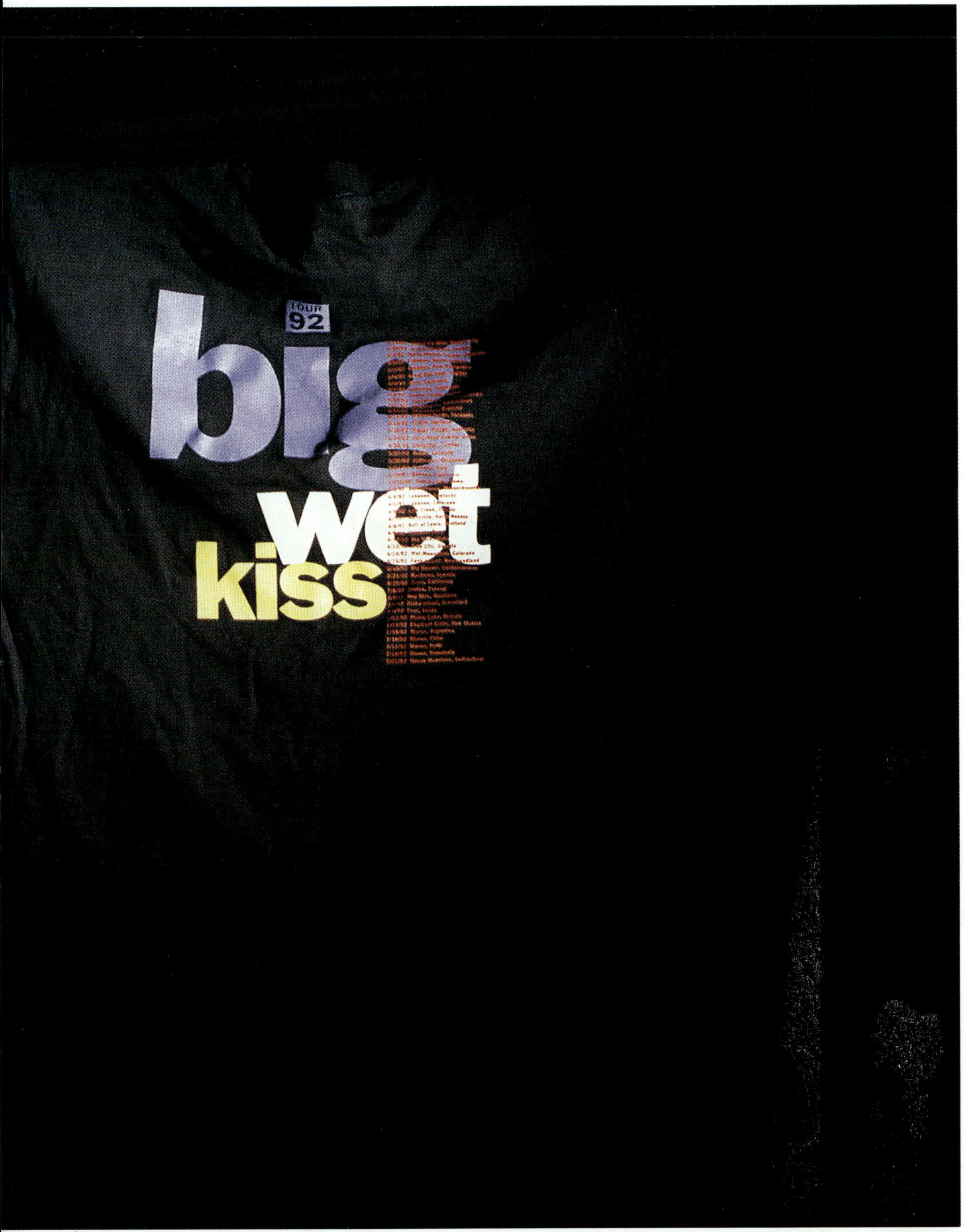

◀ facing page
Design Firm: Morla Design
Art Director: Jennifer Morla
Designer: Jennifer Morla
Illustrator: Jennifer Morla
Client: ESPRIT De Corp
Purpose or Occasion:
Designed as ESPRIT's contribution of
exculsive T-shirts for Bloomingdale's
"California"promotion
Number of Colors: 5

◀

Design Firm: Visual Dialogue
Art Director: Fritz Klaetke
Designer: Fritz Klaetke
Client: Enuffa-My-Butt Productions
Purpose or Occasion:
Chucklehead's "Big Wet Kiss" Tour
Number of Colors: 4

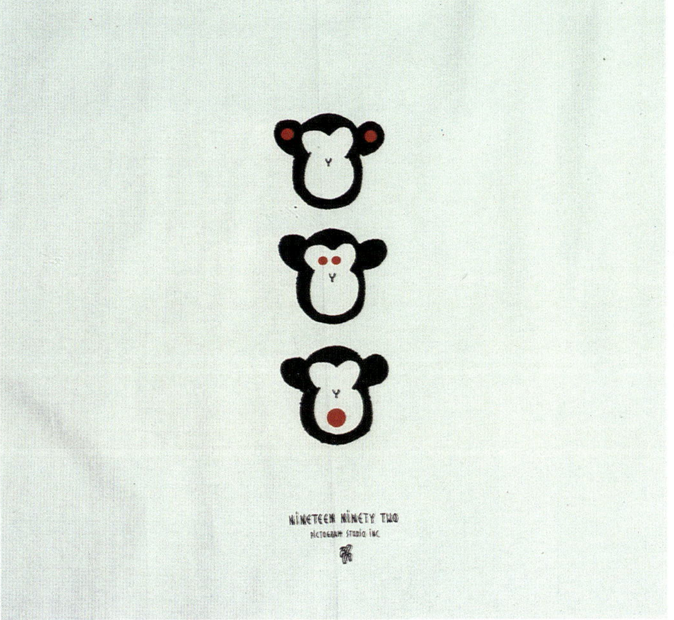

◀
Design Firm: Pictogram Studios
Art Director: Stephanie Hooton
Designer: Hien Nguyen/
Stephanie Hooton
Illustrator: Hien Nguyen
Client: Pictogram Studio
Purpose or Occasion:
Self Promotion
Number of Colors: 2
The year of the monkey.

▶

Design Firm: WGBH Design
Art Director: Chris Pullman
Designer: Chris Pullman
Illustrator: Mark Fisher
Client: MYSTERY!/WGBH
Number of Colors: 2

▼ bottom left

Design Firm: WGBH Design
Art Director: Chris Pullman
Designer: Chris Pullman
Photo: Tom Sumida
Number of Colors: 2

▼ bottom right

Design Firm: WGBH Design
Art Director: Chris Pullman
Designer: Chris Pullman
Logo Design: Gene Mackles
Client: Last Chance Garage/WGBH
Number of Colors: 4

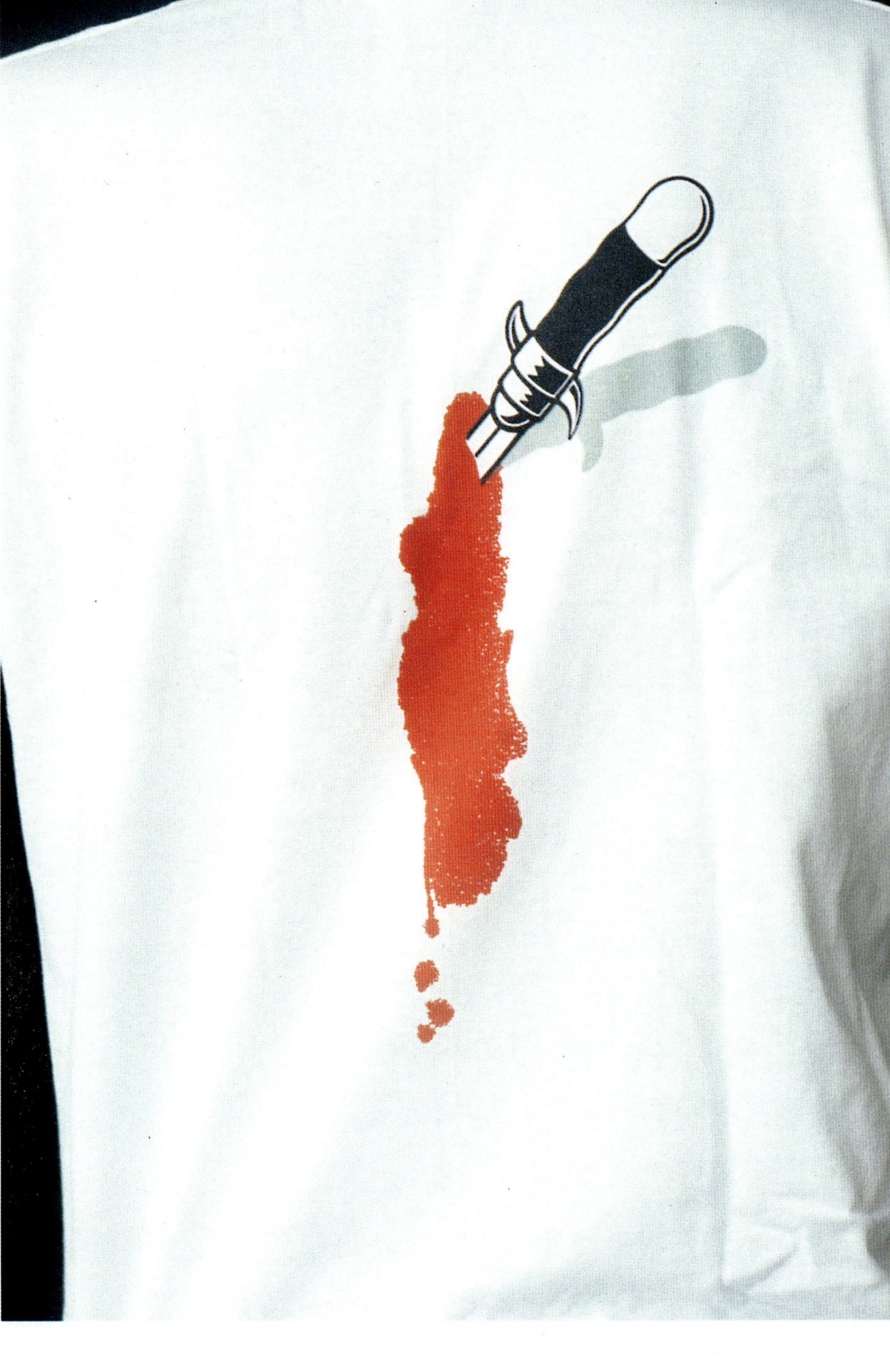

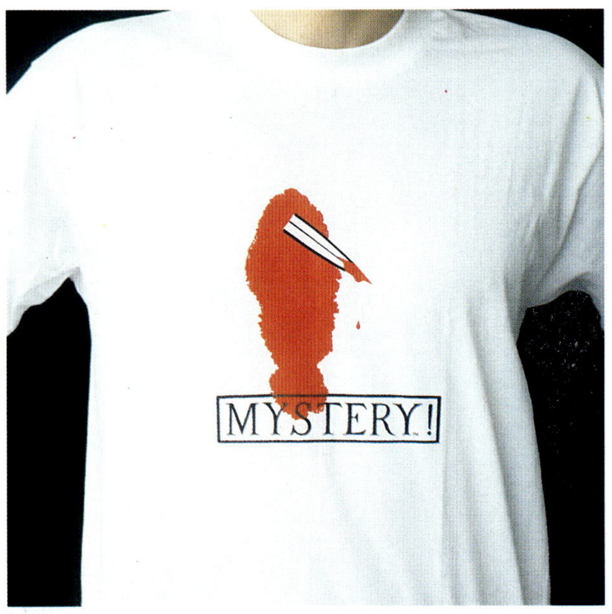

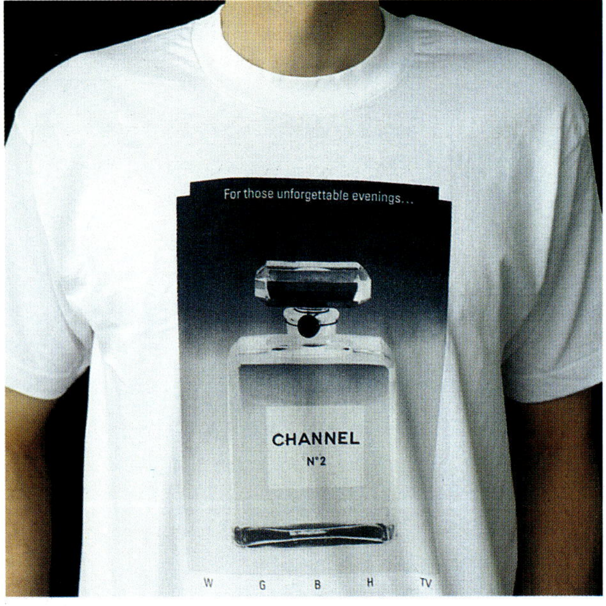

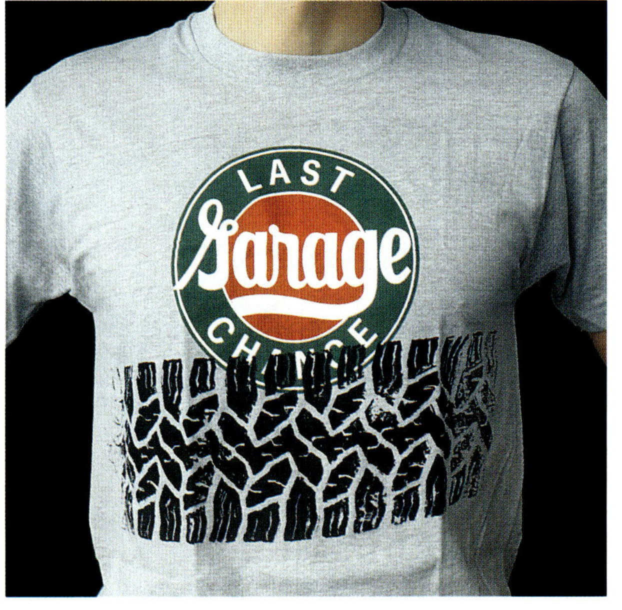

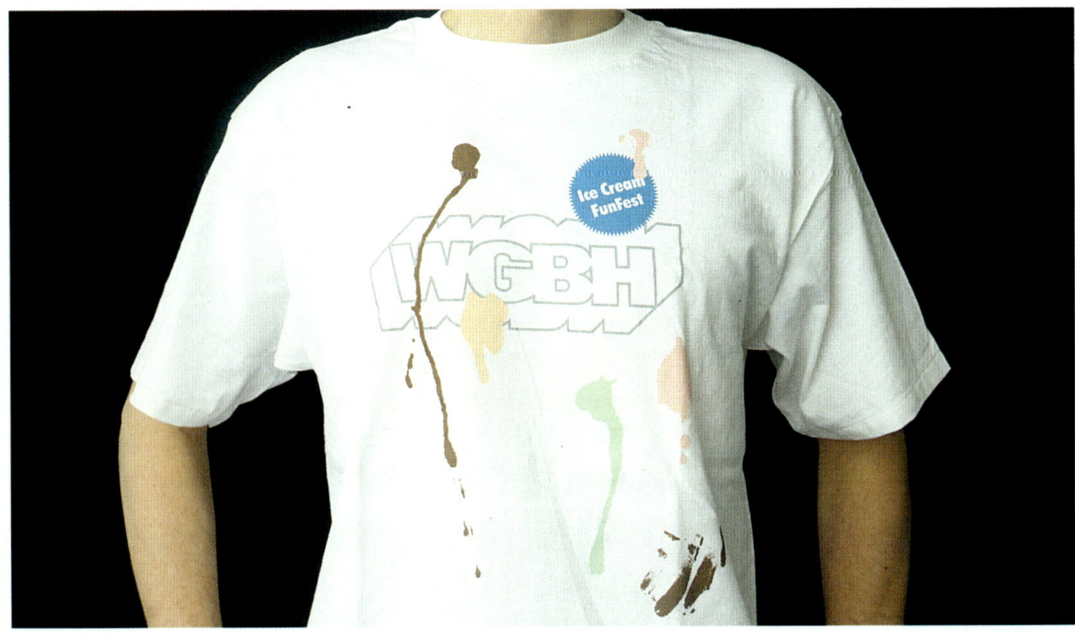

◄

Design Firm: WGBH Design
Art Director: Chris Pullman
Designer: Chris Pullman
Client: Ice Cream Fun Fest
Number of Colors: 5

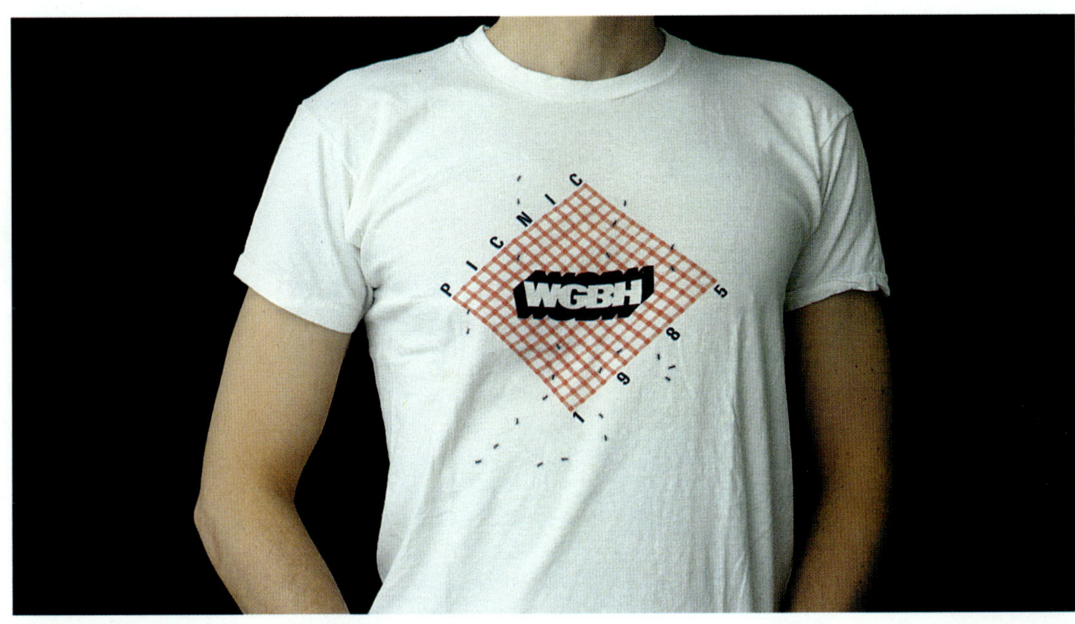

◄

Design Firm: WGBH Design
Art Director: Paul Souza
Designer: Mary Salvadore
Client: WGBH Picnic
Number of Colors: 2

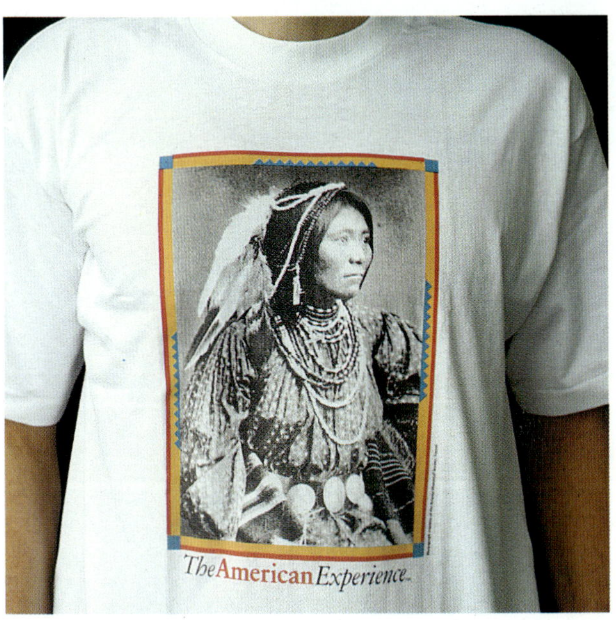

◄

Design Firm: WGBH Design
Art Director: Alison Kennedy
Designer: Elles Gianocostas
Photo: Arizona Historical Society
Client: The American Experience/WGBH
Number of Colors: 4

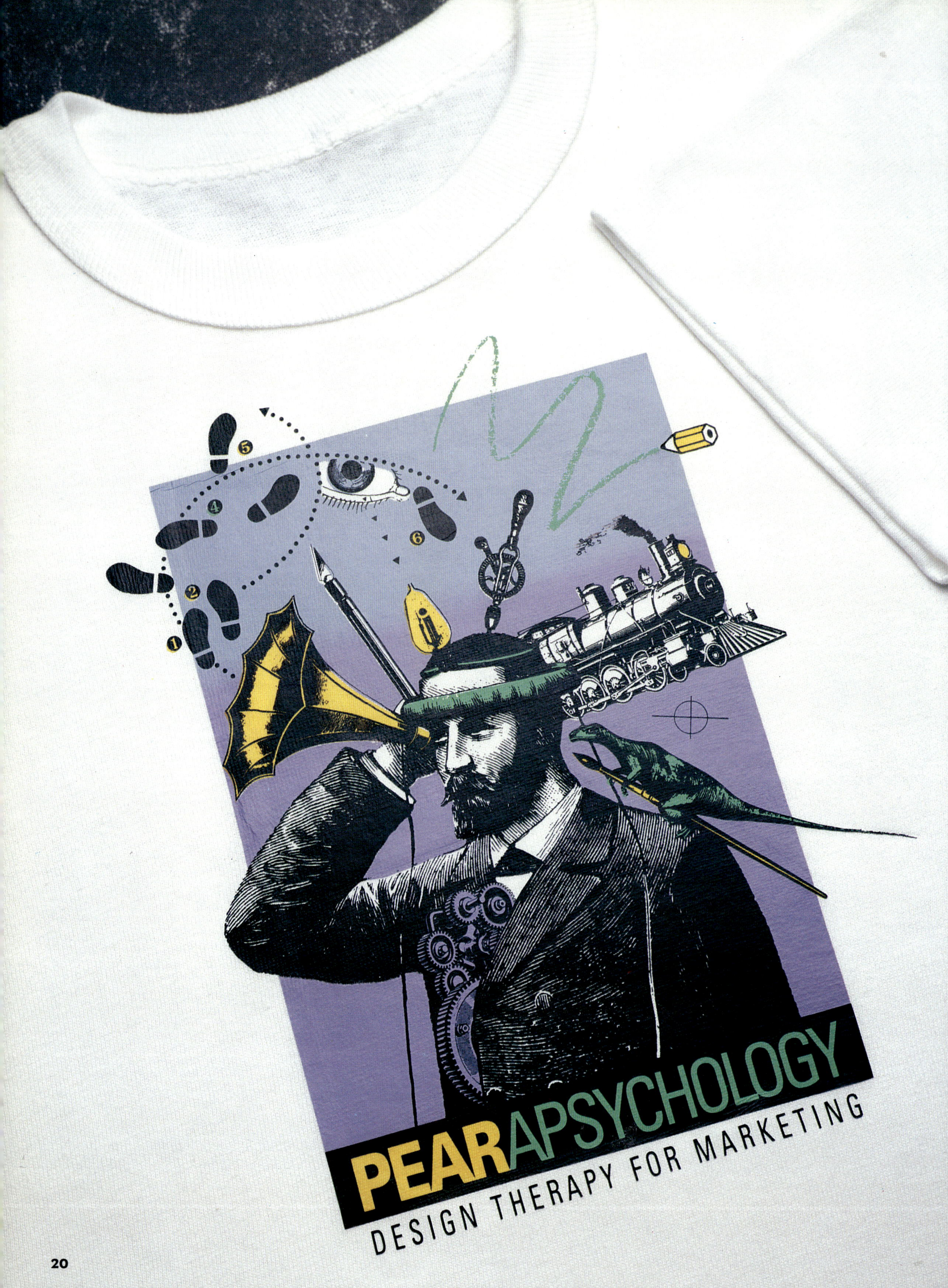
PEARAPSYCHOLOGY
DESIGN THERAPY FOR MARKETING

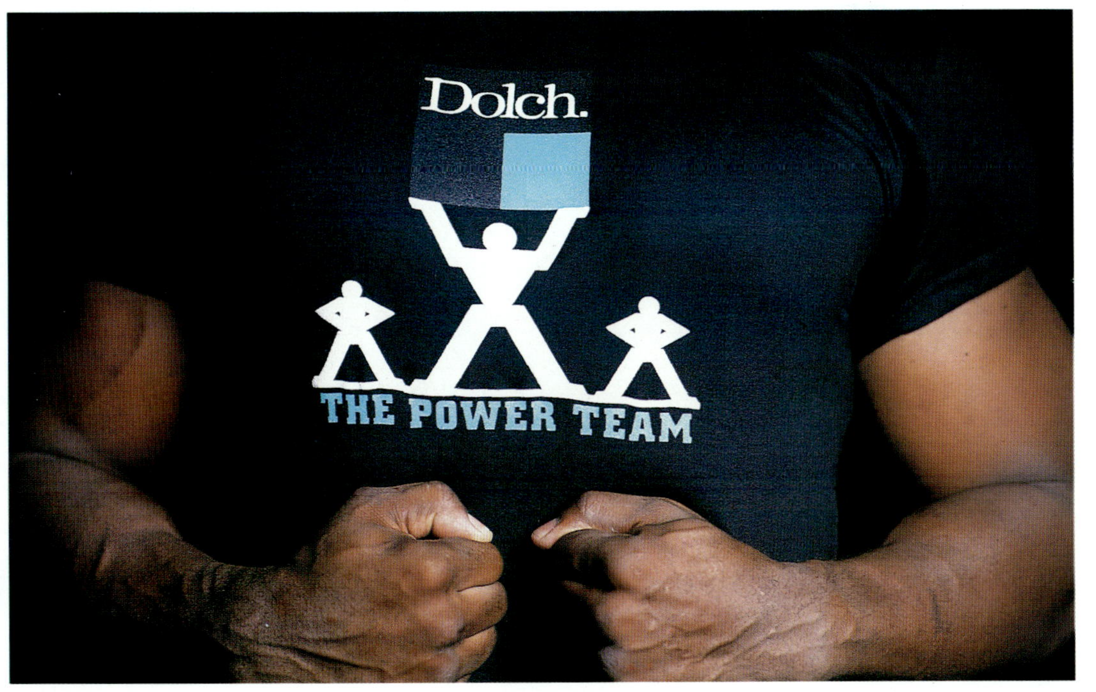

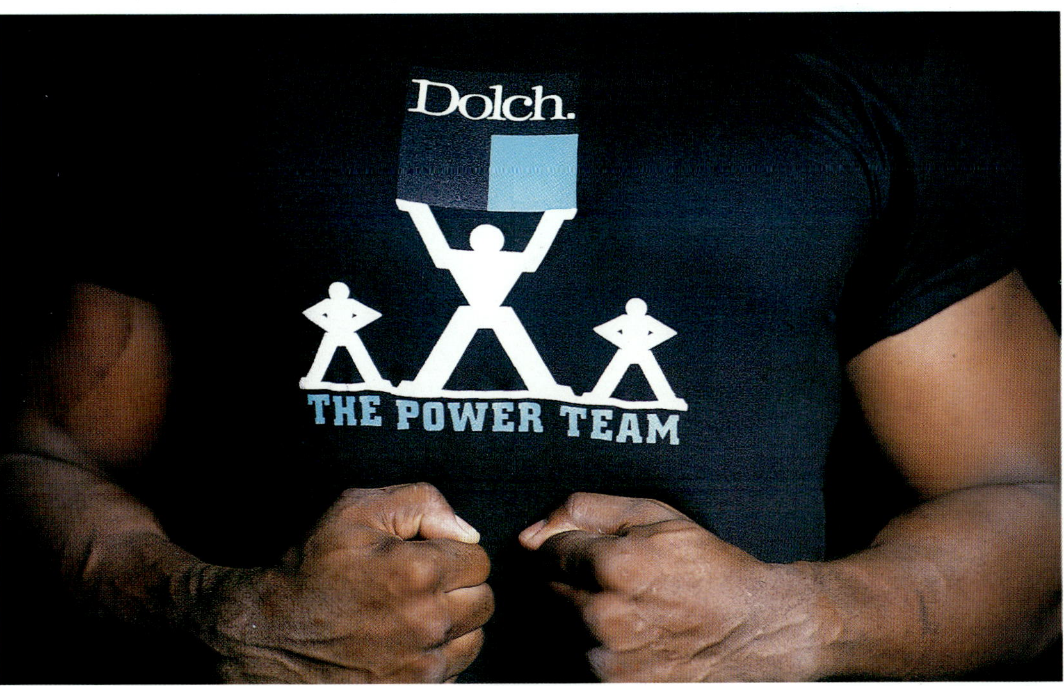

◀ facing page

Design Firm: Pear Graphics
Art Director: Mike Wesko
Designer: Kim A. Farnham
Illustrator: Kim A. Farnham
Client: Pear Graphics, Inc.
Purpose or Occasion:
Self Promotion
Number of Colors: 4

◀

Design Firm: THARP DID IT
Art Director: Rick Tharp
Designer: Rick Tharp
Illustrator: Jean Mogannam
Client: Dolch Computers
Purpose or Occasion:
Employee Ts
Number of Colors: 3

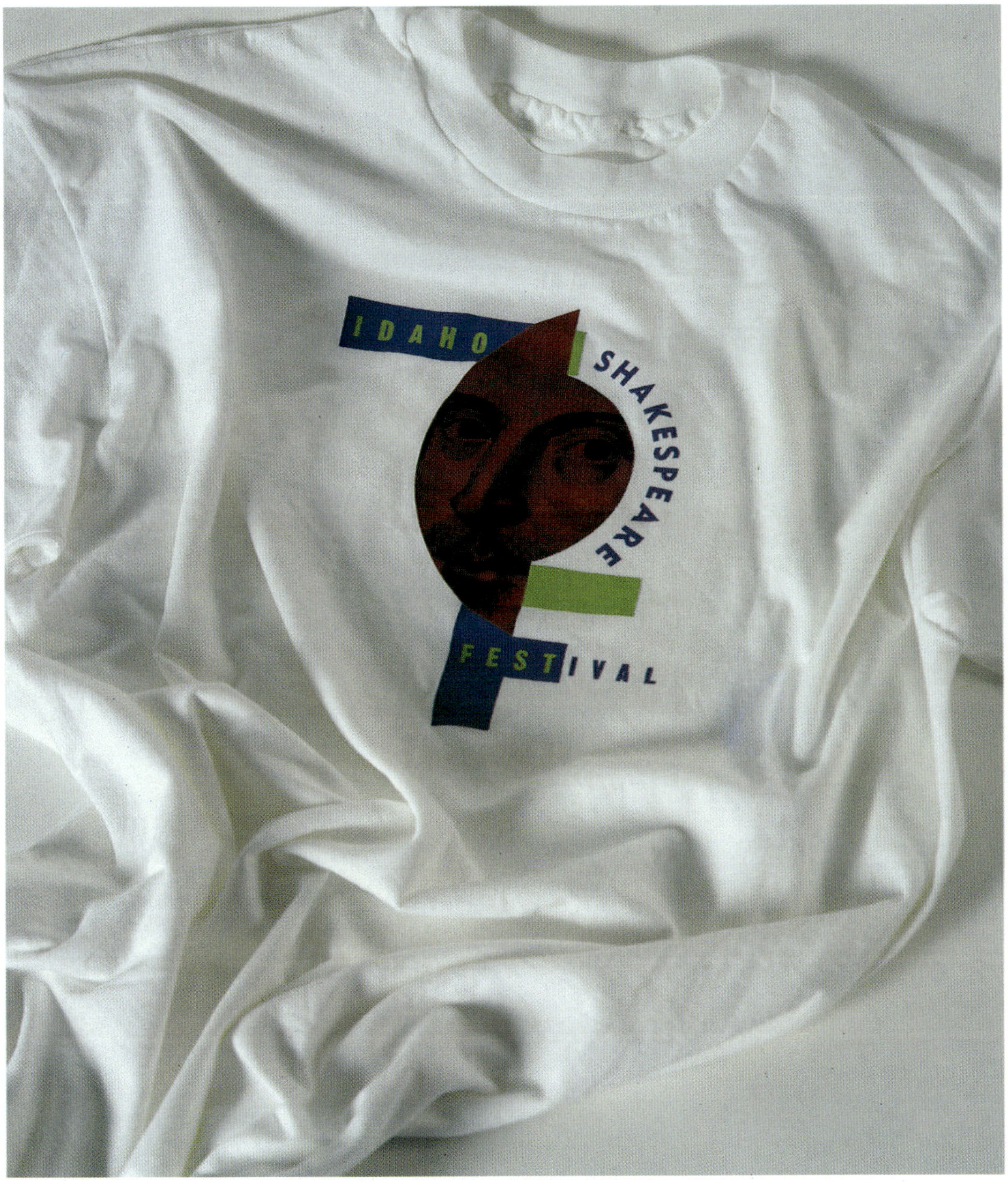

◀

Design Firm: Temel West Inc.
Art Director: Roy DeYoung
Designer: Chris Blakeman
Illustrator: Chris Blakeman
Client: Idaho Shakespeare Festival
Purpose or Occasion:
Promotional
Number of Colors: 4

▼

Design Firm: Creative Arts Group
Art Director: Gaylord Bennitt
Designer: Gaylord Bennitt
Illustrator: Gaylord Bennitt
Client: International Canoe Federation
World Championships
Purpose or Occasion: Retail
Number of Colors: 6

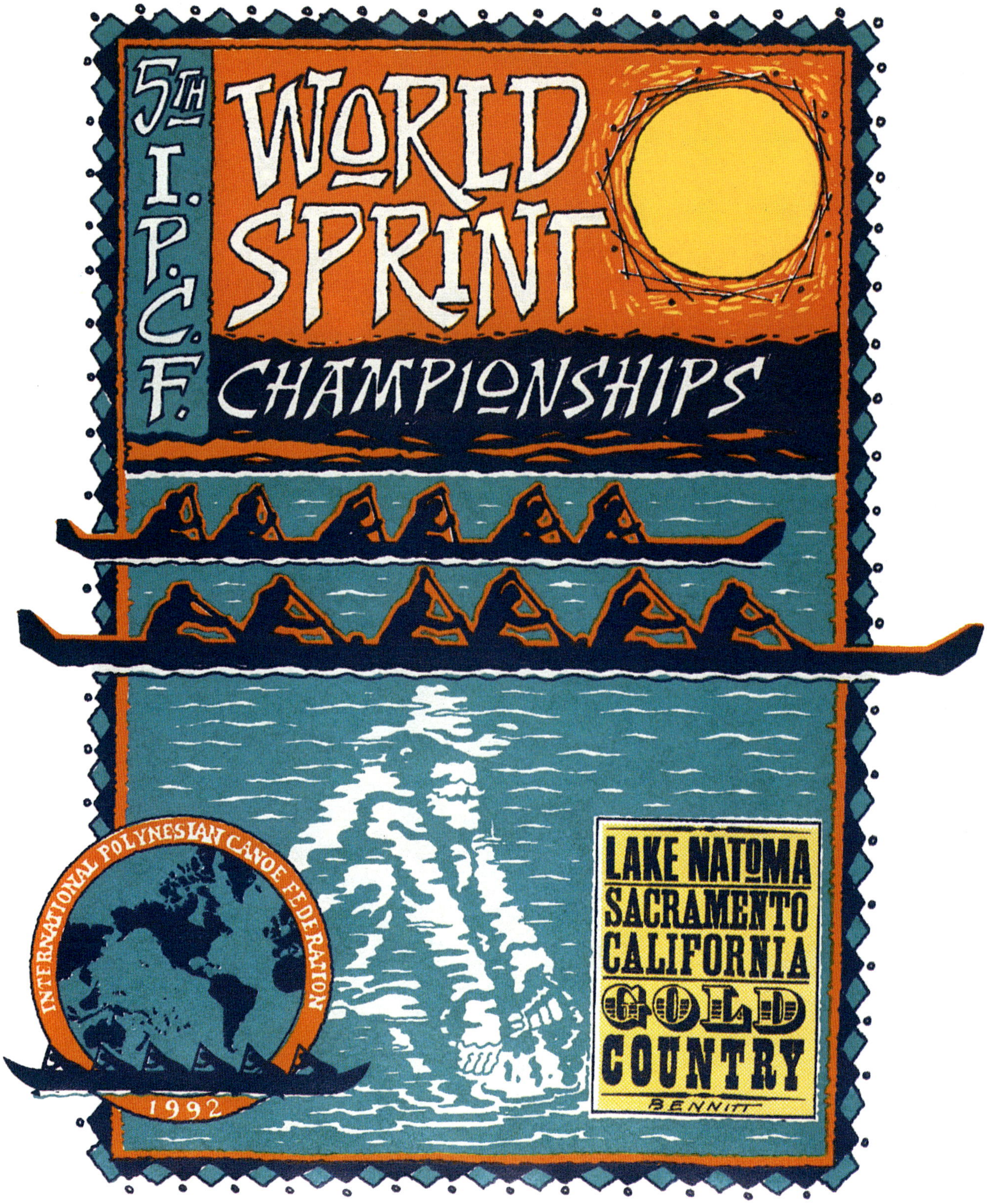

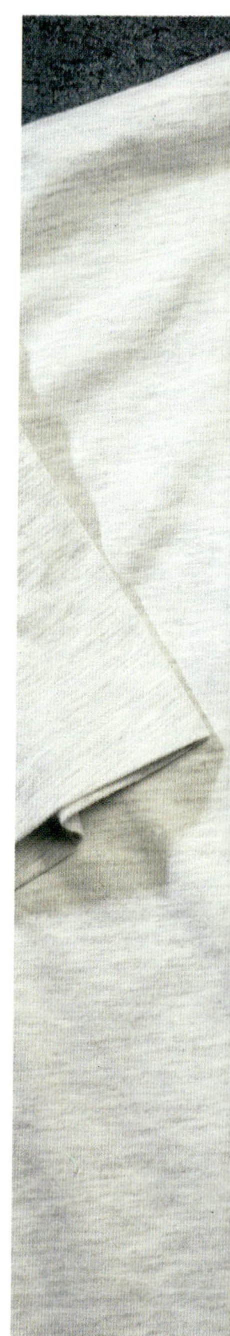

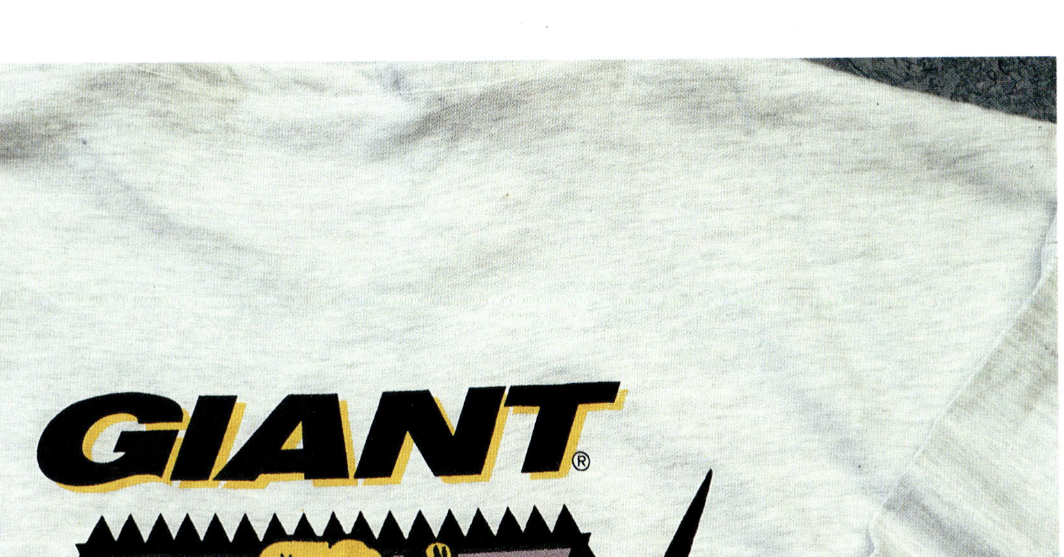

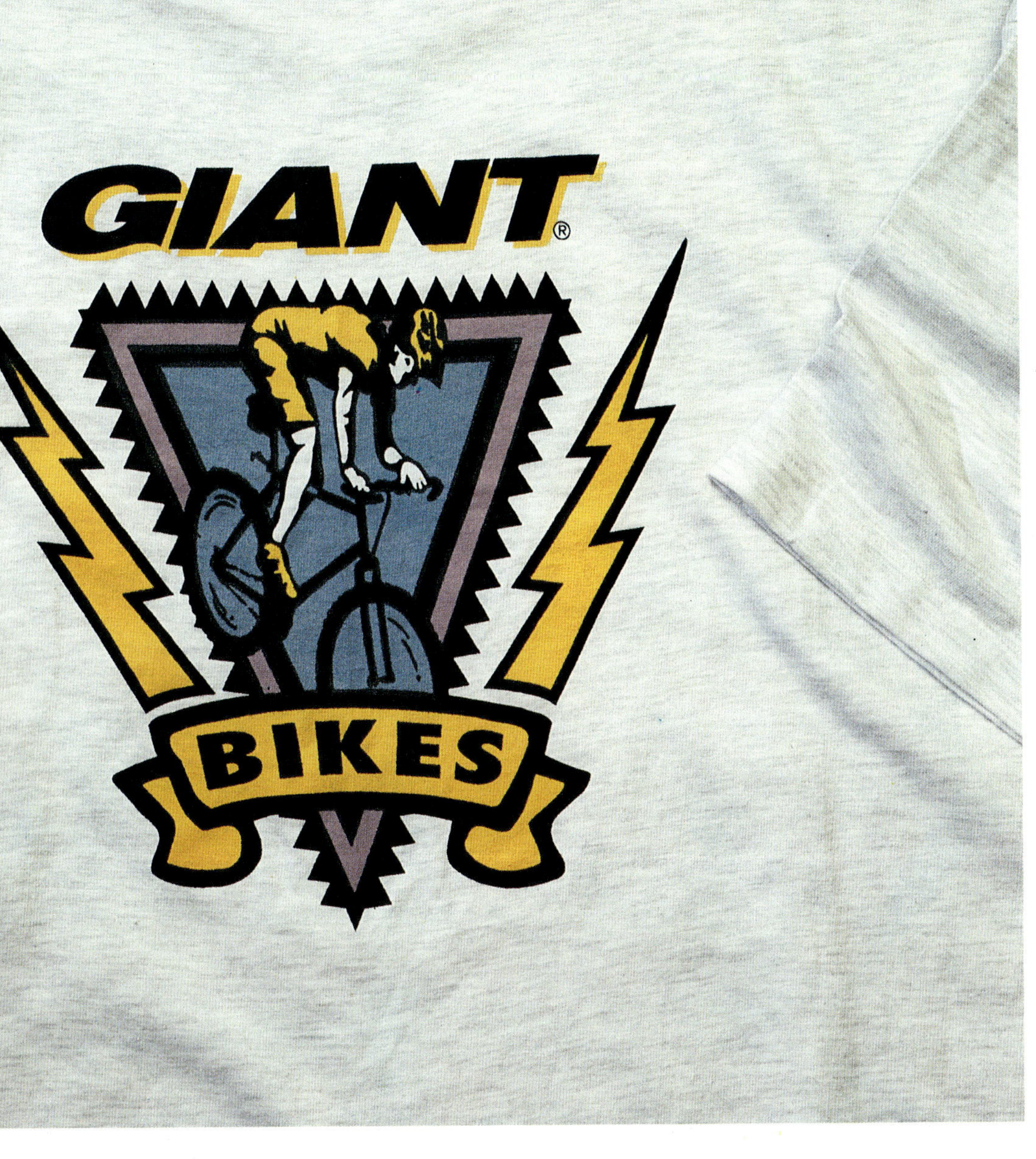

◀

Design Firm: Bright & Associates
Art Director: Konrad Bright
Designer: Konrad Bright
Client: Ketchum Advertisng
Purpose or Occasion: Logo
Number of Colors: 4

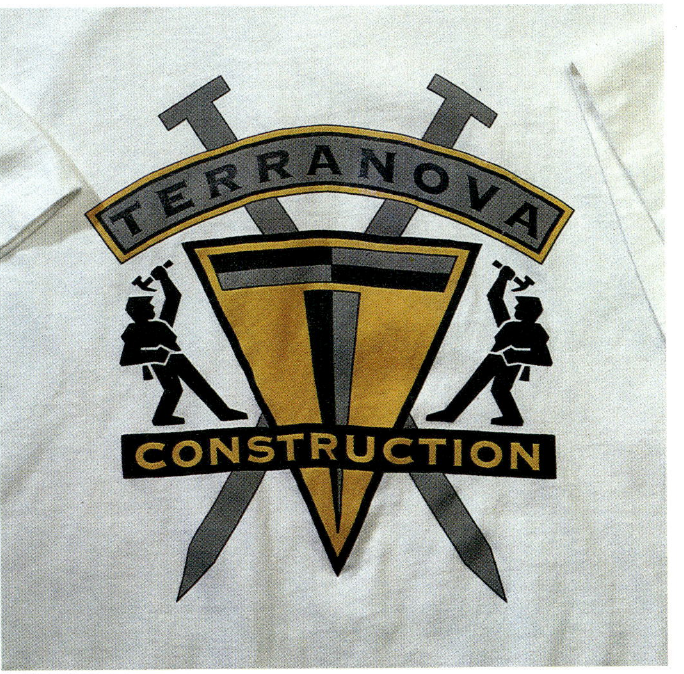

◀

Design Firm: Bright & Associates
Art Director: Konrad Bright
Designer: Konrad Bright
Illustrator: Konrad Bright
Client: Terranova Construction
Purpose or Occasion:
Logo for company
Number of Colors: 3

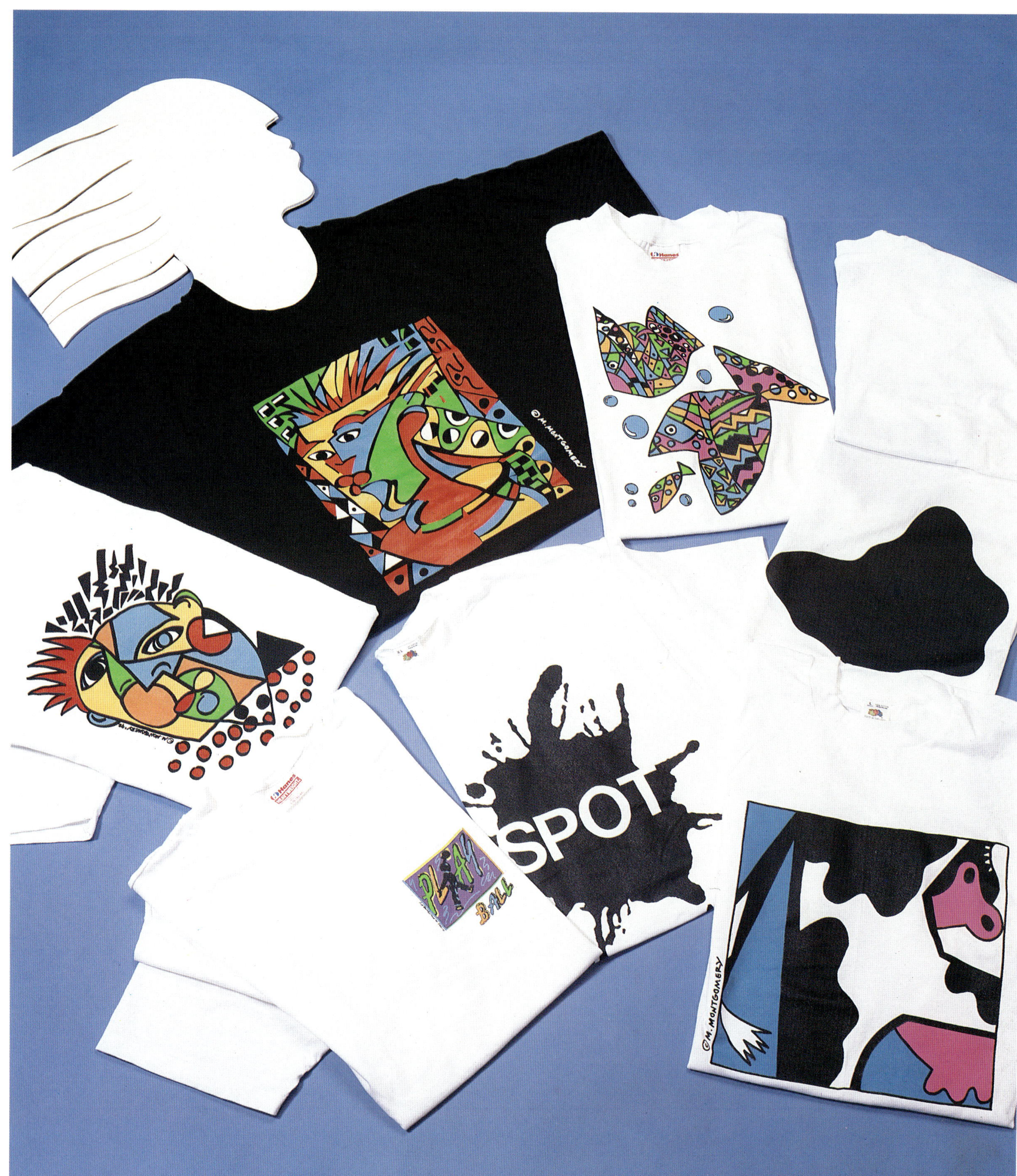

▲

Design Firm: Marlene Montgomery Design
Art Director: Marlene Montgomery
Designer: Marlene Montgomery
Illustrator: Marlene Montgomery
Client: Marlene Montgomery Design
Purpose or Occasion: Retail
Wrap-around and front and back designs.

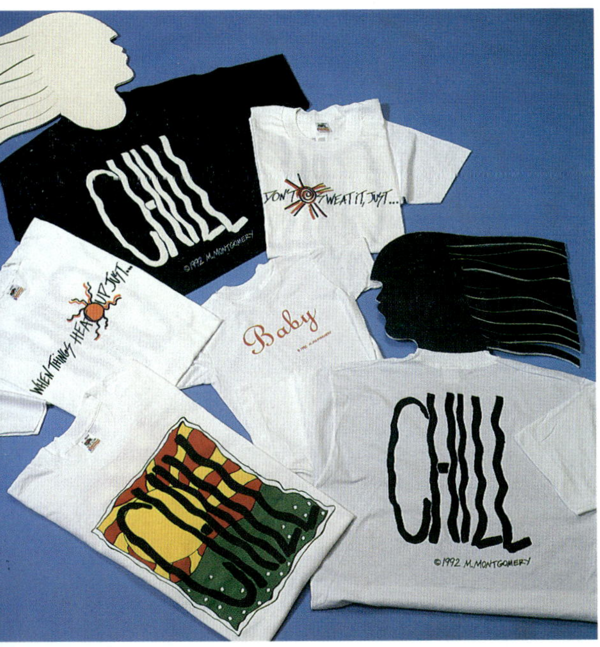

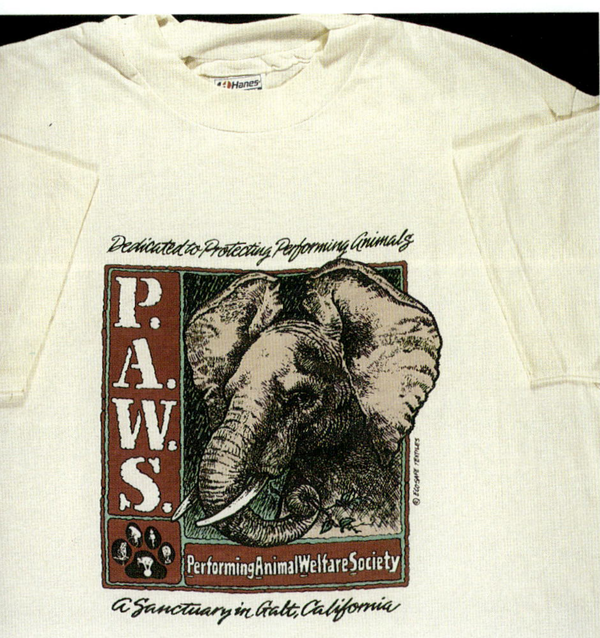

◀ top

Design Firm:
Marlene Montgomery Design
Art Director: Marlene Montgomery
Designer: Marlene Montgomery
Illustrator: Marlene Montgomery
Client: Marlene Montgomery Design
Purpose or Occasion: Retail
Number of Colors: 2
Wrap-around and front and back designs.

◀ center

Design Firm: The Bennitt Group
Art Director: Dave Dittman
Designer: Gaylord Bennitt
Illustrator: Gaylord Bennitt
Client: Eco-Safe Textiles
Purpose or Occasion:
P.A.W.S. Fundraiser
Number of Colors: 4
Water base ink - no solvents
bio-degradeable shirt.

▼ bottom

Design Firm:
Hornall Anderson Design Works
Art Director: Jack Anderson
Designer: Jack Anderson/
Julia LaPine/Lian Ng
Illustrator: Julia LaPine/Brian O'Neill
Client: Washington Software Association
Purpose or Occasion:
Fourth Annual WSA Halloween Ball
Number of Colors: 2

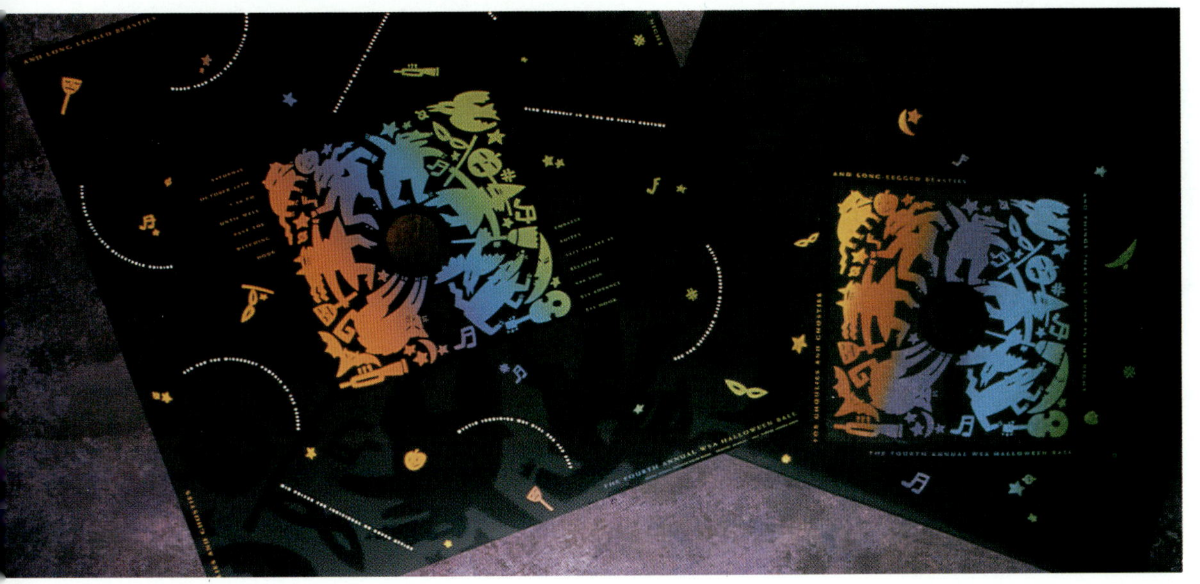

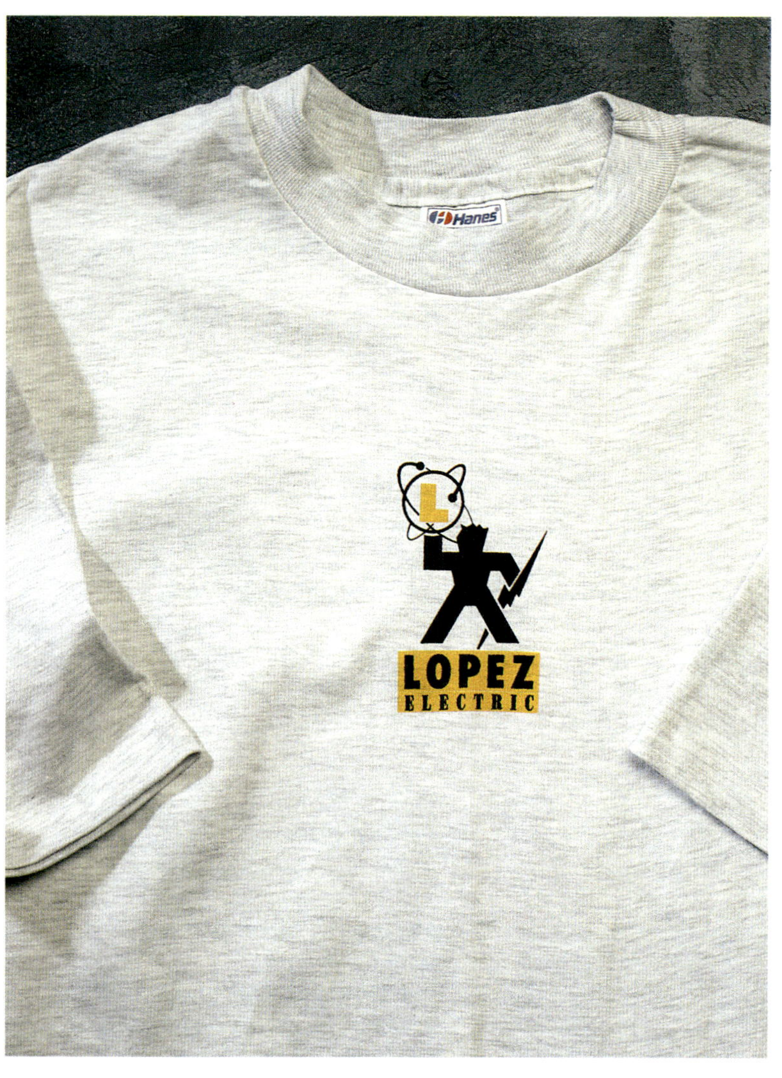

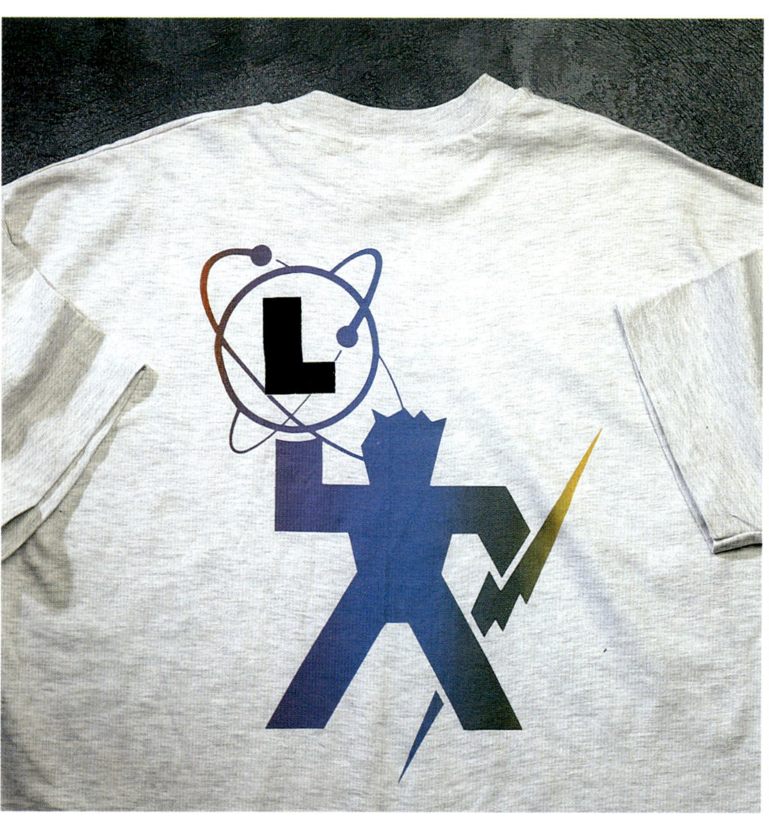

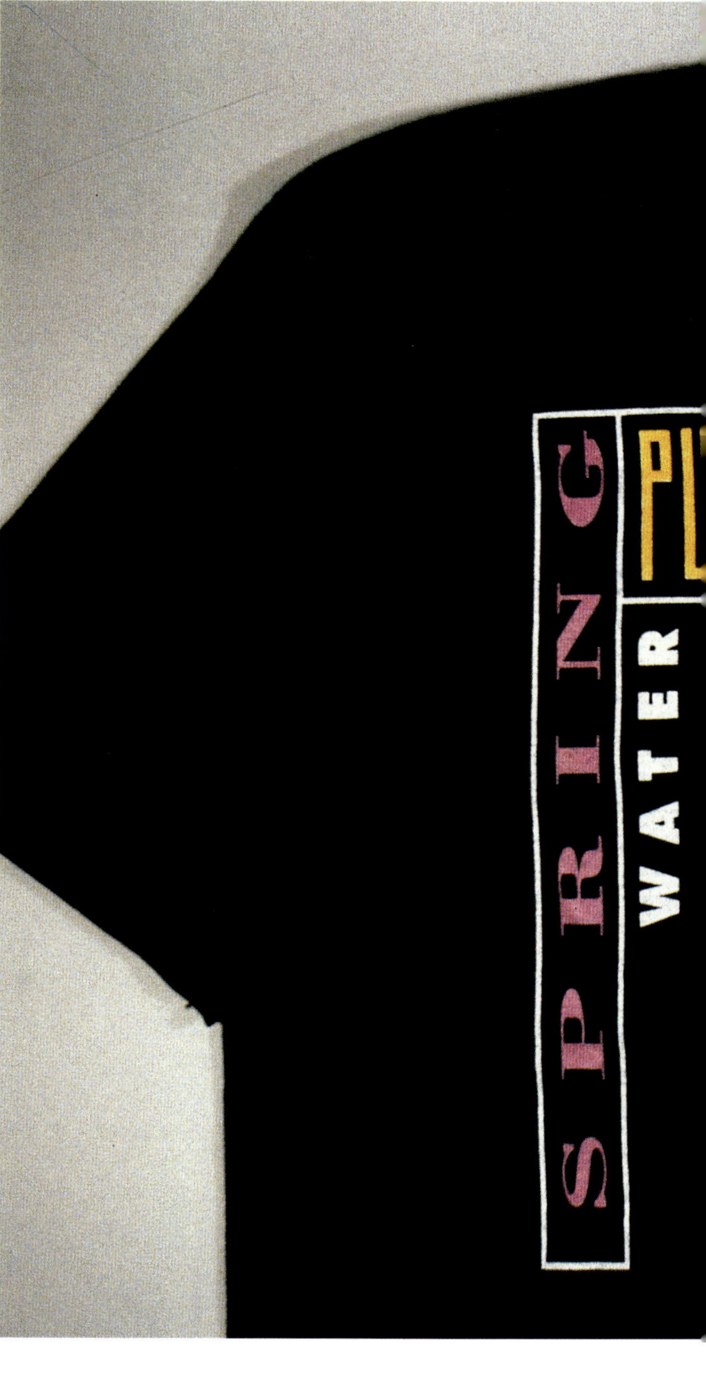

◄

Design Firm: Bright & Associates
Art Director: Konrad Bright
Designer: Konrad Bright
Illustrator: Konrad Bright
Client: Lopez Electric
Purpose or Occasion: Logo
Number of Colors: 4 on back, 2 on front

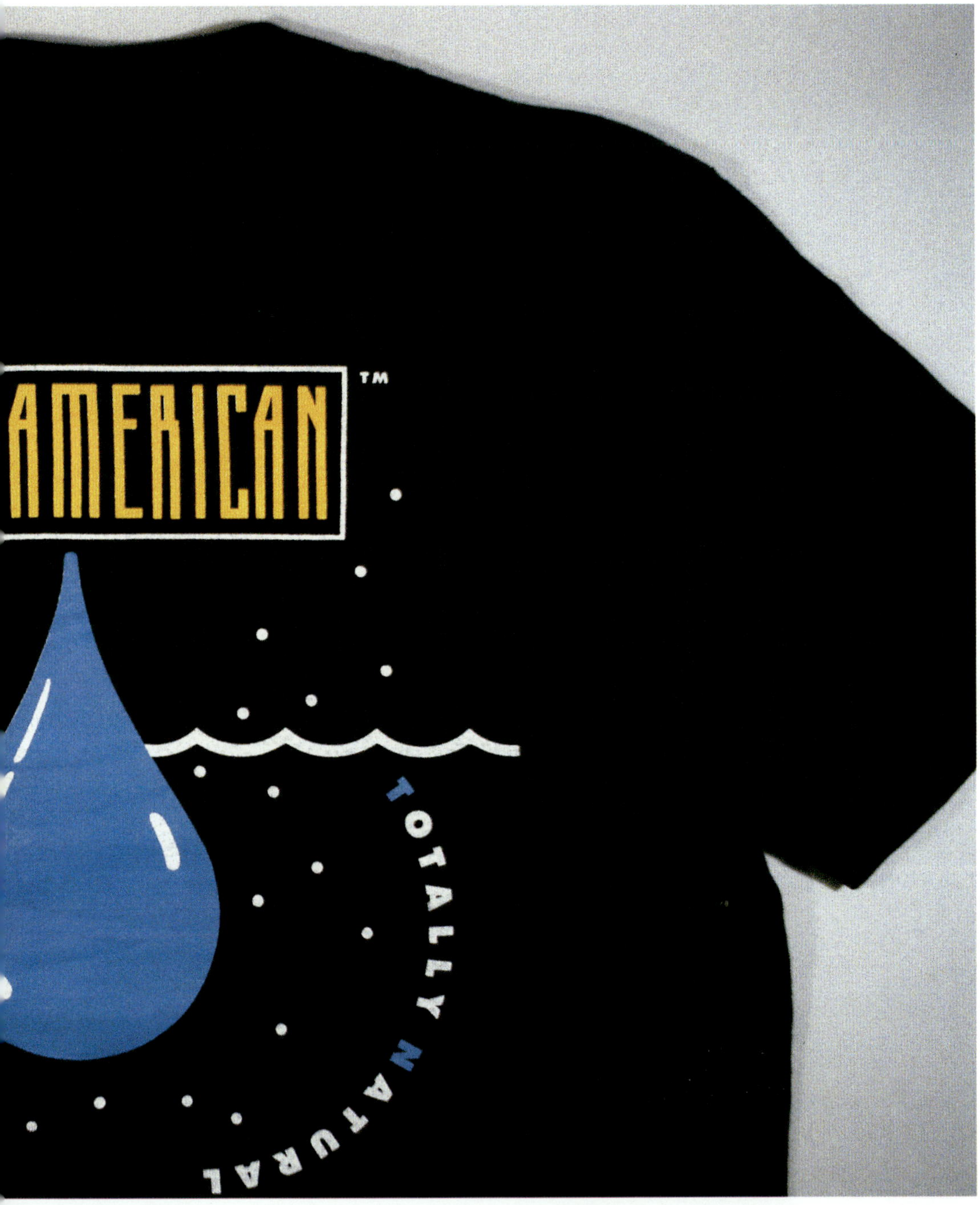

Design Firm: Sommese Design
Art Director:
Kristin Sommese/Lanny Sommese
Designer: Kristin Sommese
Illustrator: Lanny Sommese
Client: Aquapenn Spring Water Co.
Purpose or Occasion: Promotional
Number of Colors: 4

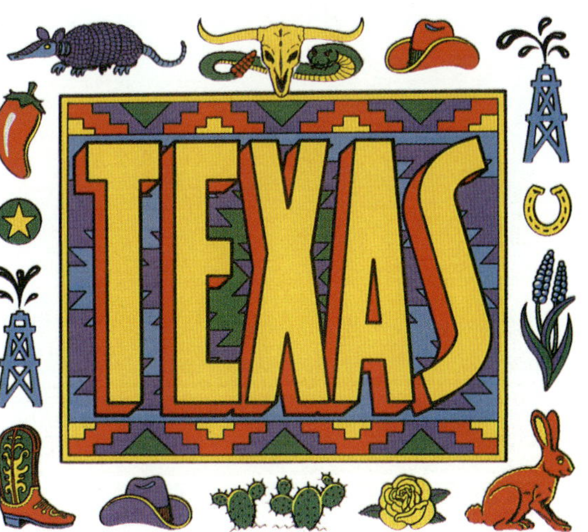

Design Firm: Aardvark Studio
Illustrator: Andy Lackow
Client: Mega Designs
Purpose or Occasion: Retail

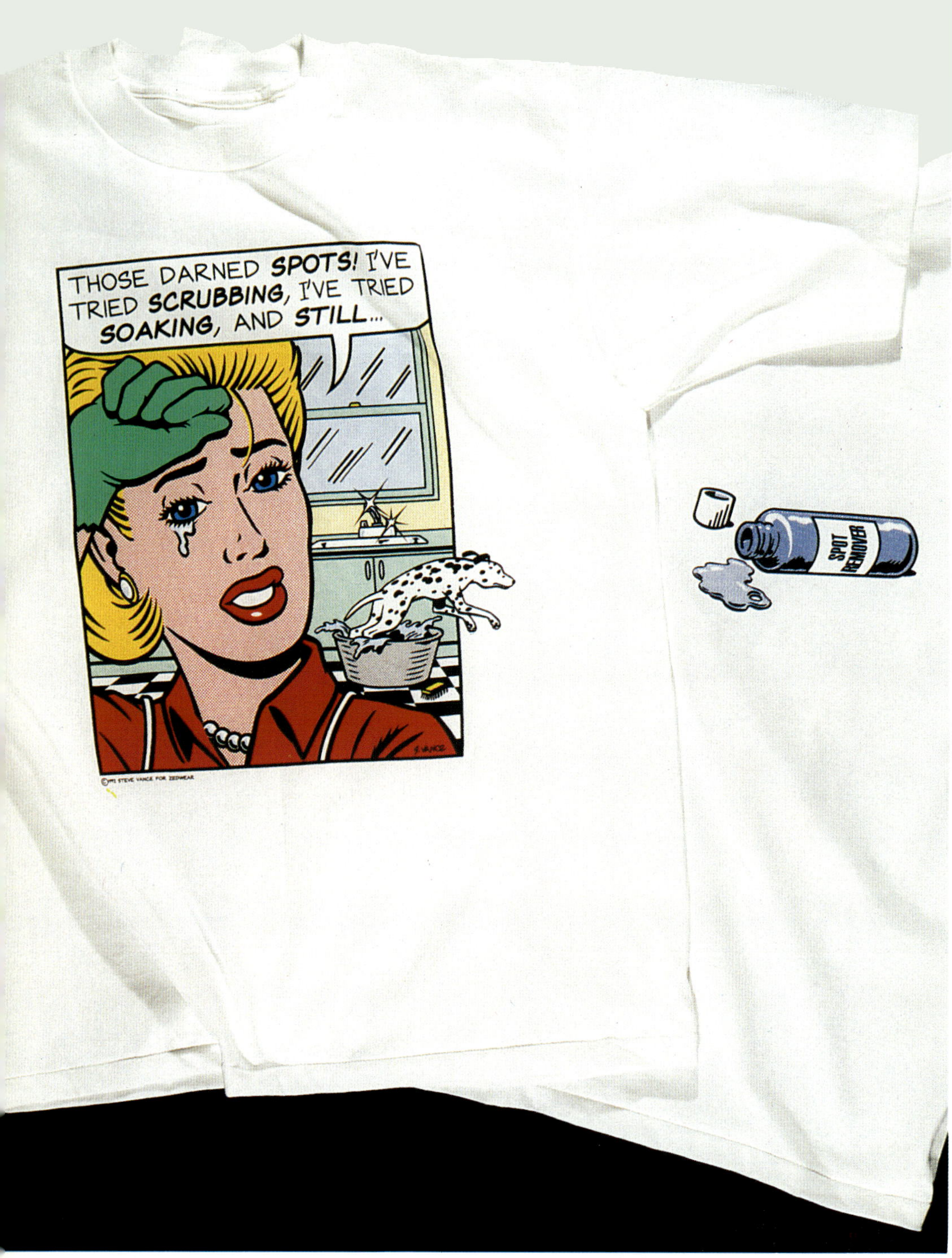

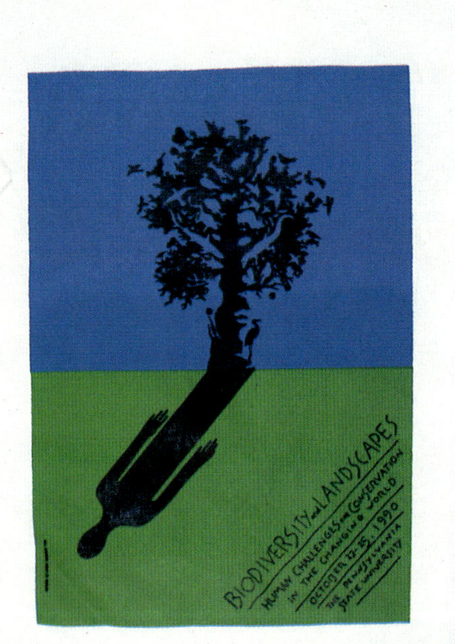

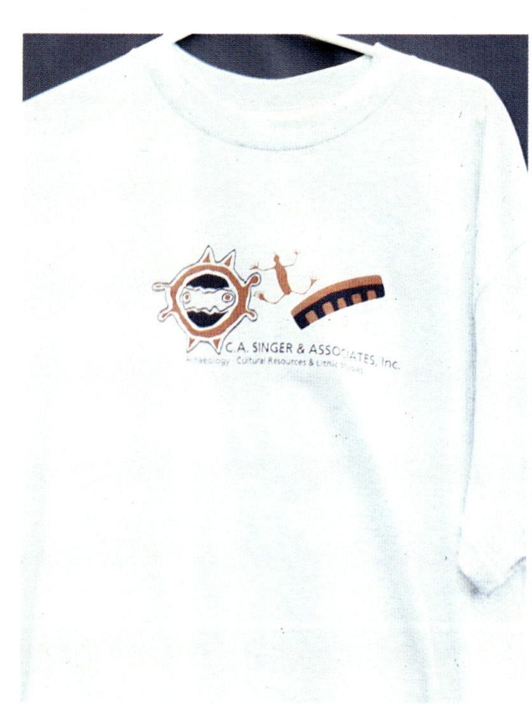

▲

Design Firm: Zedwear
Art Director: John Klaja/
George Mimnaugh
Designer: John Klaja/George Mimnaugh
Illustrator: Steve Vance
Client: Zedwear
Purpose or Occasion: Retail
Number of Colors: 5
Title: "Spot Remover"

▼

Design Firm: Gunnar Swanson
Design Office
Art Director: Gunnar Swanson
Designer: Gunnar Swanson
Illustrator: Gunnar Swanson
Client: C.A. Singer & Associates
Number of Colors: 2

▶

Design Firm: Sommese Design
Art Director: Lanny Sommese
Designer: Lanny Sommese
Illustrator: Lanny Sommese
Client: Penn State University
Purpose or Occasion: Conference
Number of Colors: 3
Shirt was given to conference participants and later sold to the public.

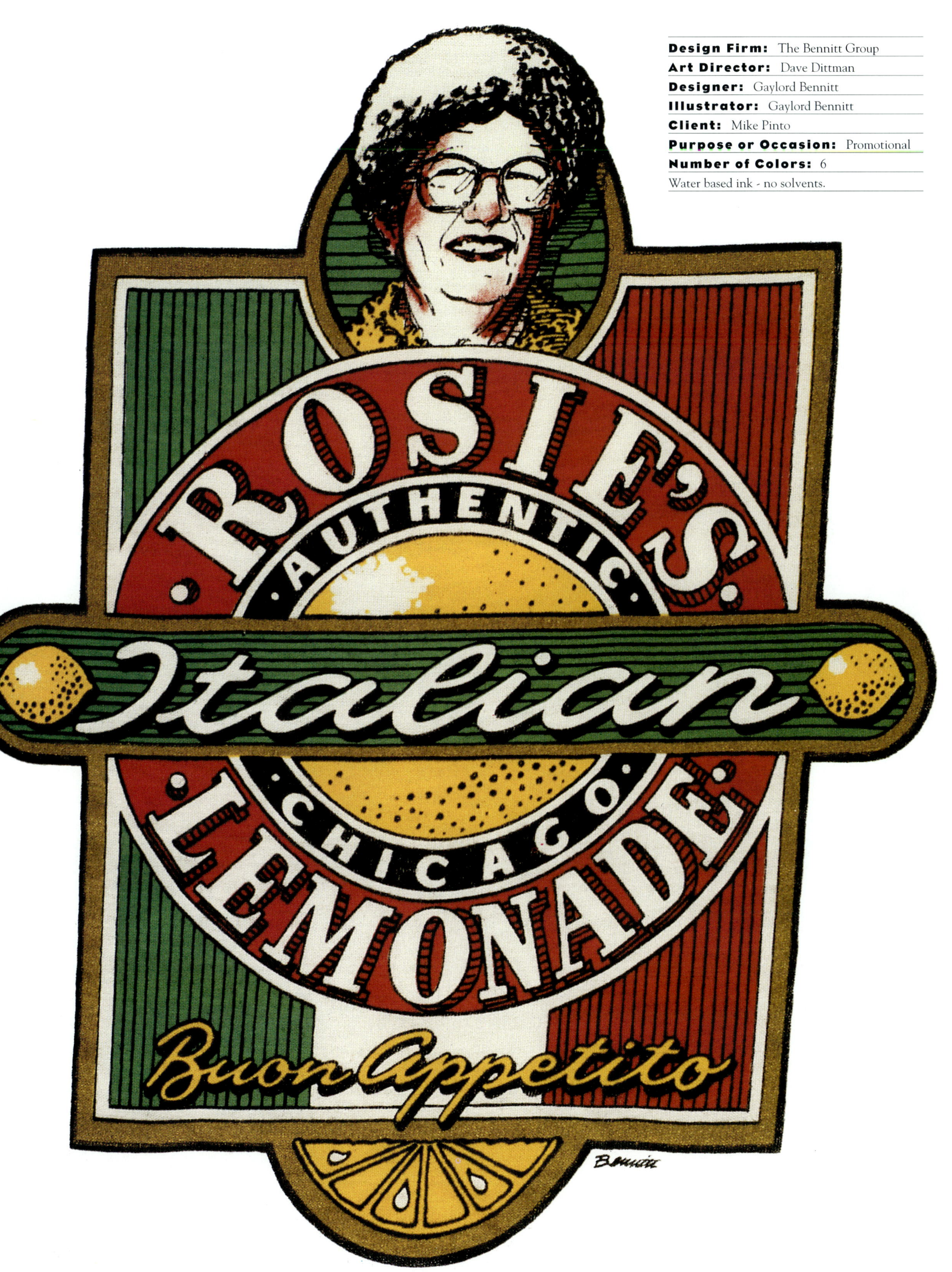

Design Firm: The Bennitt Group
Art Director: Dave Dittman
Designer: Gaylord Bennitt
Illustrator: Gaylord Bennitt
Client: Mike Pinto
Purpose or Occasion: Promotional
Number of Colors: 6
Water based ink - no solvents.

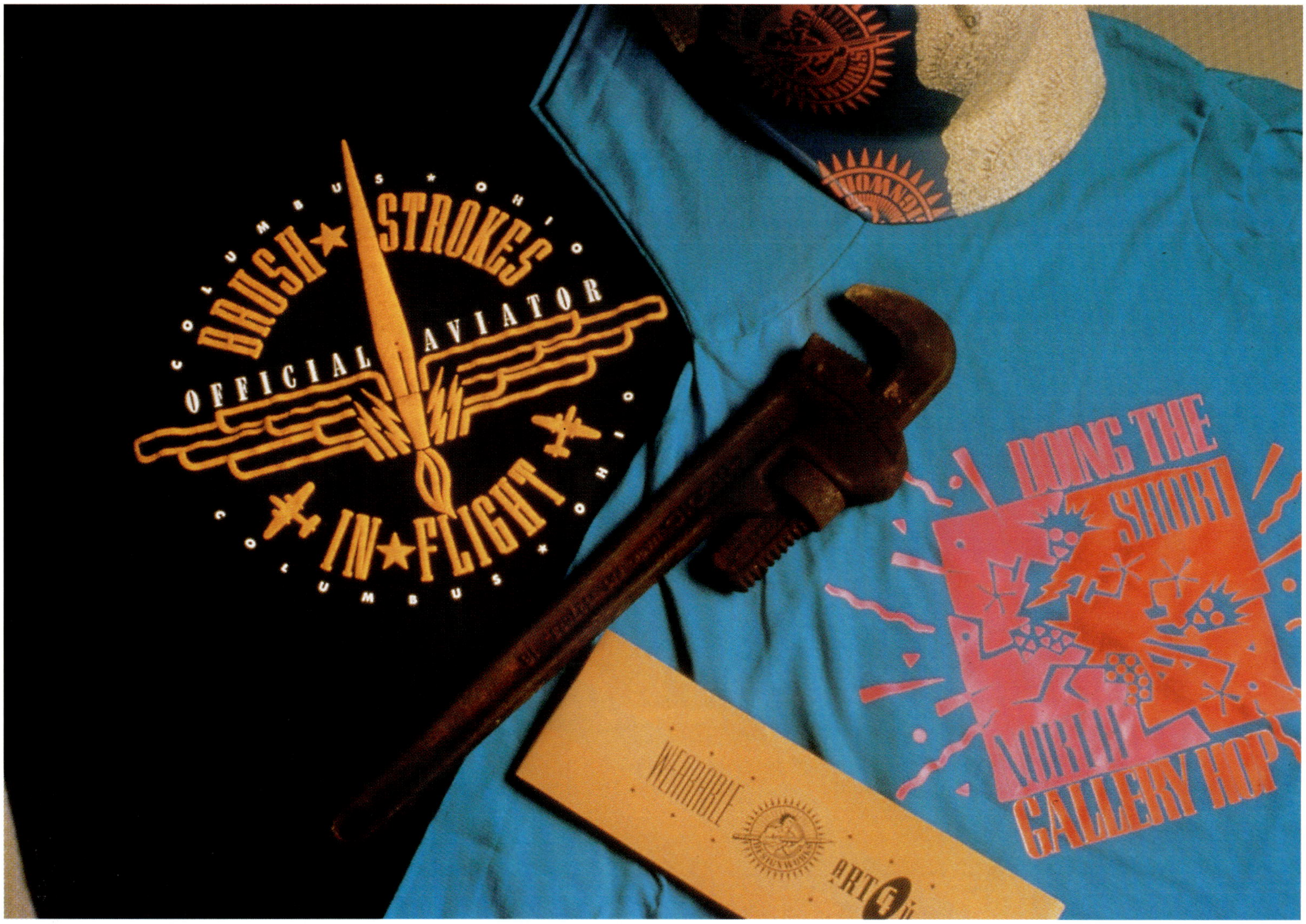

Design Firm: Rickabaugh Graphics
All Design: Eric Rickabaugh
Illustrators: Eric Rickabaugh, Tony Meuser
Client: Rickabaugh Graphics/Design Works
Purpose or Occasion: Retail
Number of Colors: 2
Two self-promotional T-shirts created for sale
in the studio's retail outlet, *Design Works*.

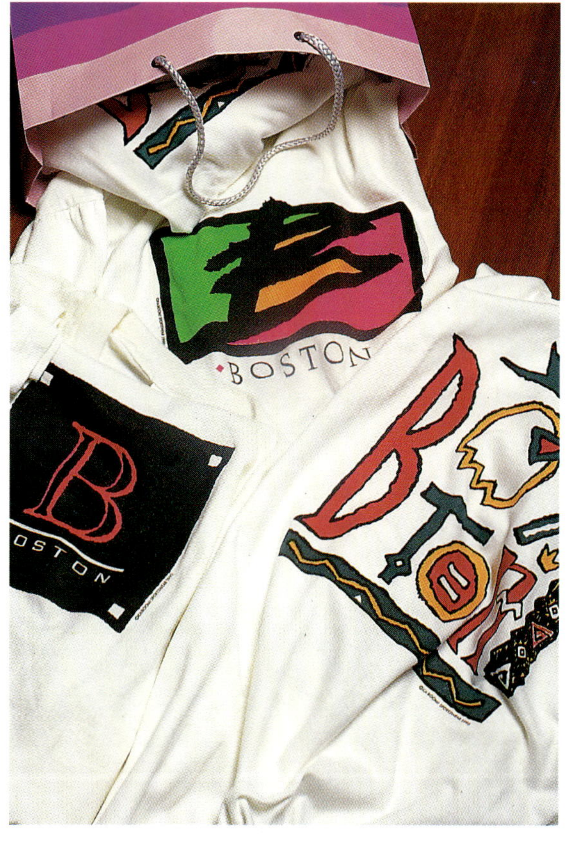

Design Firm: PandaMonium Designs
All Design: Raymond Yu
Client: Ka-Boom! Sportswear
Purpose or Occasion: Retail
Number of Colors: 5
A variety of T-shirts designed for retail sale
targeted at the tourism market.

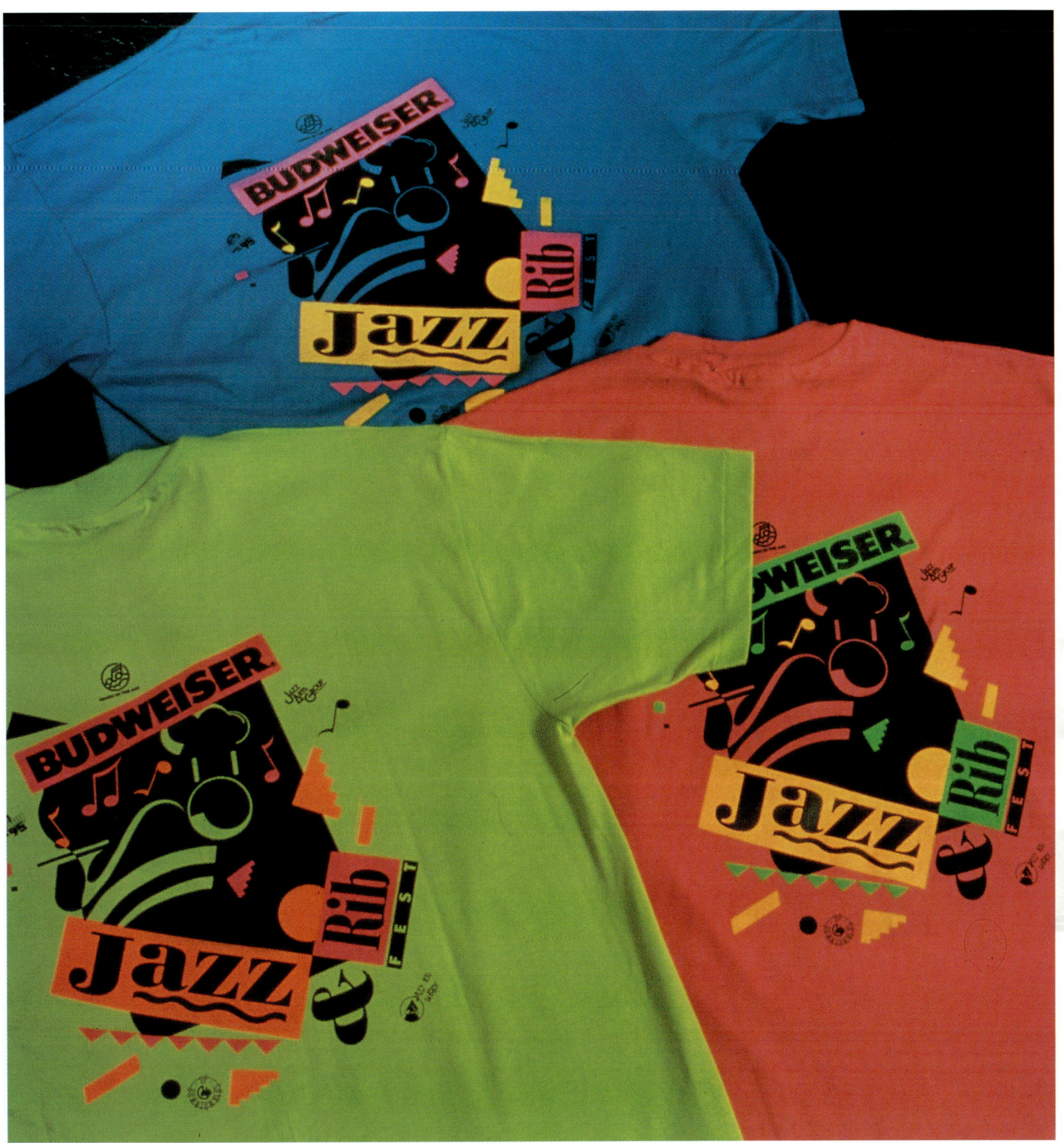

Design Firm: Rickabaugh Graphics
All Design: Mark Krumel
Client: City of Columbus—Recreation & Parks Department
Purpose or Occasion: Jazz & Rib Festival
Number of Colors: 3

The festival logo was broken apart to create some movement and energy. The shirts were sold to raise money for the Recreation and Parks Department and to create awareness.

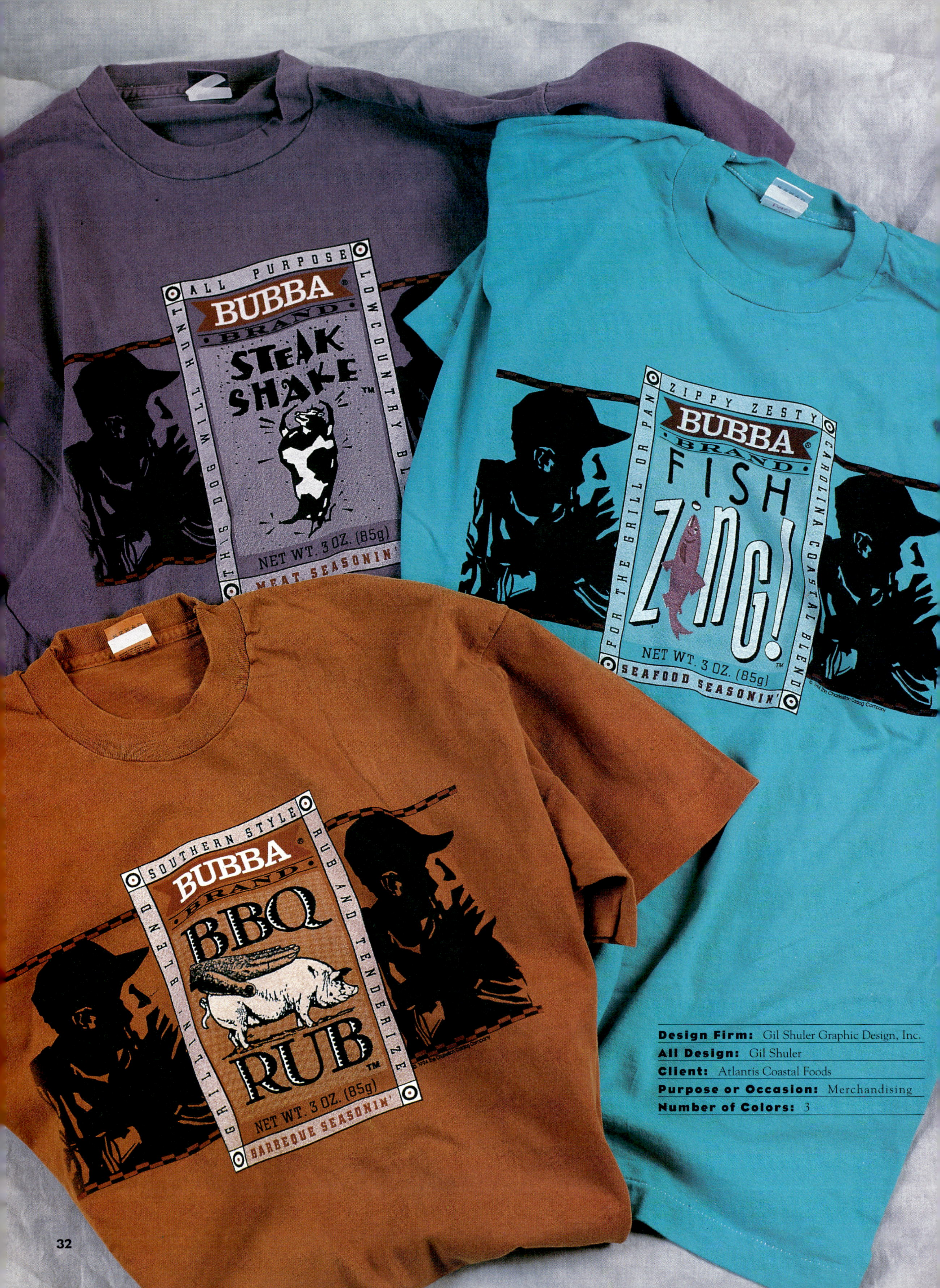

Design Firm: Gil Shuler Graphic Design, Inc.
All Design: Gil Shuler
Client: Atlantis Coastal Foods
Purpose or Occasion: Merchandising
Number of Colors: 3

Design Firm: ZEDWEAR
All Design: John Klaja
Client: ZEDWEAR
Purpose or Occasion: Retail
Number of Colors: 2

The *Champion Breed* emblem was printed on micro-stripe T-shirts and is part of the design company's dalmatian-inspired sportswear.

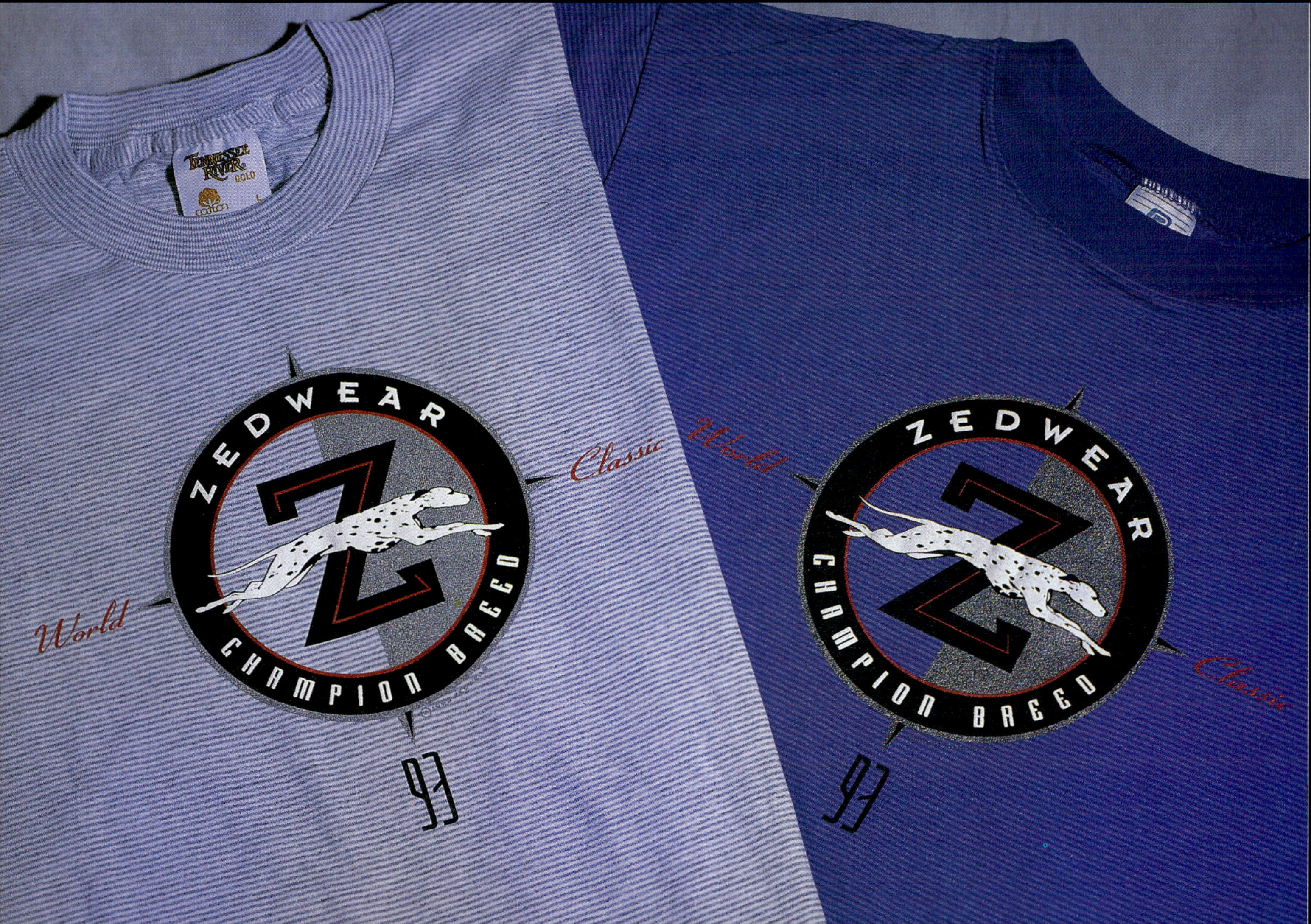

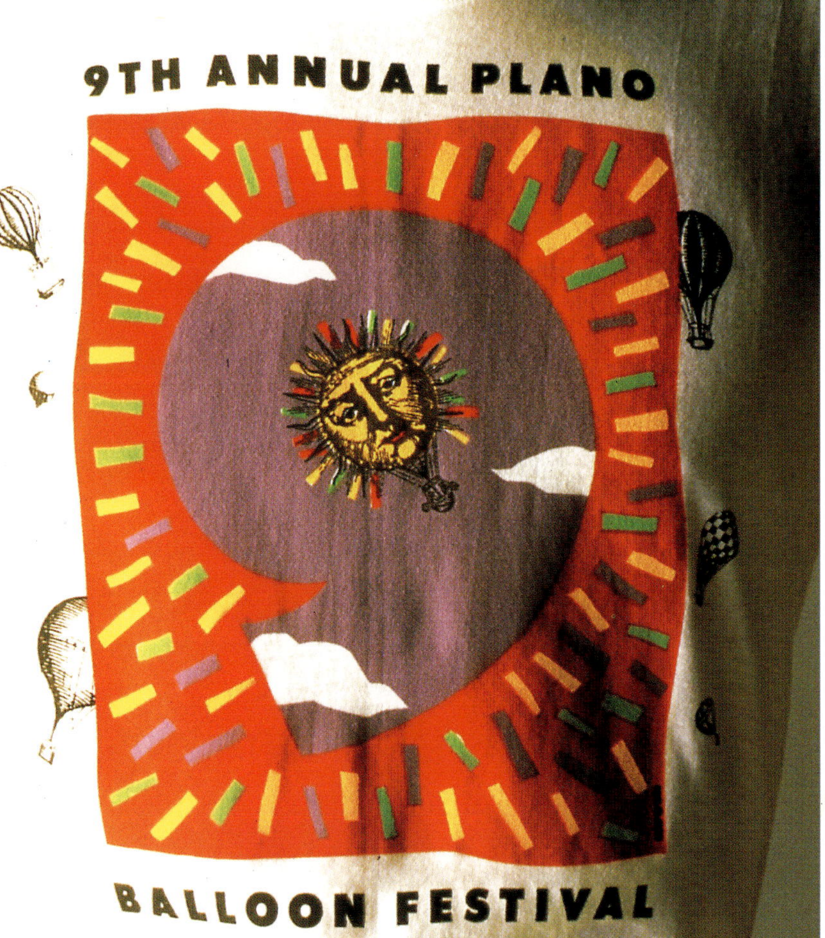

Design Firm: SullivanPerkins
Art Directors: Ron Sullivan, Art Garcia
Designer: Art Garcia
Client: Plano Balloon Festival Committee
Purpose or Occasion: Ninth annual Plano Balloon Festival
Number of Colors: 5

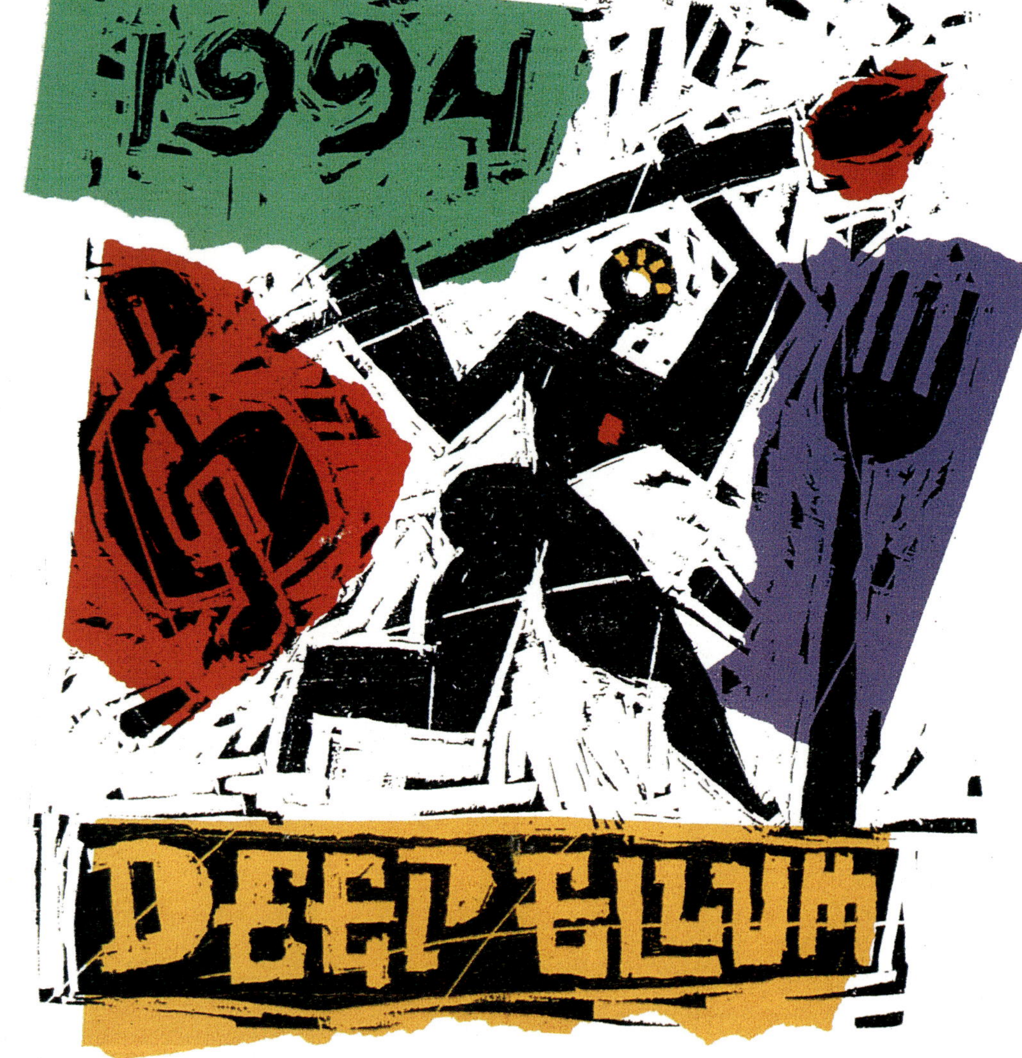

Design Firm: John Evans Design
All Design: John Evans
Client: Deep Ellum Association
Purpose or Occasion: Fund-raiser
Number of Colors: 6

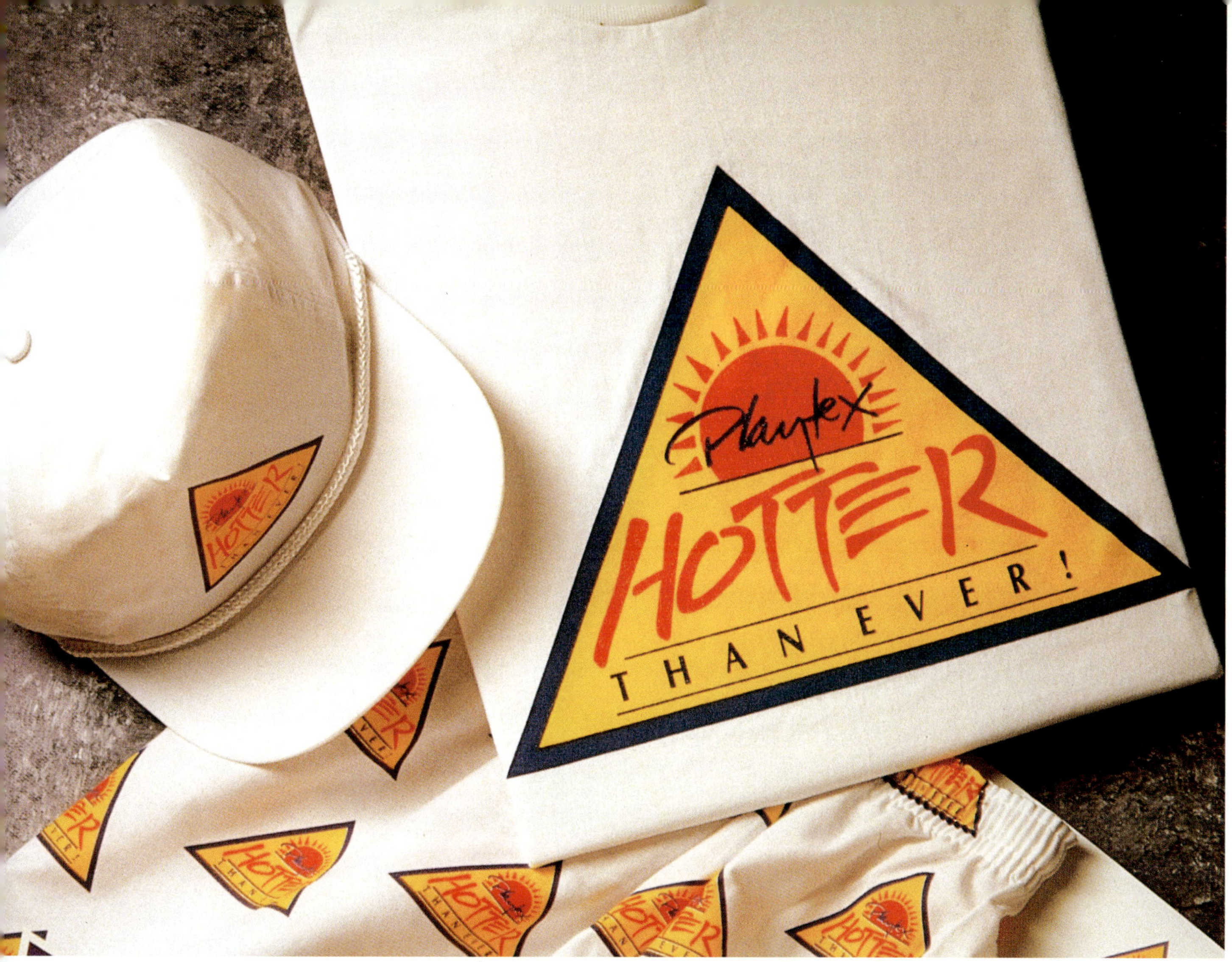

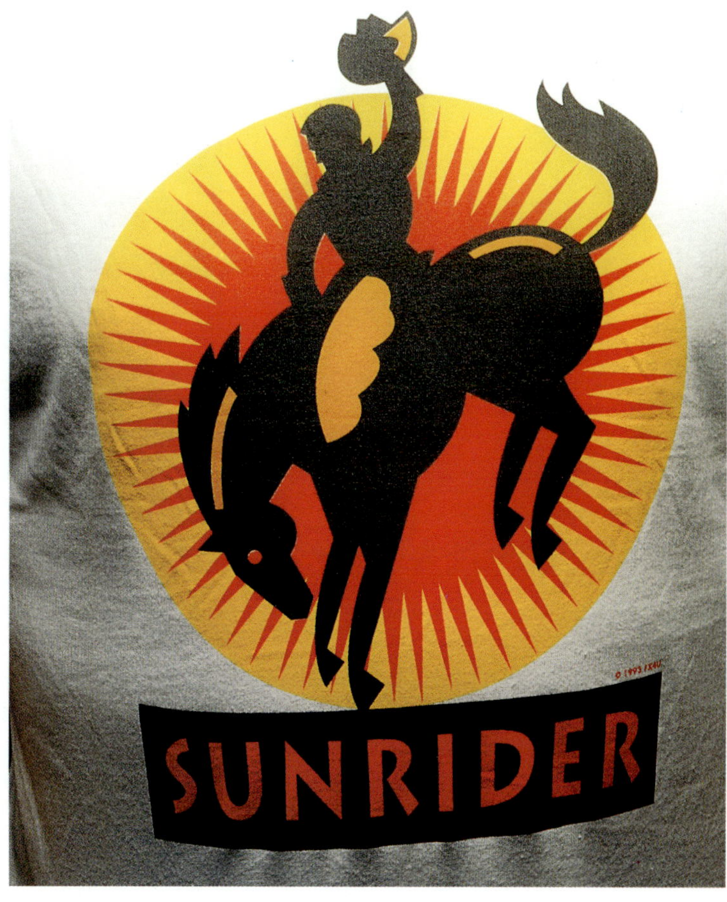

▲

Design Firm: Baldino Design
All Design: Patt Baldino
Client: Playtex
Purpose or Occasion: Promotion
Number of Colors: 3
T-shirts were created as promotional pieces for
sales meetings which took place in Acapulco.

▶

Design Firm: Lehner & Whyte
Art Directors: Donna Lehner, Hugh Whyte
Designers: Hugh Whyte, Donna Lehner
Illustrator: Hugh Whyte
Client: FX4U
Purpose or Occasion: Retail
Number of Colors: 3

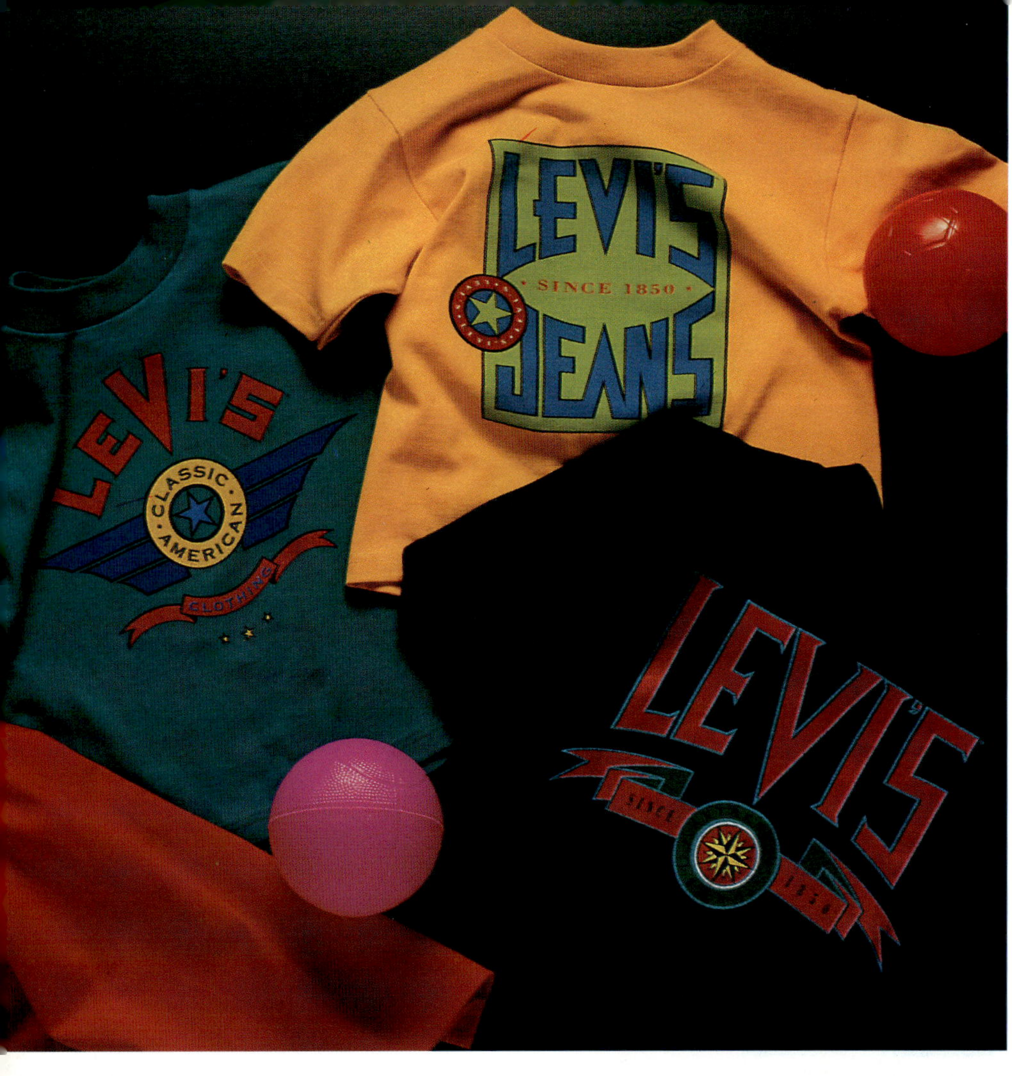

◄

Design Firm: Sackett Design
Art Director: Mark Sackett
Designers: Mark Sackett, Wayne Sakamoto
Client: Levi Strauss & Co.—*Little Levi's*
Purpose or Occasion: Promotion
Number of Colors: 2 and 3

These T-shirts promote *Little Levi's*, a new line of clothing for children aged 4-6.

▶

Design Firm: Sackett Design
All Design: Mark Sackett
Client: Mervyn's IMI Apparel
Purpose or Occasion: Promotion
Number of Colors: 3 and 4

These T-shirts promote a new line of apparel for young girls.

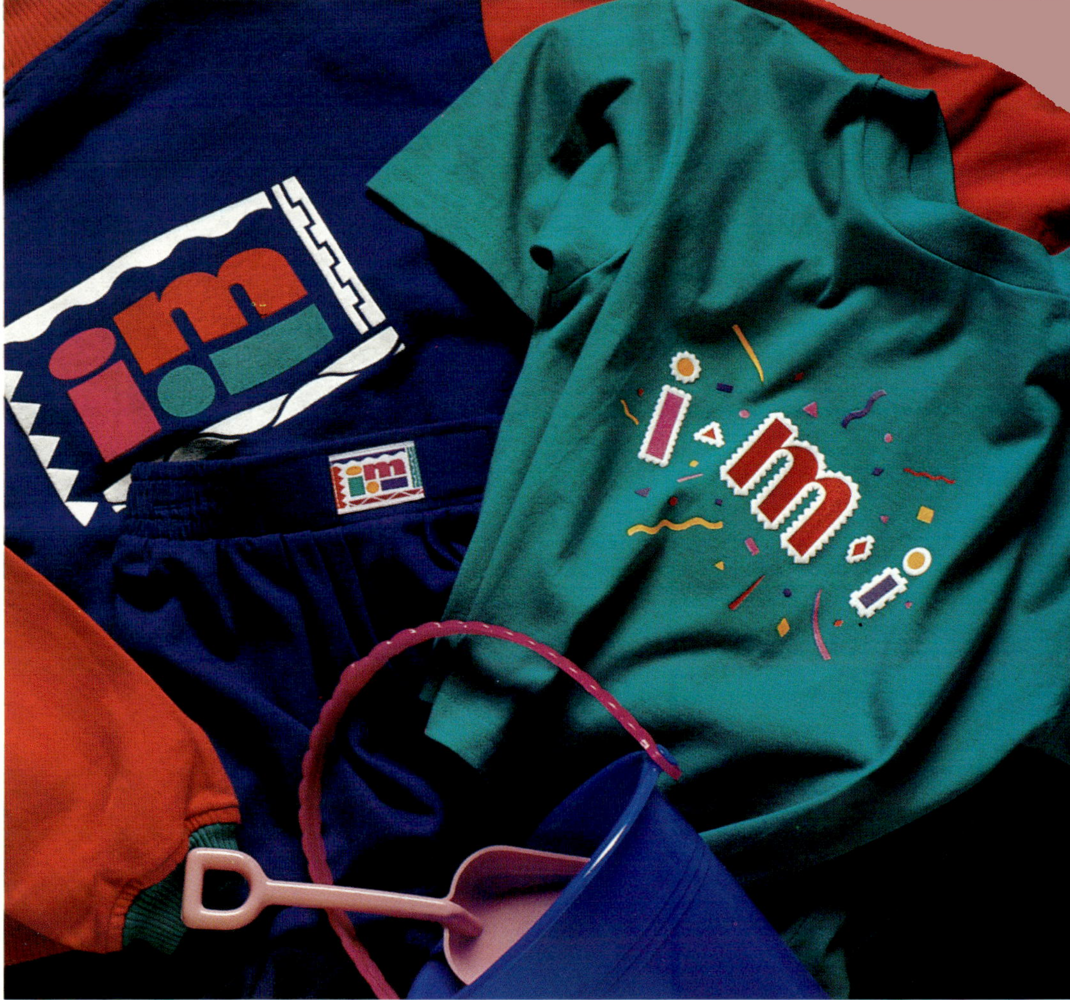

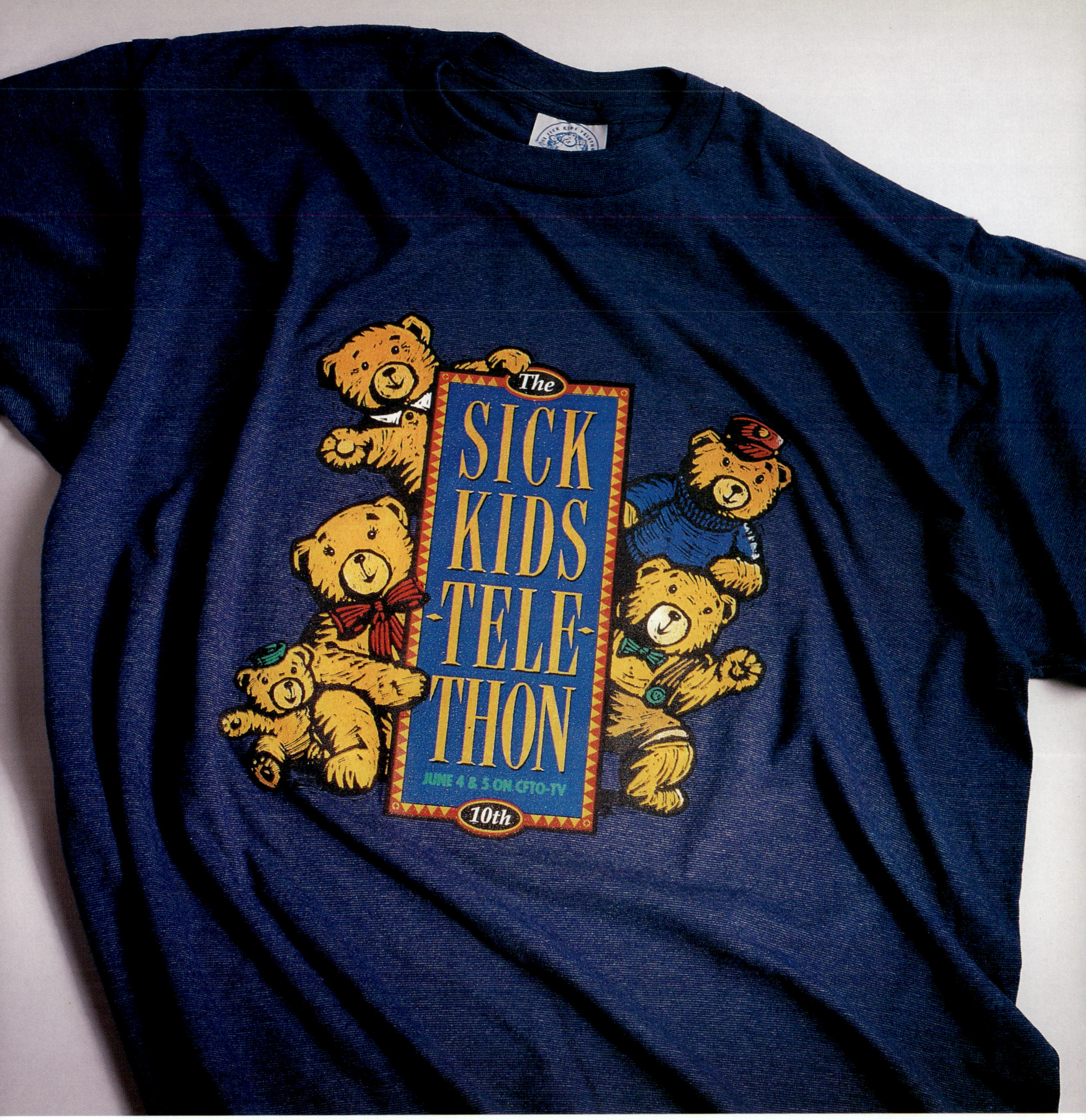

Design Firm: The Riordon Design Group, Inc.
Art Director: Ric Riordon
Illustrator: Dan Wheaton
Client: Toronto Sick Kids Hospital
Purpose or Occasion: CFTO-TV telethon
Number of Colors: 7

Produced to give-away to telethon contributors, this T-shirt helped raise funds for Sick Kids Hospital.

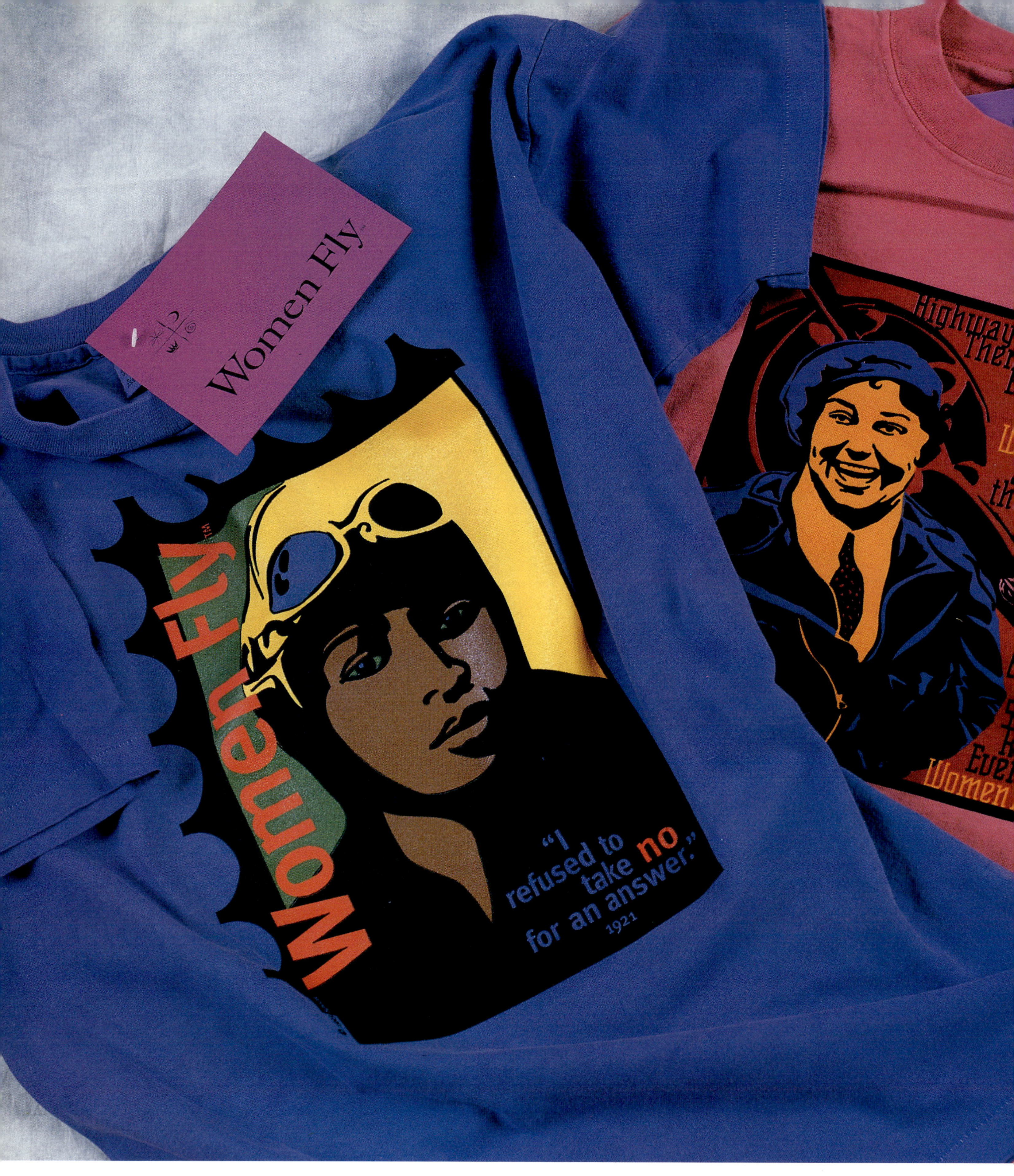

Women Fly.
Women Fly
"I refused to take no for an answer."
1921
Highway
Them
Ever
Women

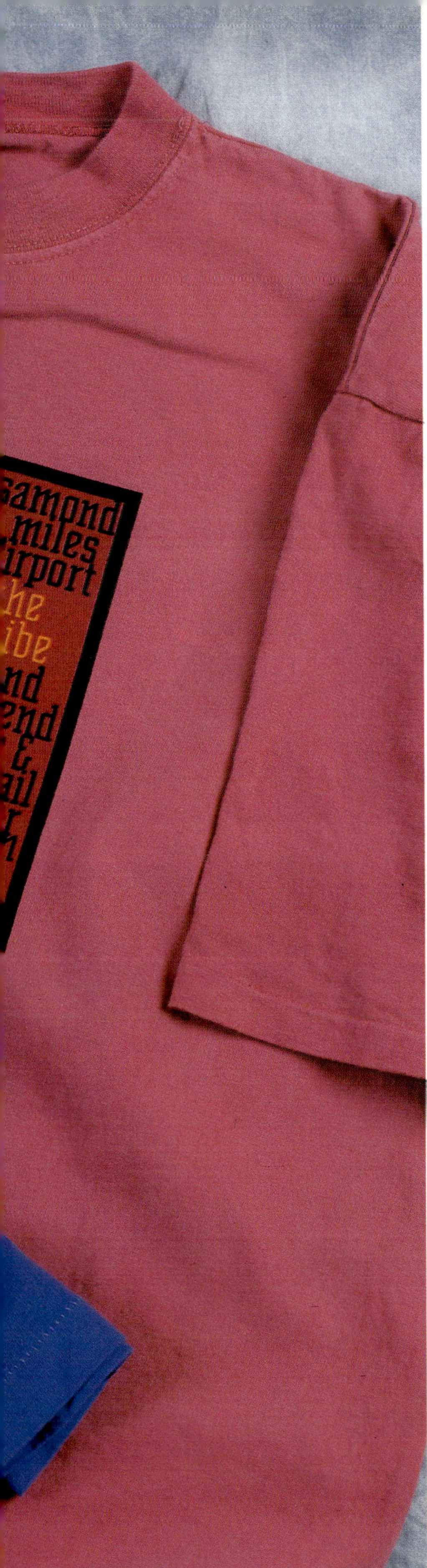

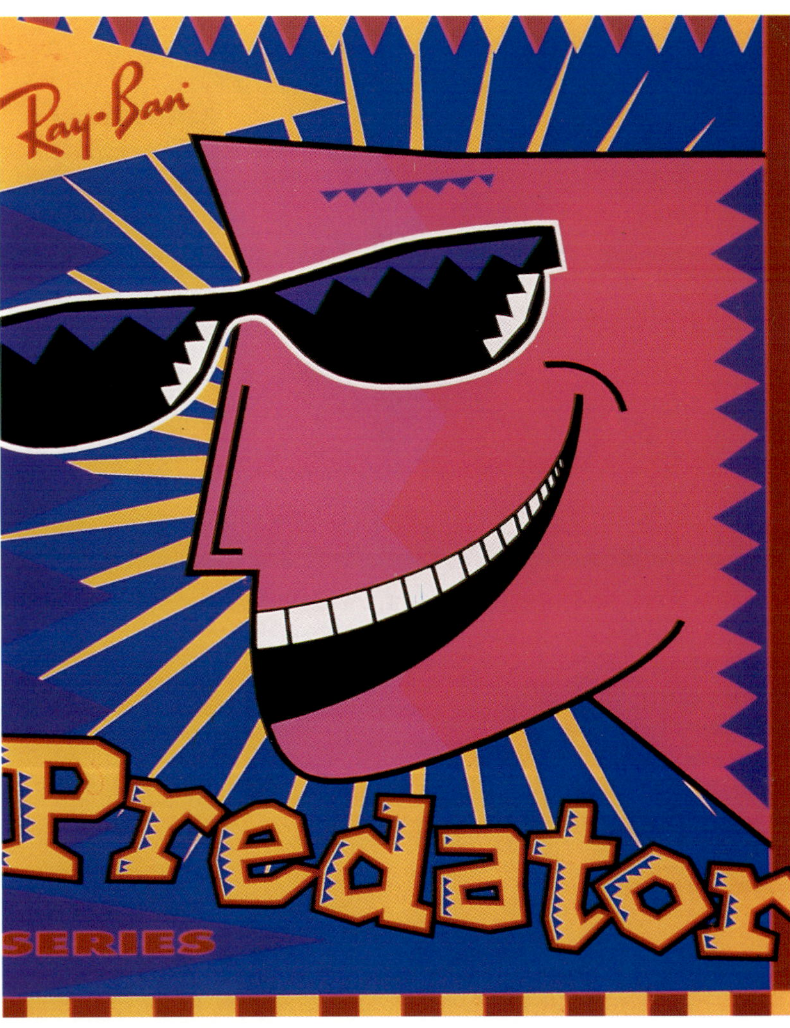

▲

Design Firm: Elton Ward Design
All Design: Jason Dominiak
Client: Ray Ban
Purpose or Occasion: Promotional give-away
Number of Colors: 4

T-shirt graphic for *Predator* series of sunglasses.

▲

Design Firm: Speak, Inc.
All Design: Amy Cahill, Chele Isaac
Client: Speak, Inc.
Purpose or Occasion: Retail

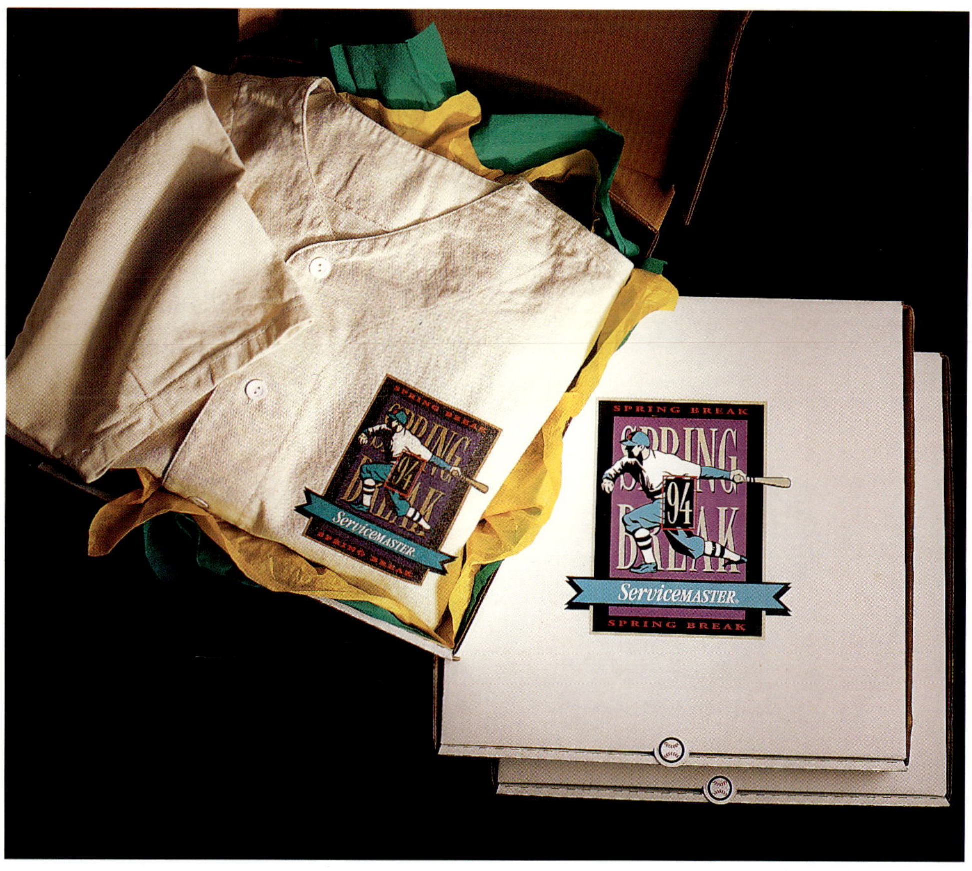

Design Firm: The Riordon Design Group, Inc.

Art Director: Ric Riordon

Designer: Dan Wheaton

Illustrator: Dan Wheaton

Client: Service Master Canada

Purpose or Occasion: Corporate performance premium

Number of Colors: 7

▶

Design Firm: Joan C. Hollingsworth

All Design: Joan C. Hollingsworth

Client: Joan C. Hollingsworth

Purpose or Occasion: Gift for artist's grandchildren

Number of Colors: 4

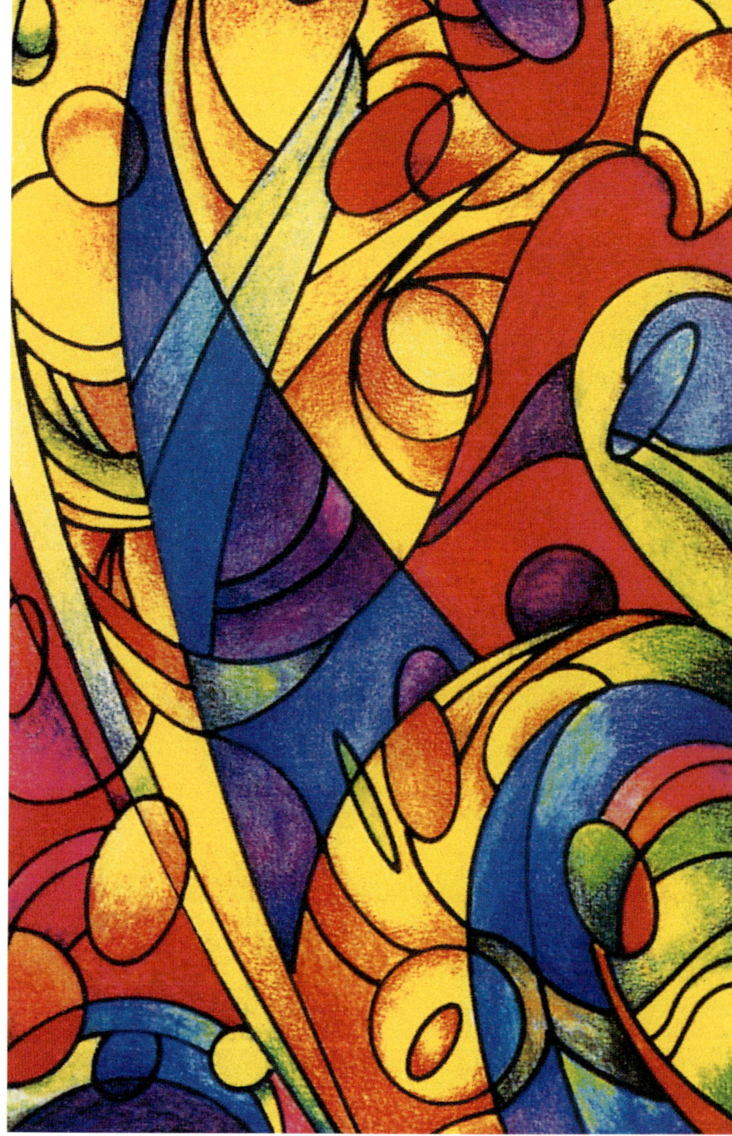

Design Firm: Ken Brown Designs
Designer: Ken Brown
Purpose or Occasion: Retail
Number of Colors: 6

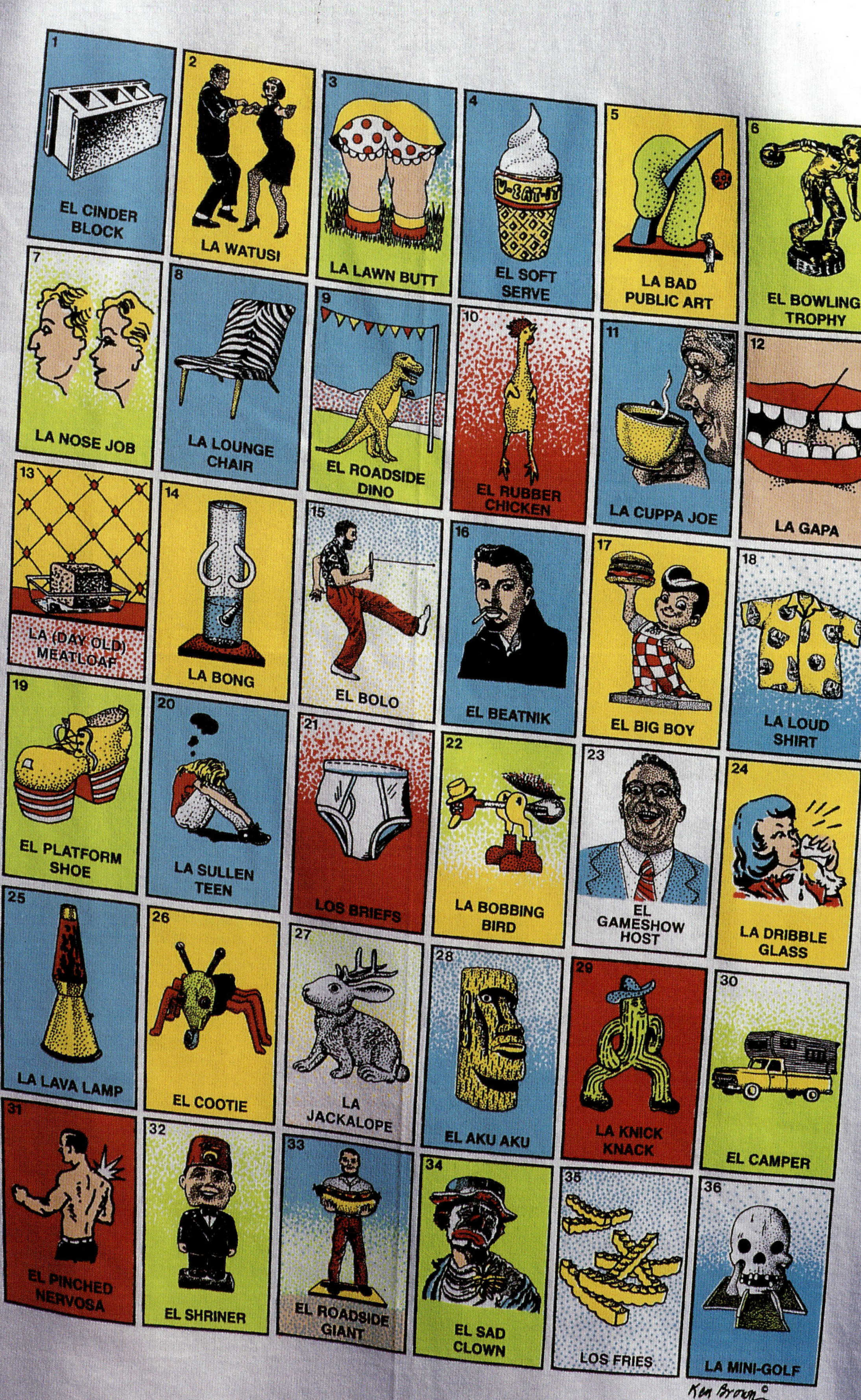

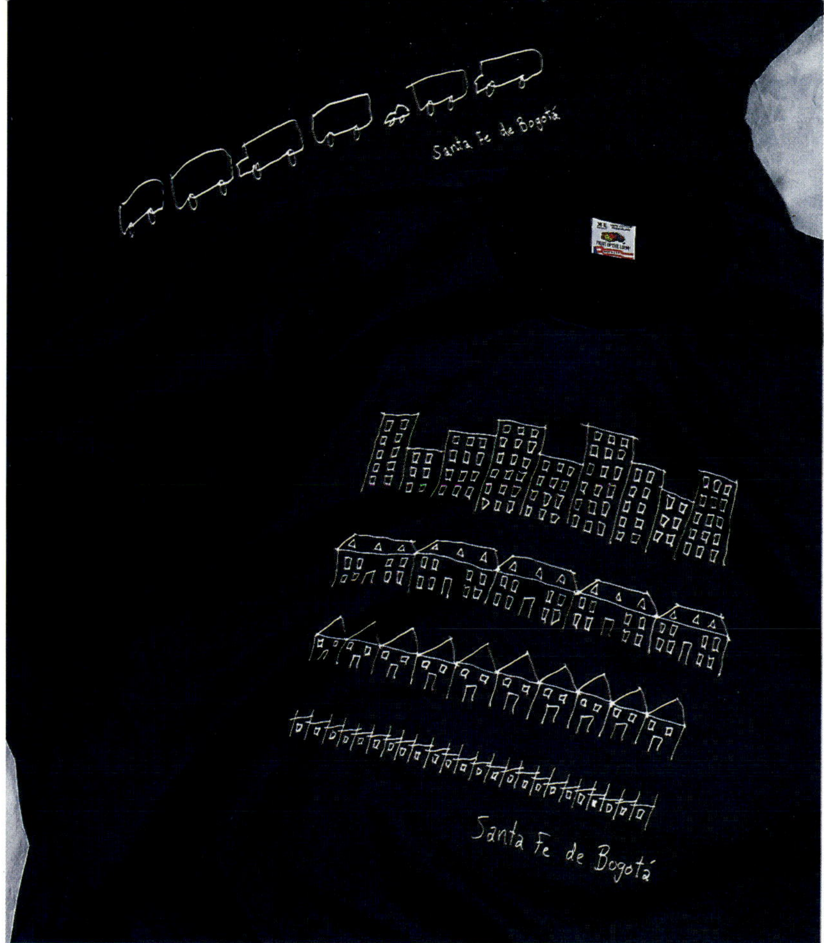

◄

Design Firm: Ricardo Beron Castro
All Design: Ricardo Beron Castro
Purpose or Occasion: Retail
Number of Colors: 1

▼

Design Firm: The Design Company
Art Director: Marcia Romanuck
Designers: Marcia Romanuck, Denise Pickering
Client: The Design Company
Purpose or Occasion: Christmas gift
Number of Colors: 1

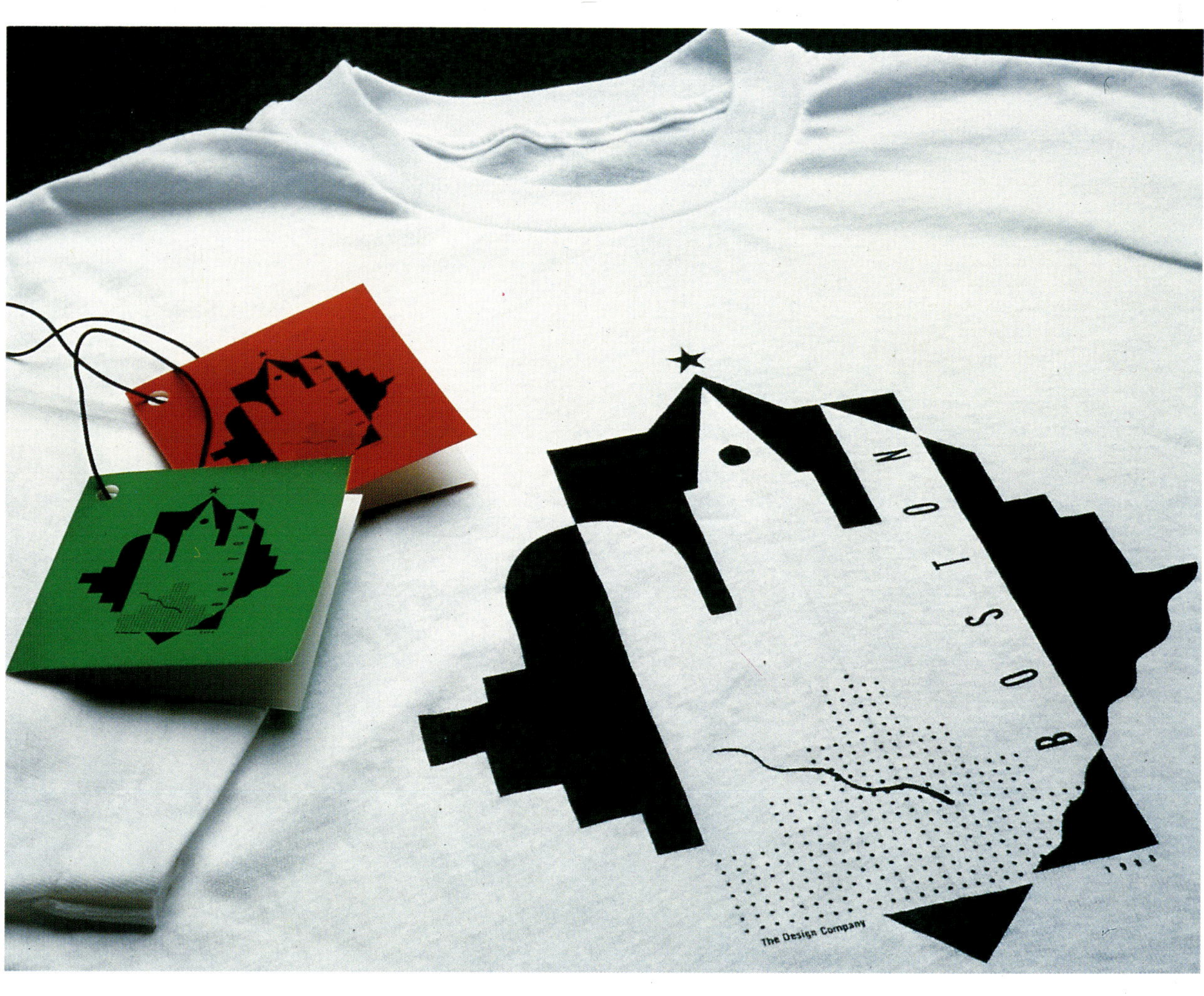

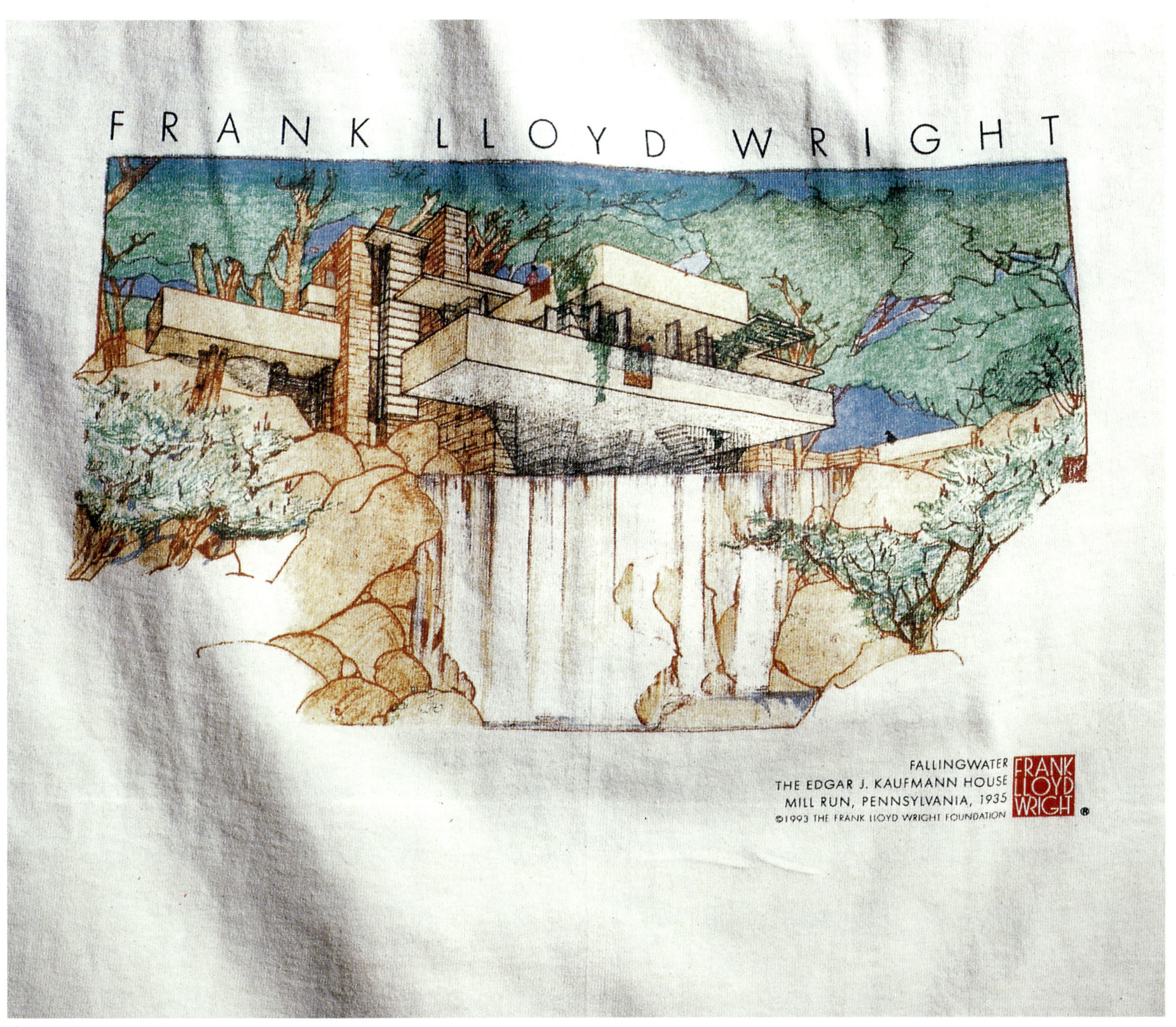

Design Firm: Fotofolio/Mirror Image, Inc.

Art Director: Ron Schick

Designer: Frank Lloyd Wright

Client: Fotofolio

Purpose or Occasion: Retail

Number of Colors: 7

Separations/Printing: Mirror Image, Inc./
Judy Winters

Design Firm: Sommese Design
All Design: Lanny Sommese
Client: Joel Confer Softball Team
Purpose or Occasion: Team jersey
Number of Colors: 2

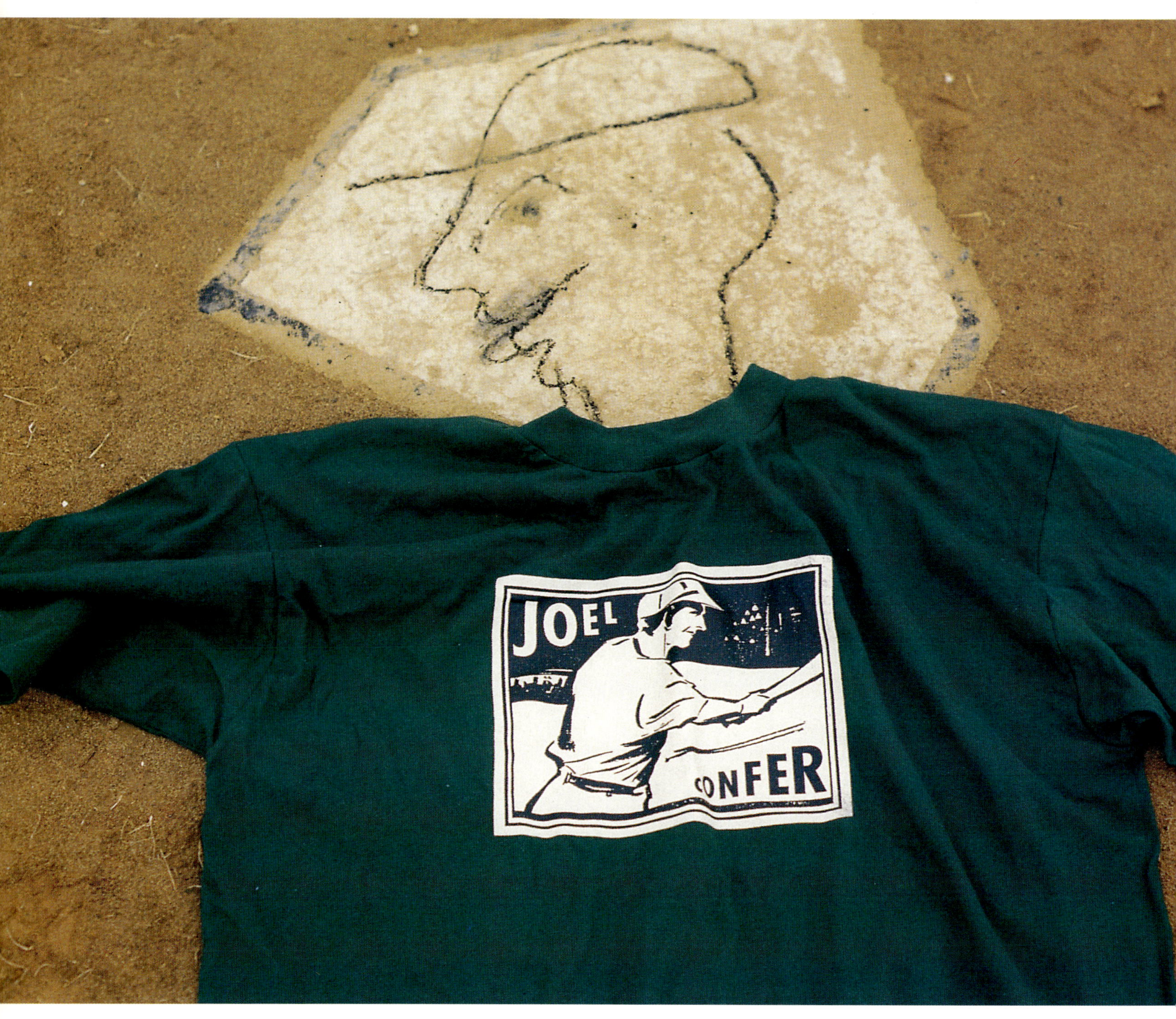

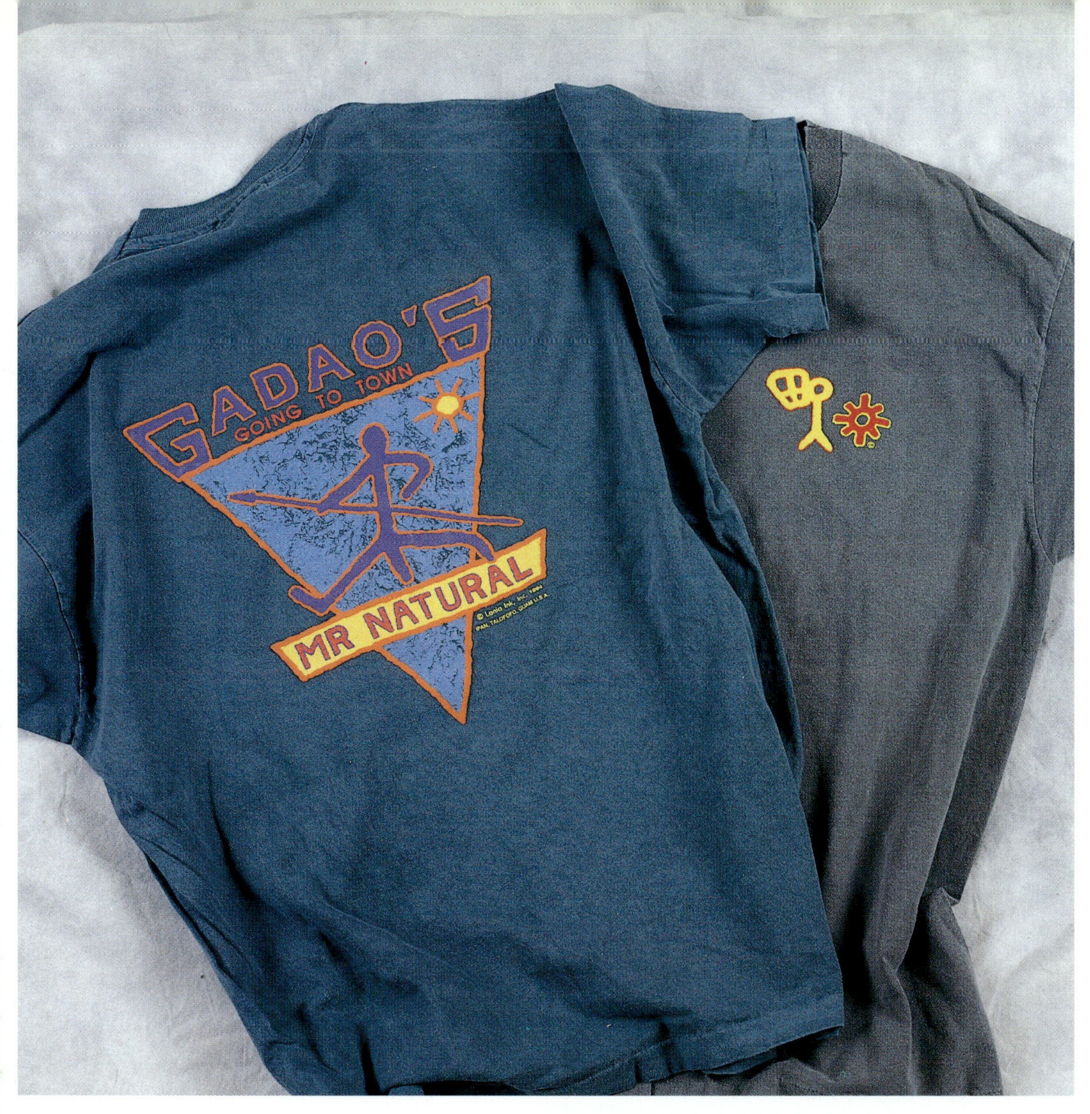

◄

Design Firm: Lania Ink, Inc.
All Design: John R. Patton
Client: Lania Ink, Inc.
Purpose or Occasion: Cultural theme awareness
Number of Colors: 6
The petroglyphs and pictographs that decorate this T-shirt are a permanent record of the traditions and the roots of image-making in the Marianas Islands.

▶

Design Firm: Sommese Design
All Design: Lanny Sommese
Client: Joel Confer Softball Team
Purpose or Occasion: Team jersey
Number of Colors: 2

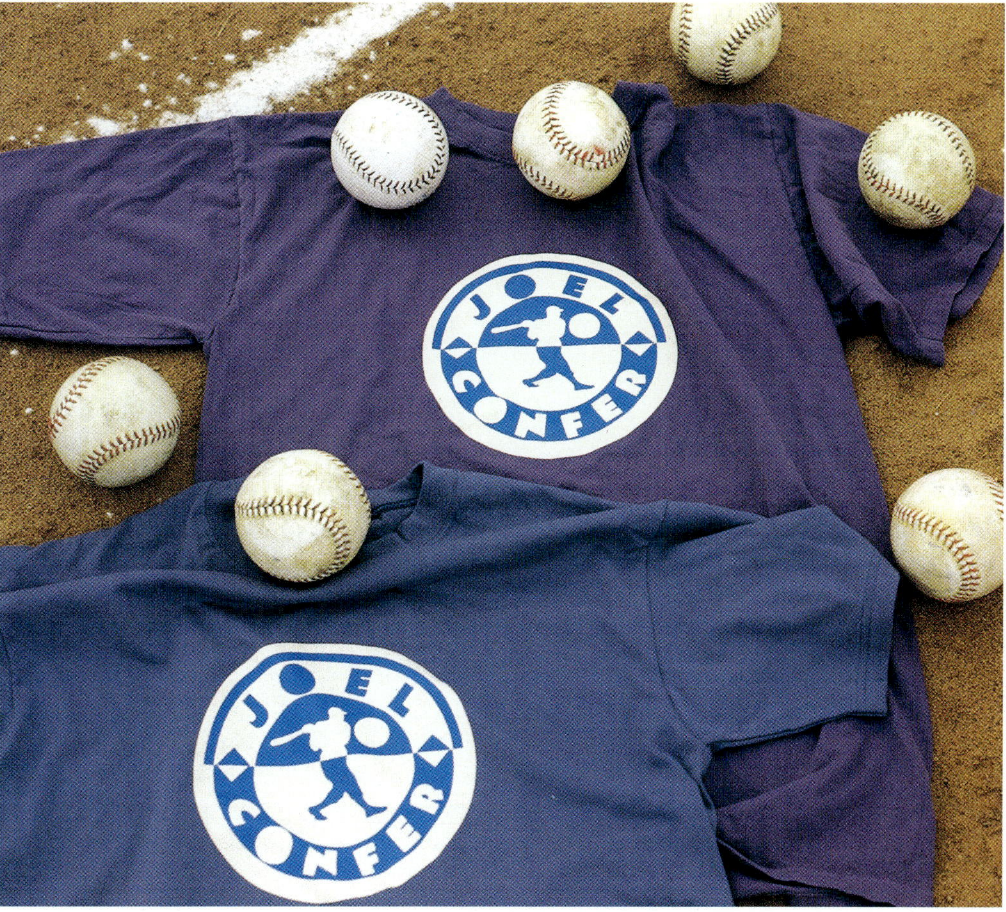

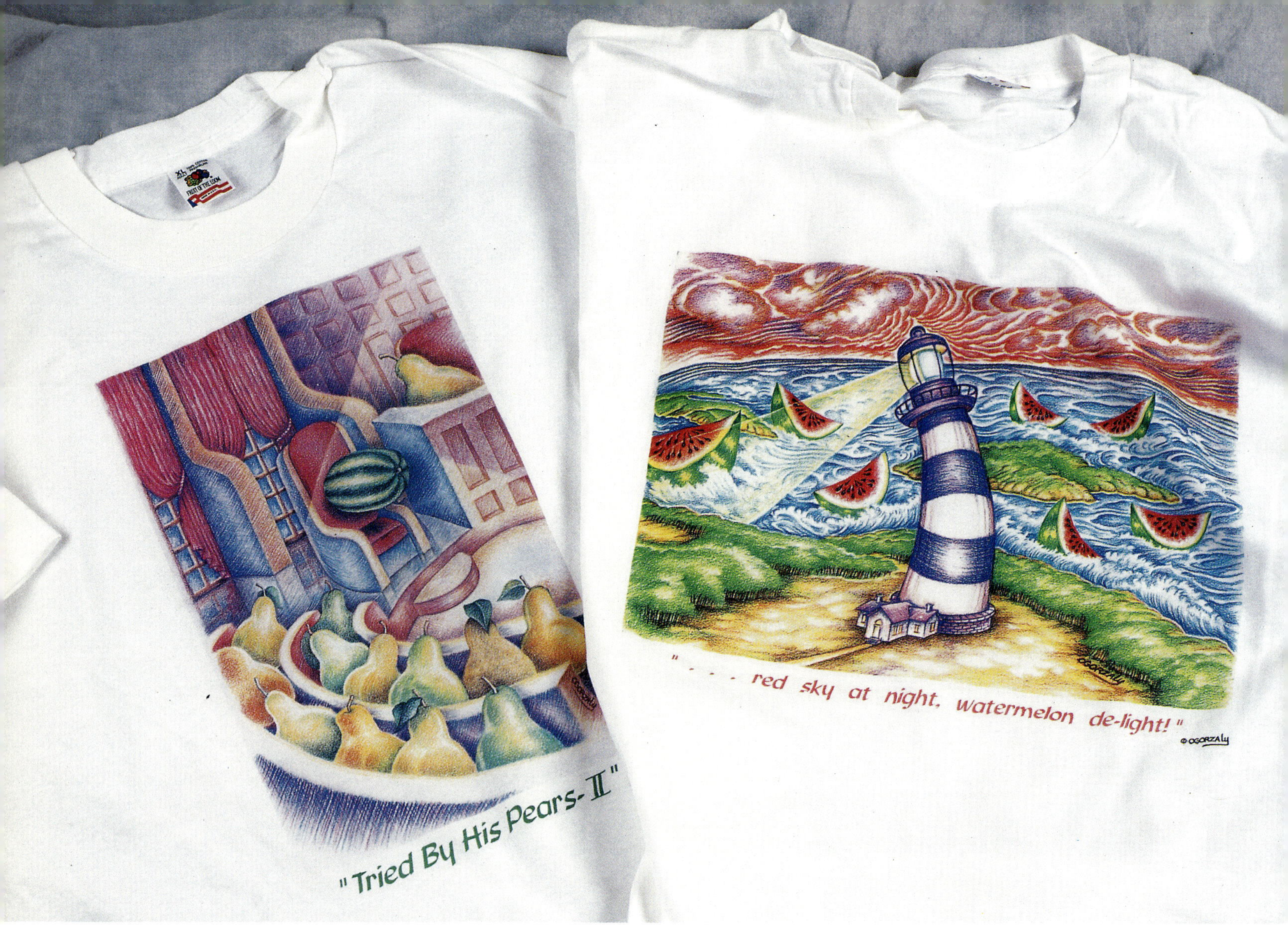

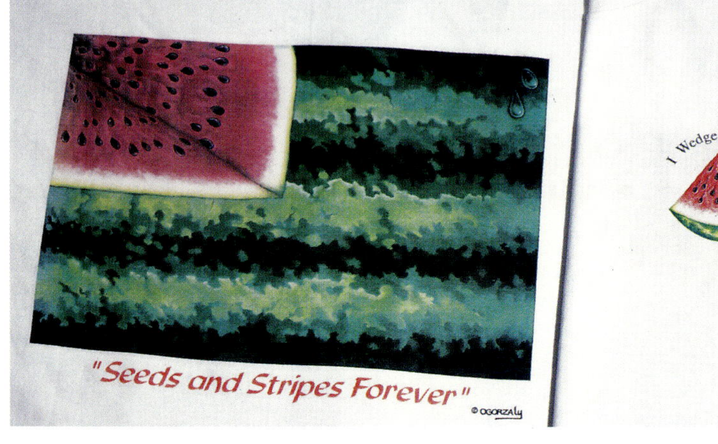

▲

Design Firm: Ogre's Alley
All Design: David J. Ogorzaly
Client: Friends, relatives, and business associates
Purpose or Occasion: Retail

The original artwork for this T-shirt was designed using colored pencils. The designer prints his watermelon art on *Fruit of the Loom* products, using laser color copier heat transfer.

▲

Design Firm: Ogre's Alley
All Design: David J. Ogorzaly
Client: Friends, relatives, and business associates
Purpose or Occasion: Retail

"I Wedge Allegiance/Seeds & Stripes Forever" fulfills the demand for having a two-sided T-shirt design. The "wedge" on the breast pocket makes viewers giggle a little—but the total concept comes to life when the watermelon flag is viewed on the back side of the T-shirt.

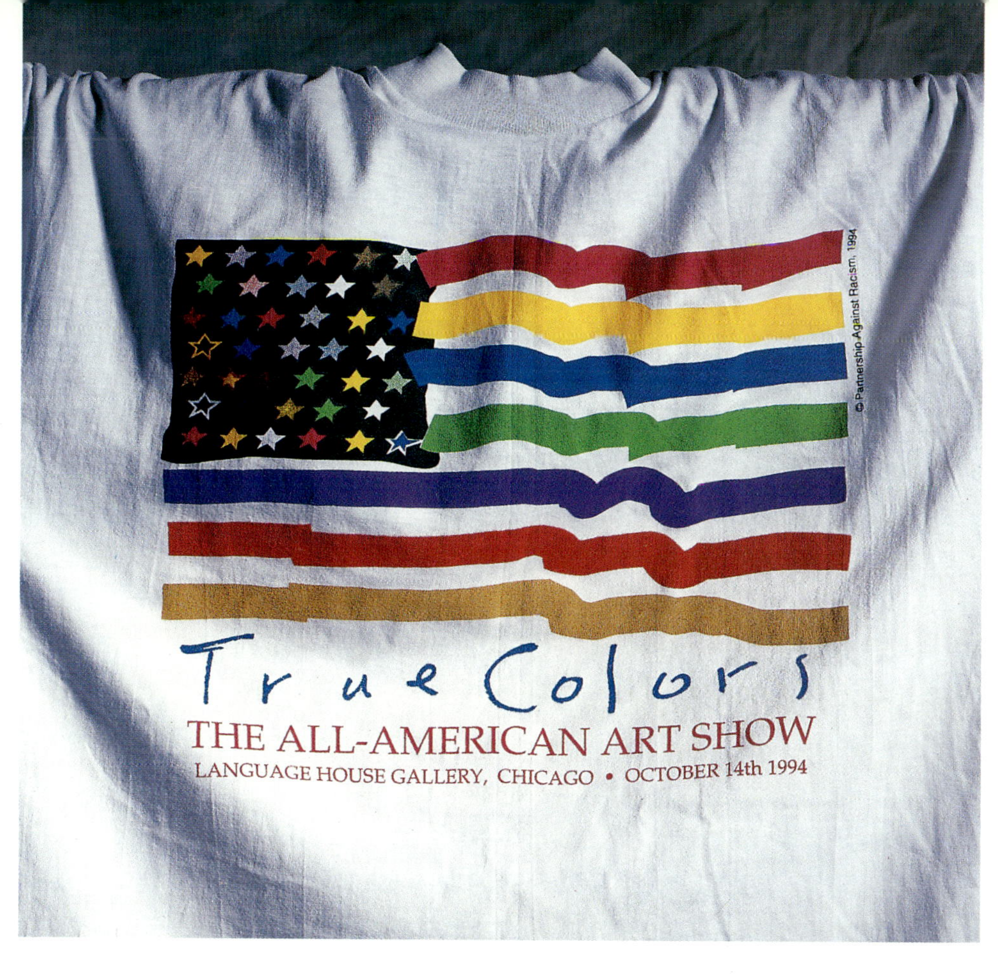

◀

Design Firm: Propaganda
Art Director: Jason Meadows
Designer: Lowell Thompson
Client: Partnership Against Racism
Purpose or Occasion: Promotion of an art show
Number of Colors: 6

▶

Design Firm: Alphawave Design
All Design: Douglas Dunebin
Client: Alphawave/Buck the System Foundation
Purpose or Occasion: Retail
Number of Colors: 4

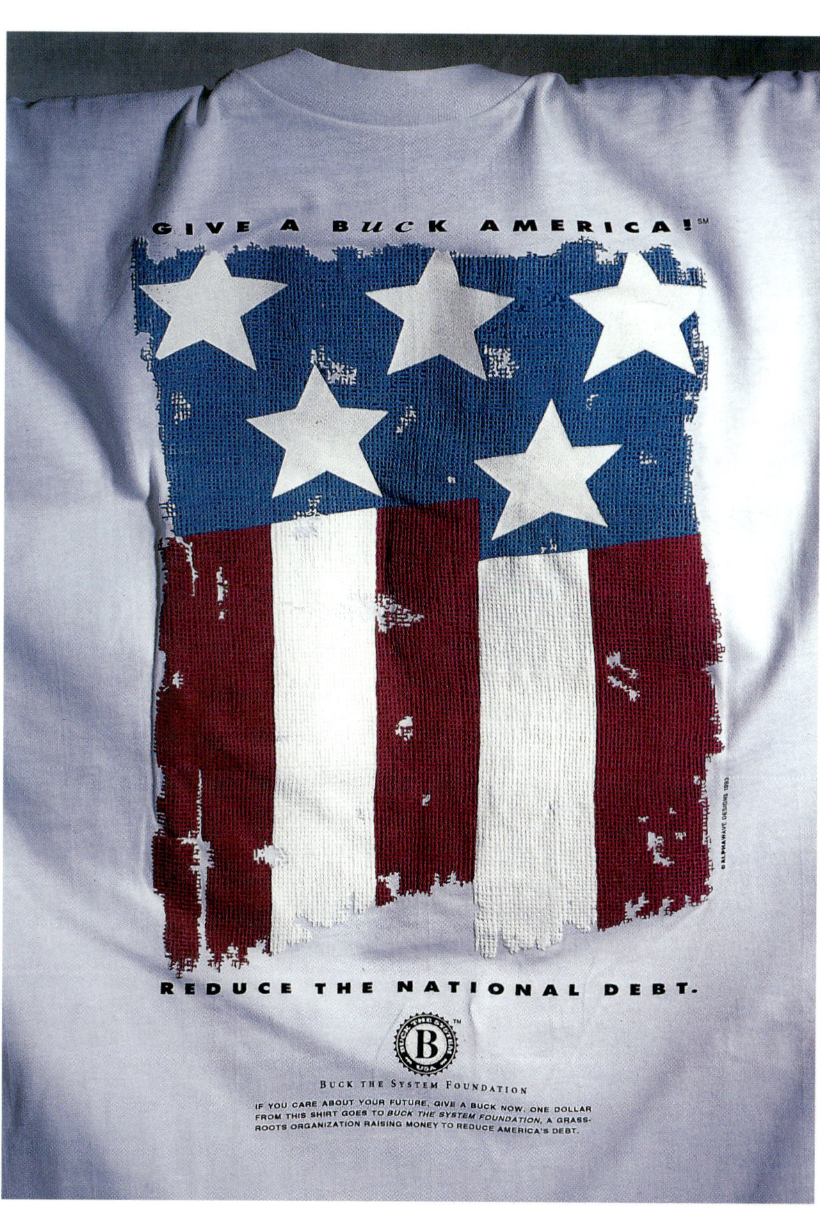

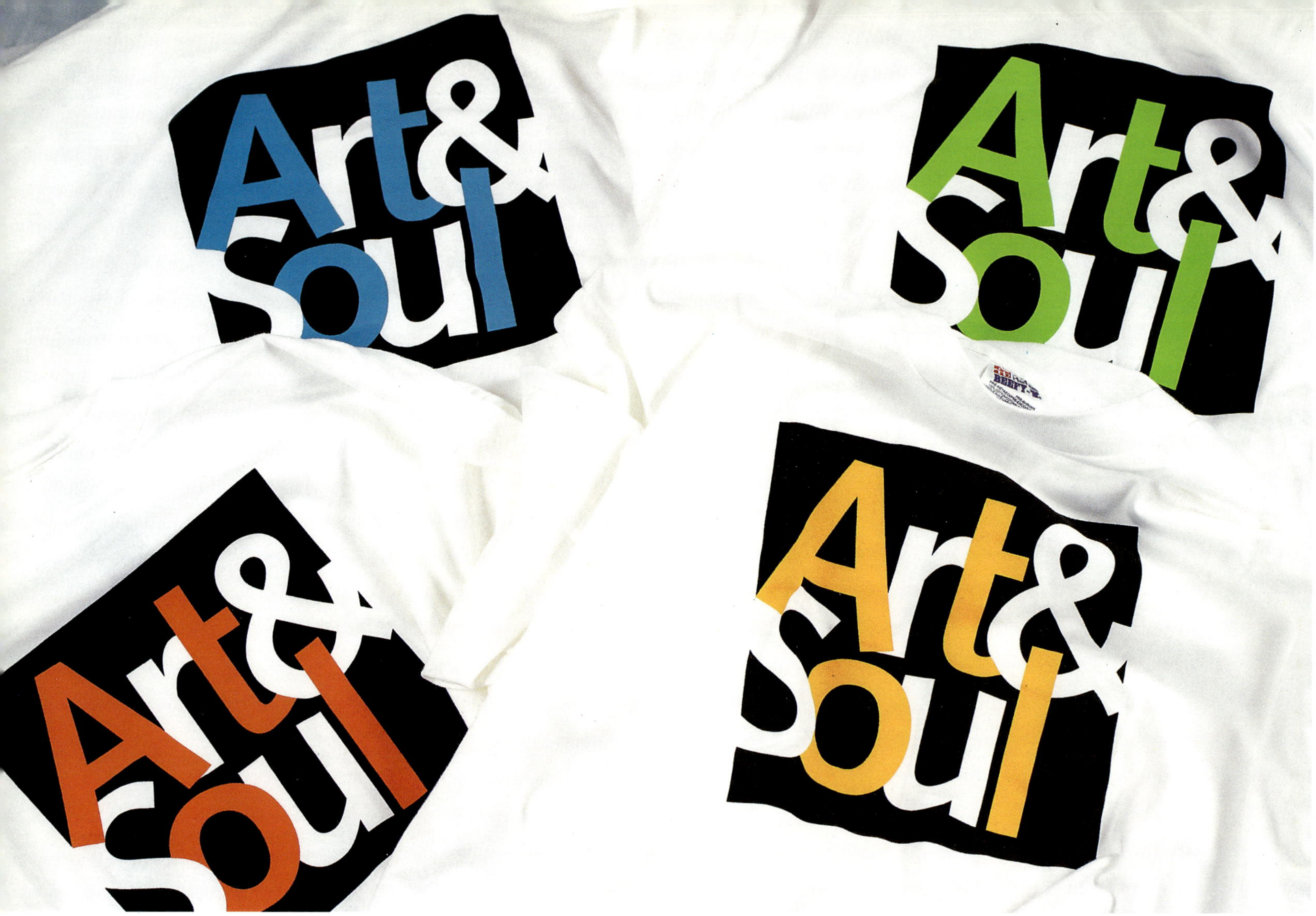

▲

Design Firm:	Mires Design, Inc.
Art Director:	John Ball
Designer:	John Ball
Production:	Miguel Perez
Client:	California Center for the Arts, Escondido
Purpose or Occasion:	Promotion
Number of Colors:	1

The T-shirt's *Art & Soul* logo promotes the grand
opening of the Center for Visual and Performing Arts.

▶

Design Firm:	Lee Reedy Design Associates
All Design:	Lee Reedy
Client:	MCI
Purpose or Occasion:	Employee incentive program
Number of Colors:	1

This oversized, knee-length shirt was used as a
promotional incentive to MCI's telemarketers.
The campaign theme was "Big" and all of the
pieces were oversized.

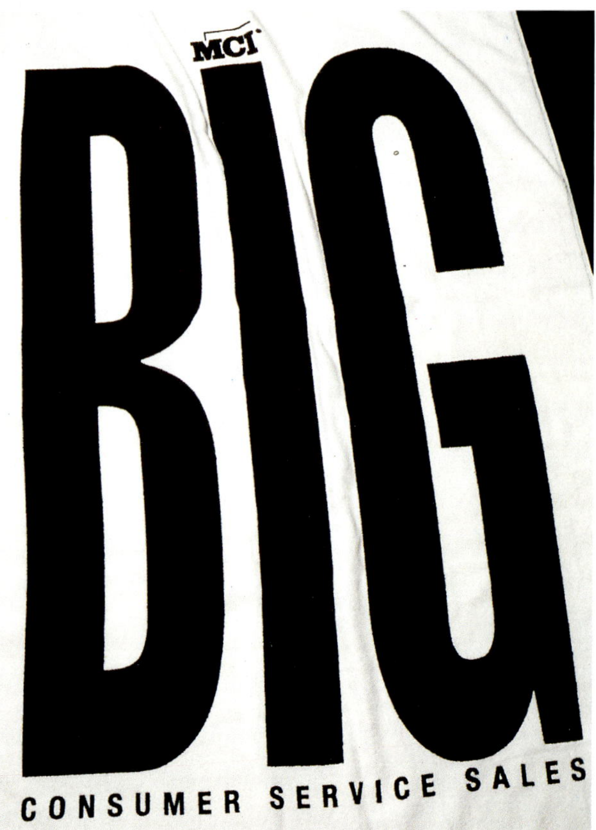

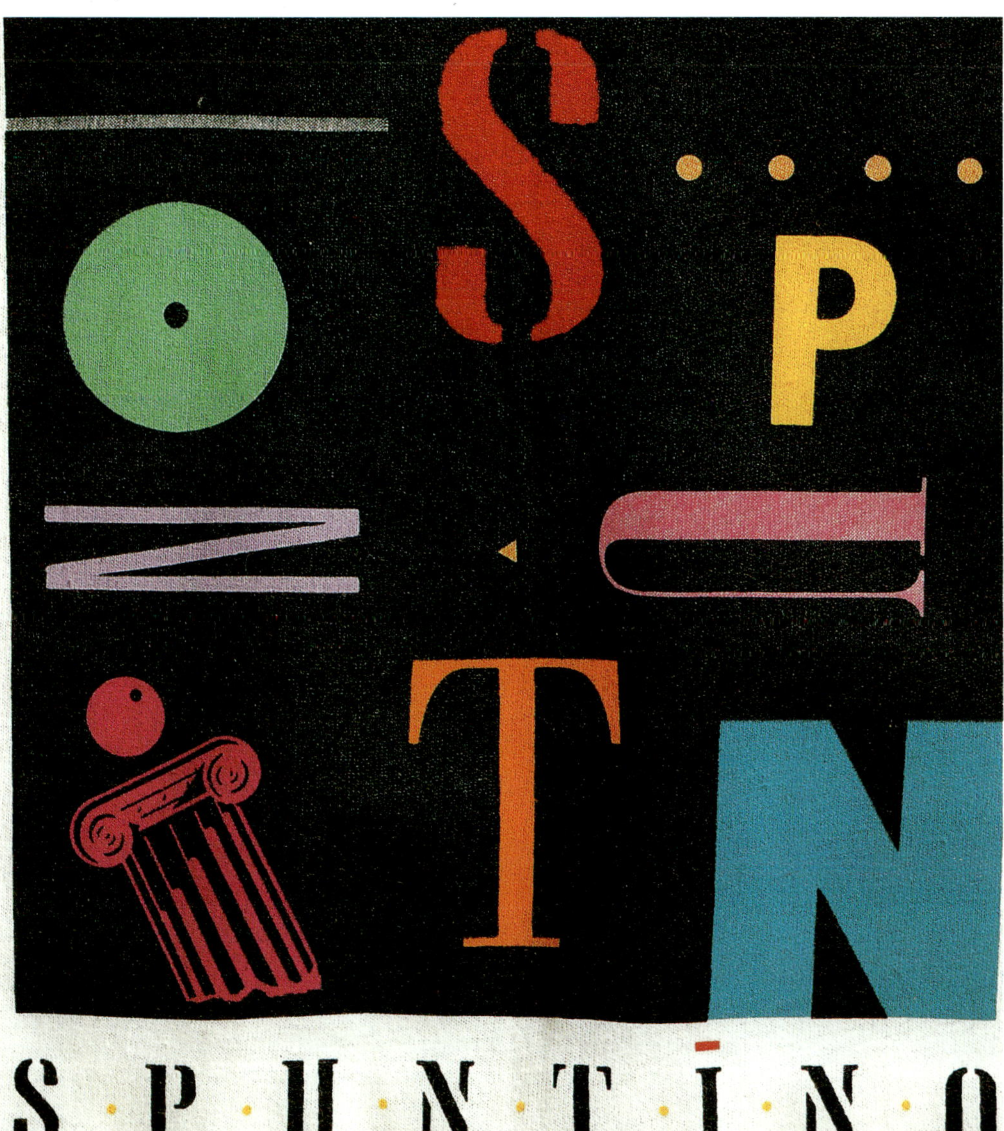

◀

Design Firm: Dyer/Mutchnick Group, Inc.
Art Director: Rod Dyer
Designer: Clive Piercy
Client: Spuntino Restaurant
Purpose or Occasion: Promotion
Number of Colors: 10

▶

Design Firm: Russell Leong Design
All Design: Russell K. Leong
Client: E-MU Systems
Purpose or Occasion: Promotion
Number of Colors: 4

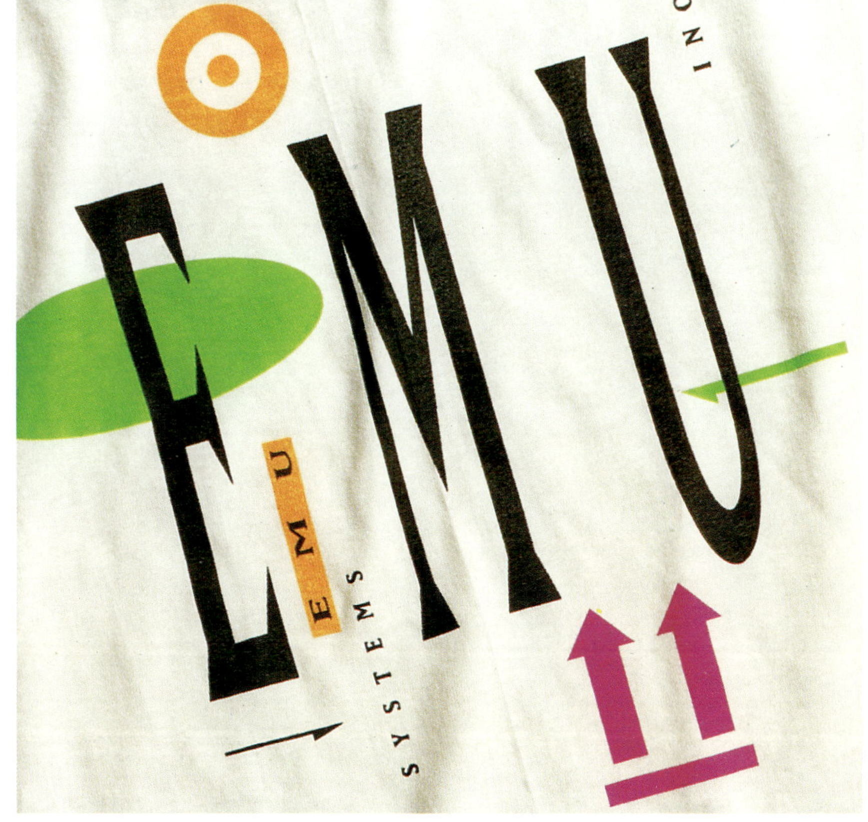

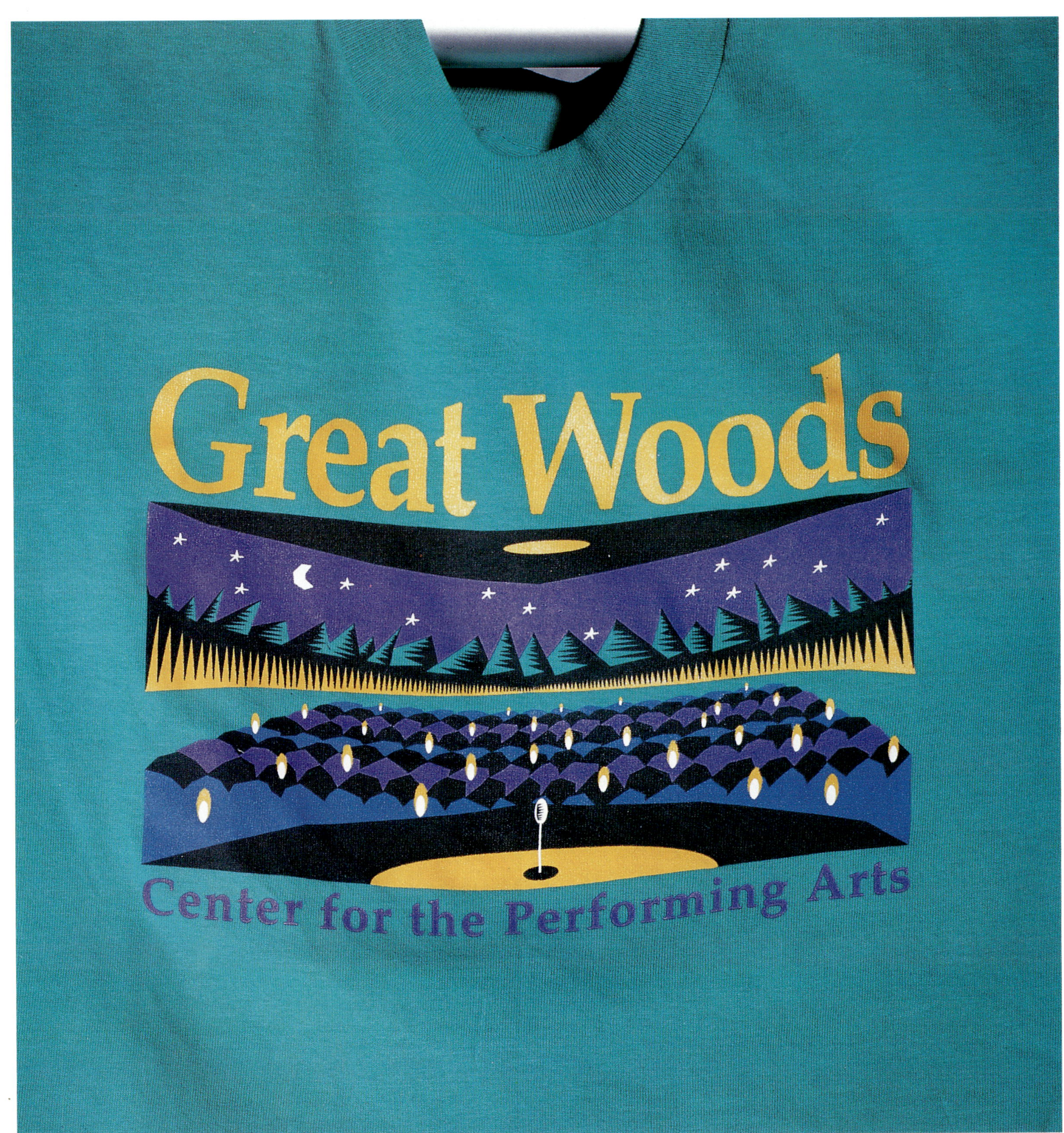

Design Firm:	Mirror Image, Inc.
Art Director:	Erica Reitmayer
Designer:	Derek Yesman
Client:	Great Woods
Purpose or Occasion:	Promotion & retail
Number of Colors:	5

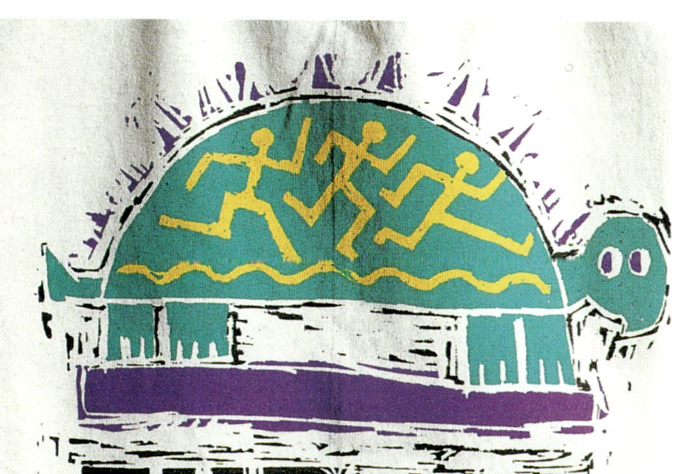

Design Firm: Sibley Peteet Design
All Design: John Evans
Client: National Kidney Foundation
Purpose or Occasion: 10K run
Number of Colors: 4

Design Firm: Lee Reedy Design Associates
All Design: Lee Reedy
Client: American Water Works Association
Purpose or Occasion: Promotion
Number of Colors: 2
This design promotes National Drinking Water Week
and the protection of clean drinking water.

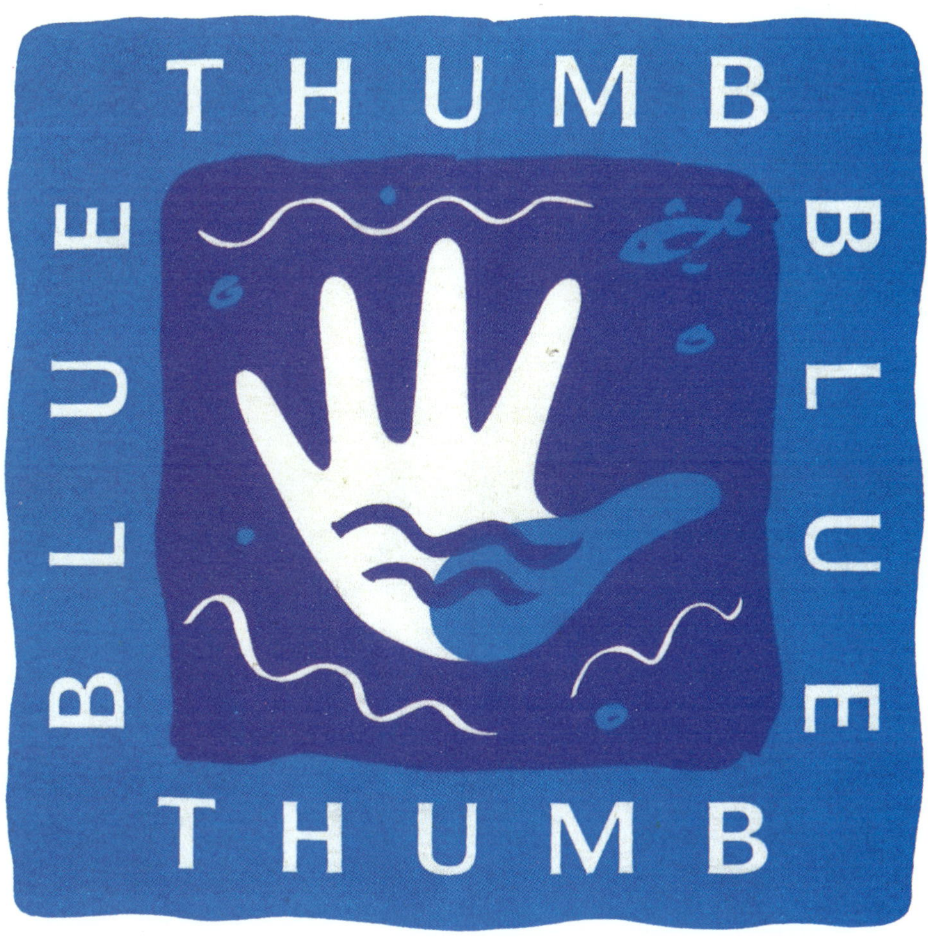

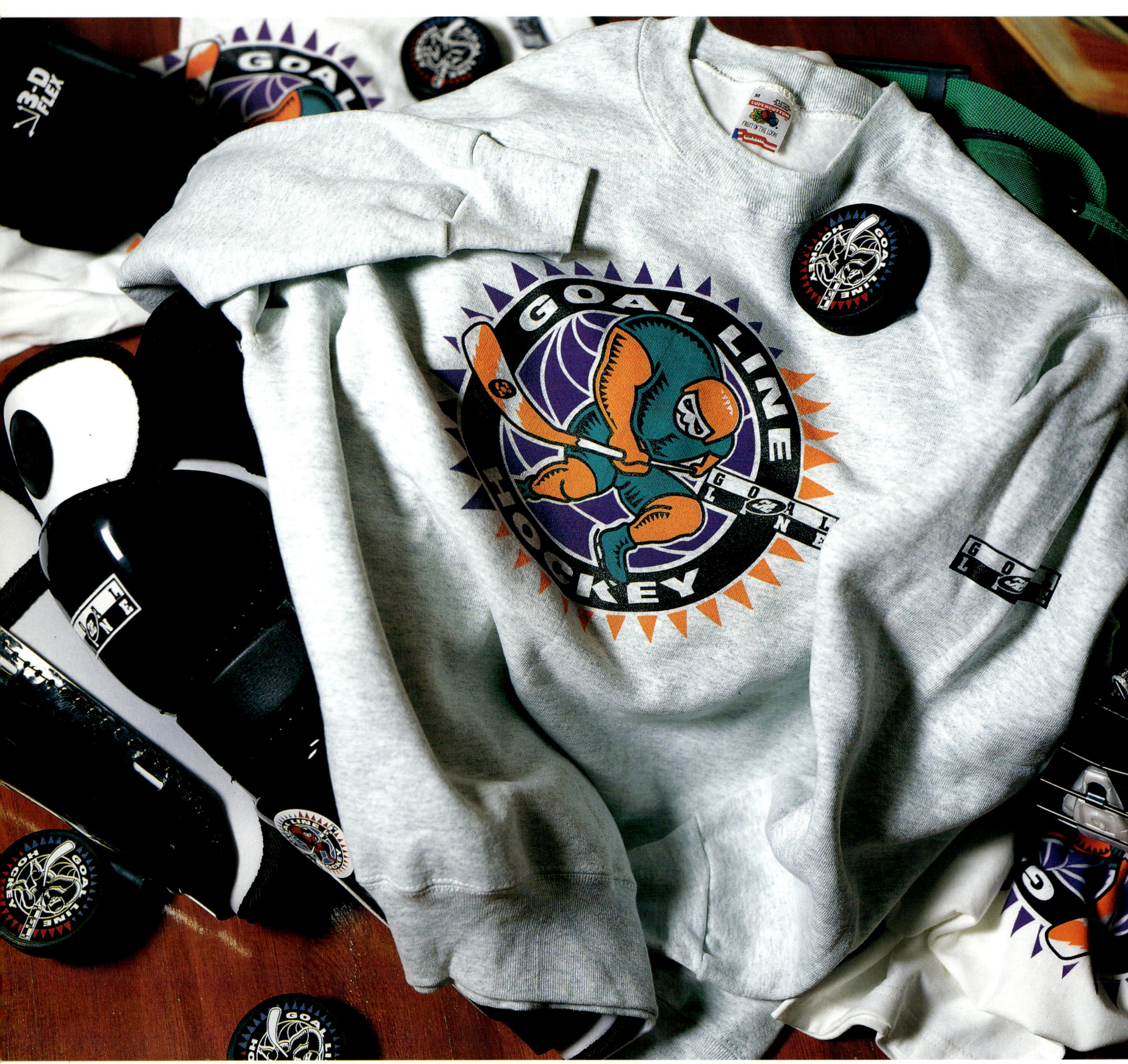

Design Firm: PandaMonium Designs
Art Director: Raymond Yu
Designers: Raymond Yu, Daniel Yee
Illustrator: Daniel Yee
Client: Goal Line Sports Equipment
Purpose or Occasion: Promotion
Number of Colors: 4

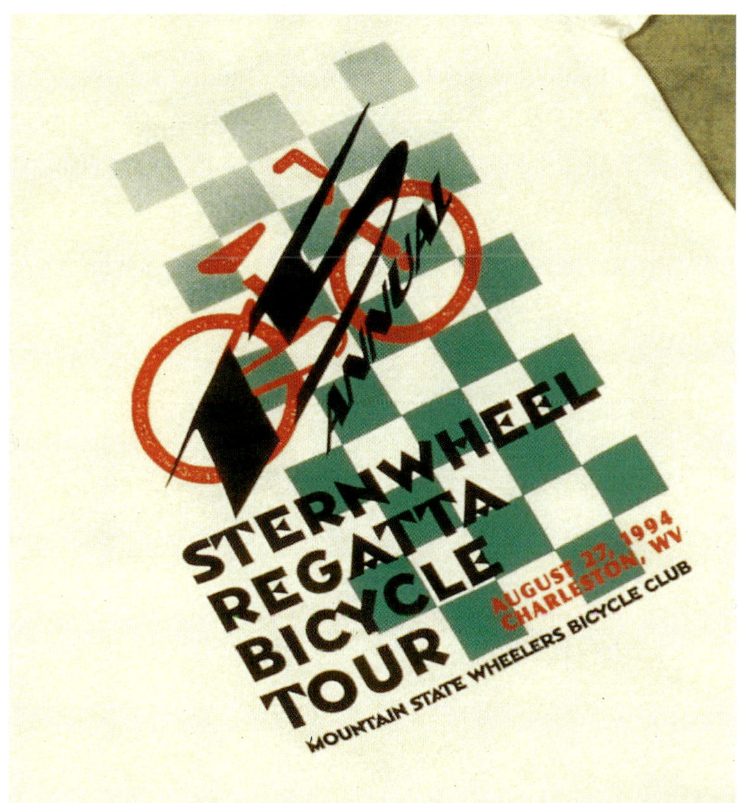

Design Firm: A.C. Designs

Designer: Anne H. Cronier

Client: Mountain State Wheelers Bicycle Club

Purpose or Occasion: Bicycle Club Ride

Number of Colors: 3

Design Firm: Alphawave Designs

All Design: Douglas Dunbebin

Client: Alphawave/National Organization
for Women

Purpose or Occasion: Fund-raiser

Number of Colors: 4

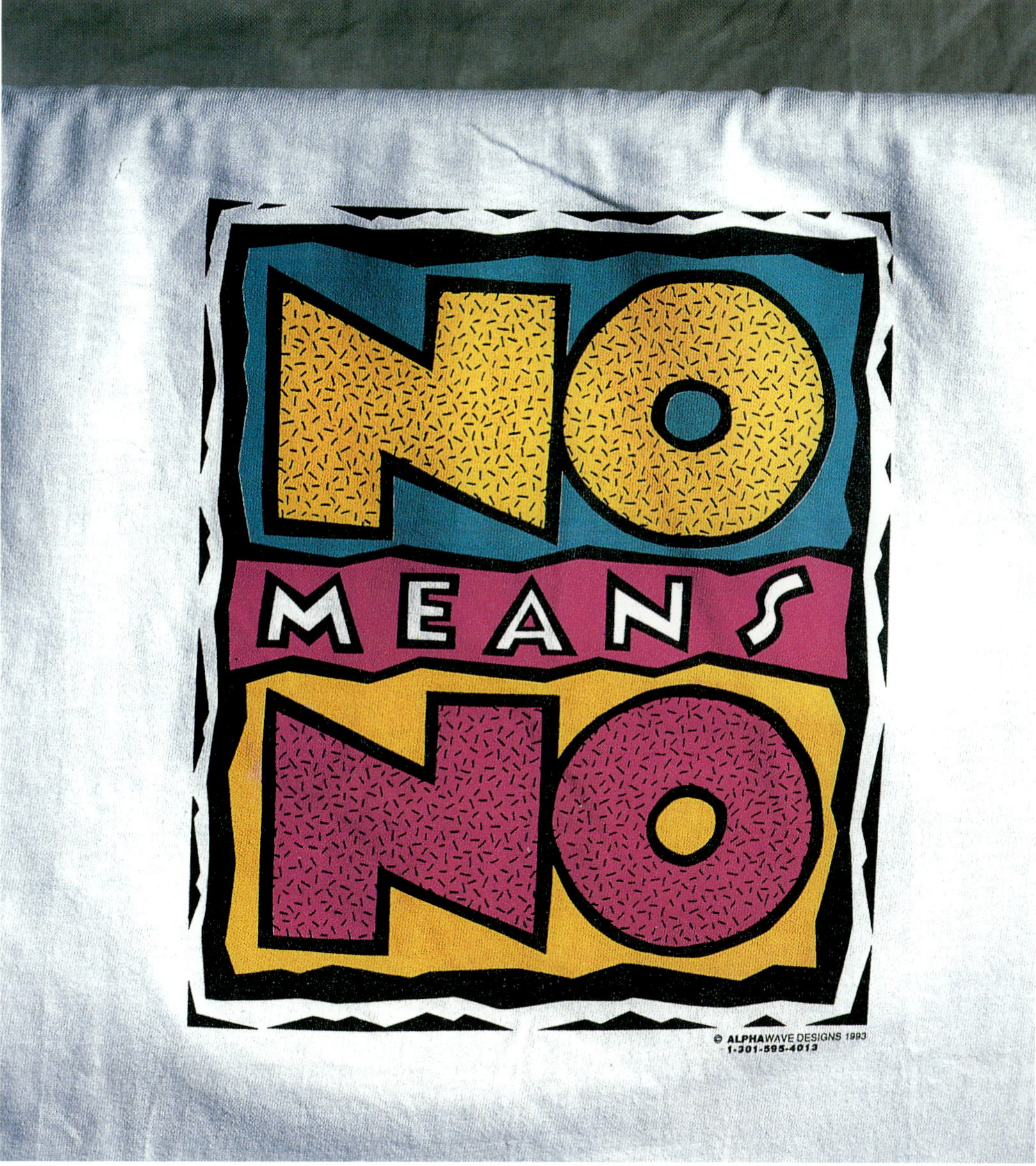

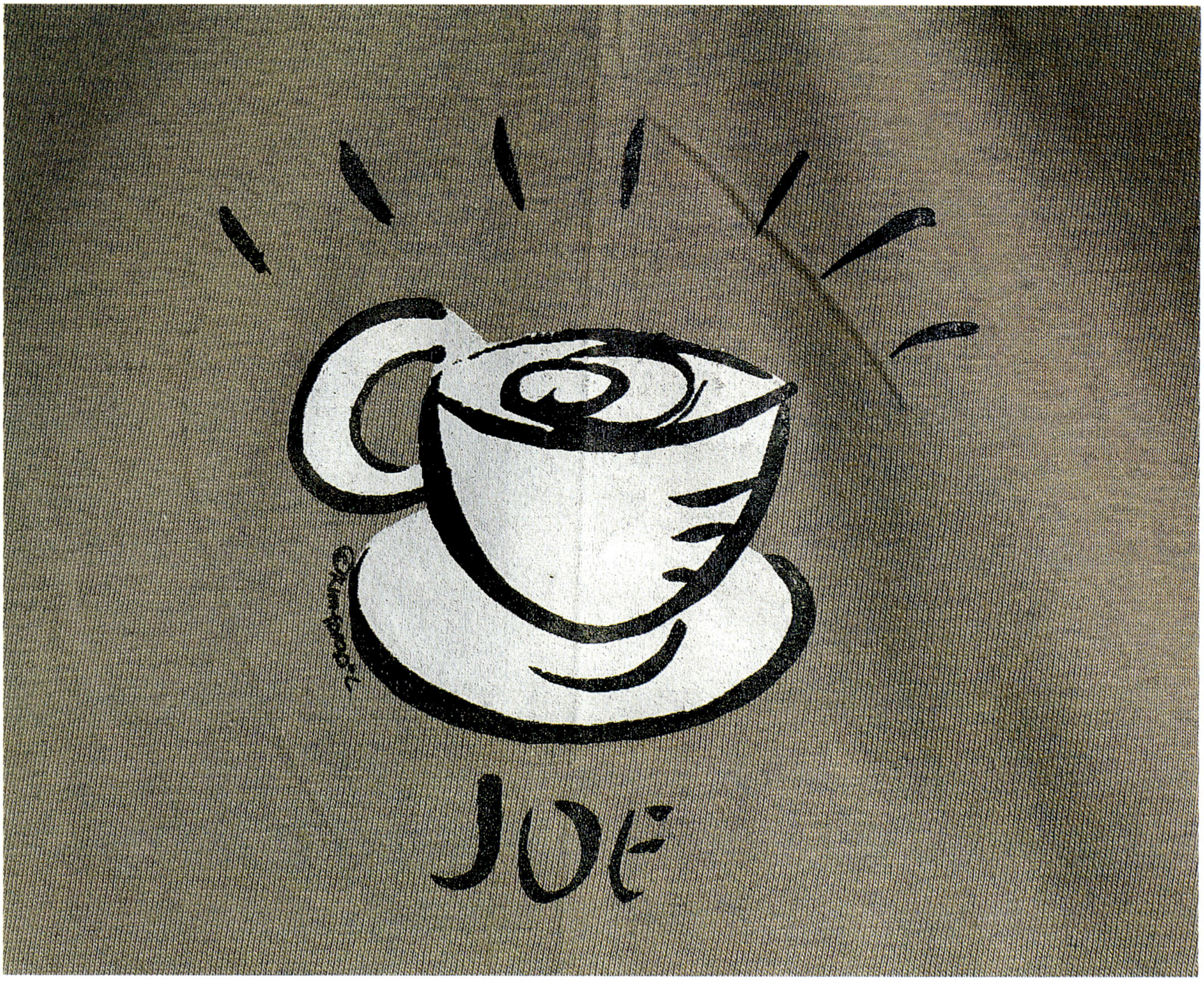

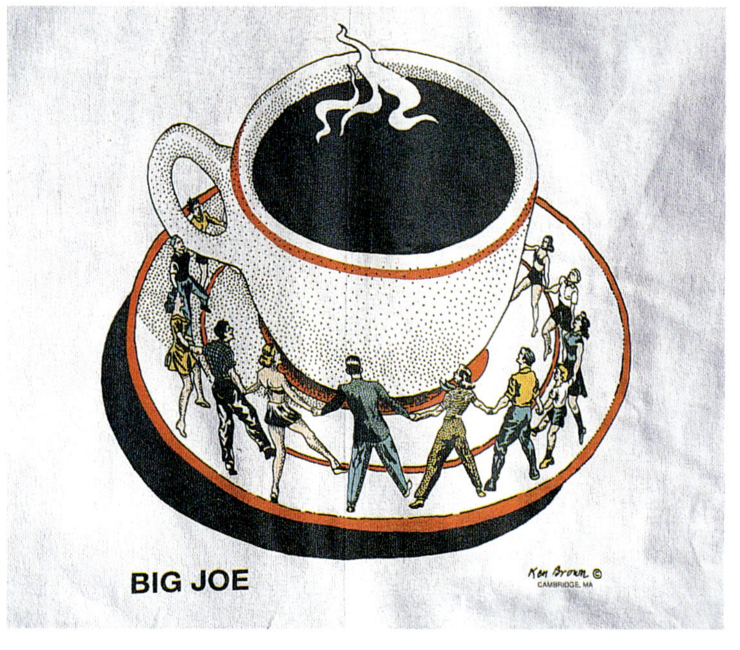

▲

Design Firm: 90° Angle
All Design: Kim Sager
Client: 90° Angle
Purpose or Occasion: Retail

◄

Design Firm: Ken Brown Designs
Designer: Ken Brown
Purpose or Occasion: Retail
Number of Colors: 5

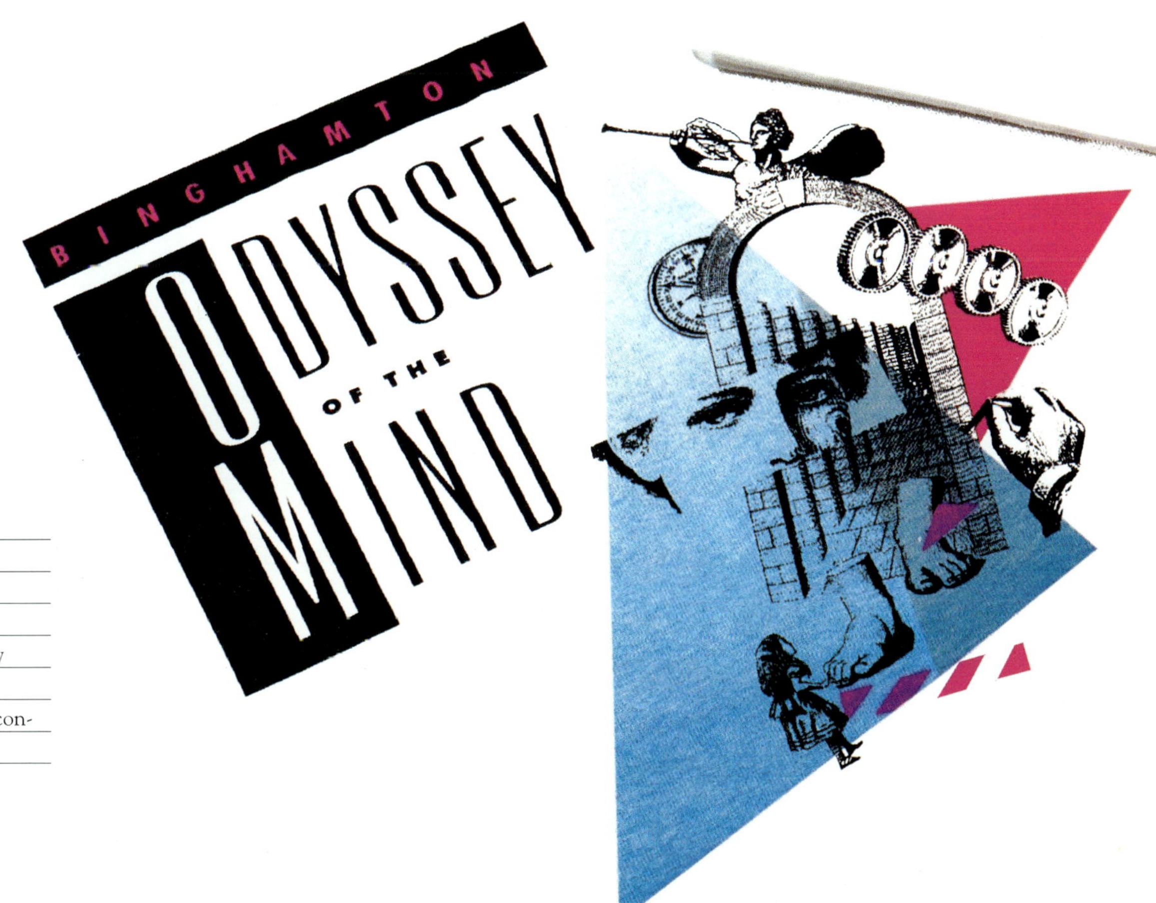

Design Firm: Cerretani Design
All Design: Janet Cerretani
Client: Binghamton High School
Purpose or Occasion: Give-away
Number of Colors: 3
Designed for a nationwide problem solving contest sponsored by a local school system.

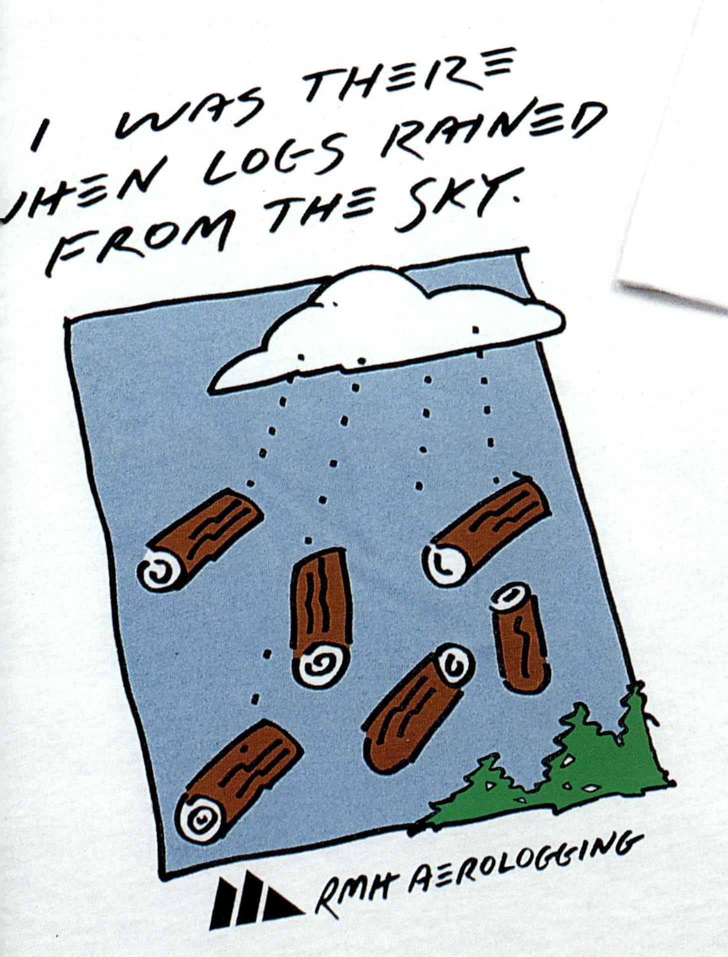

Design Firm: Cerretani Design
All Design: Janet Cerretani
Client: Rocky Mountain Helicopters
Purpose or Occasion: Give-away
Number of Colors: 4
The shirt was a gift to helicopter operators for the end-of-the-season logging push in Alaska.

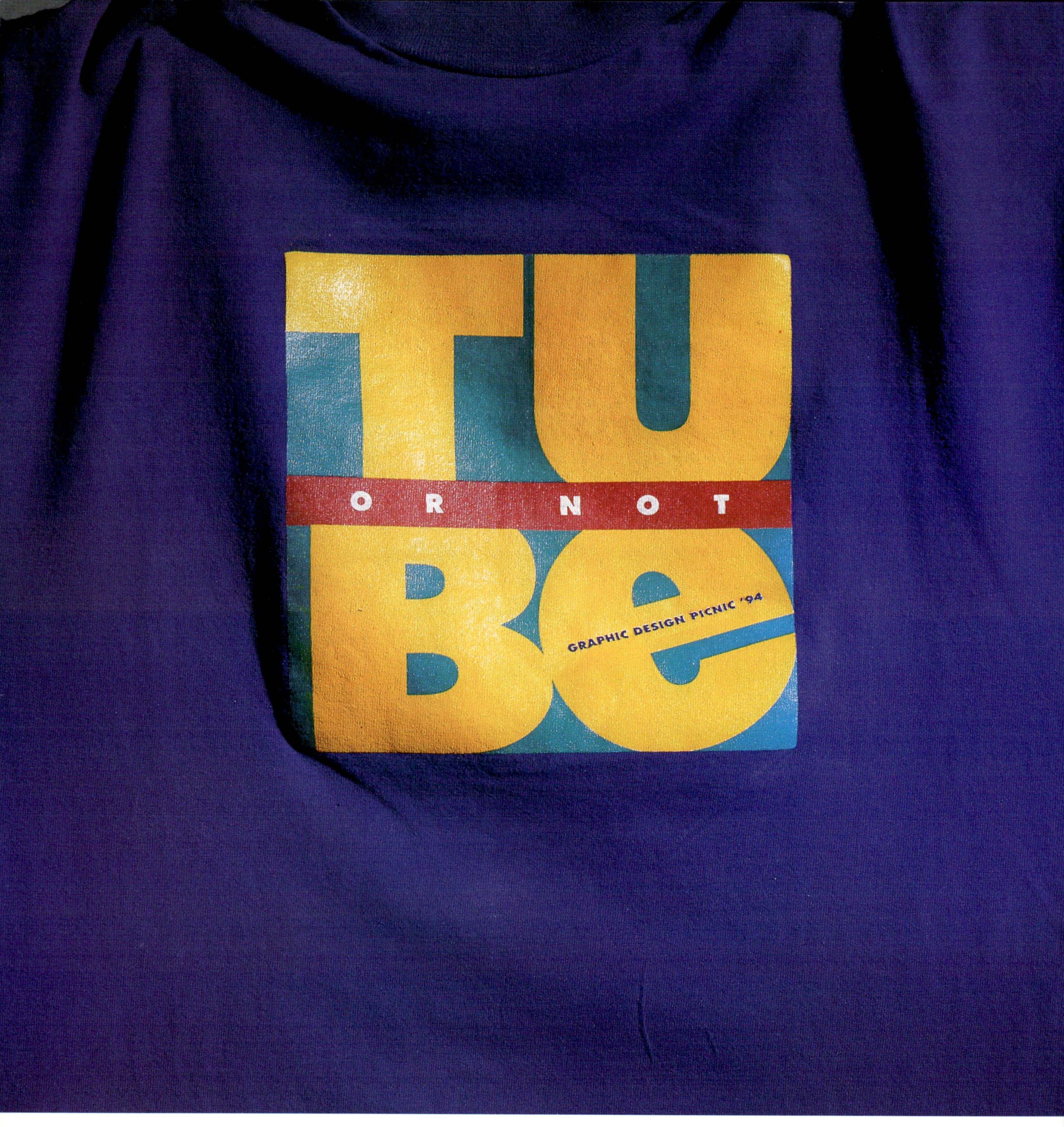

Design Firm: Alex Paradowski Graphic Design
Art Director: Alex Paradowski
Designer: Stephen Cox
Illustrator: Stephen Cox
Client: Alex Paradowski Graphic Design
Purpose or Occasion: Company float trip
Number of Colors: 4

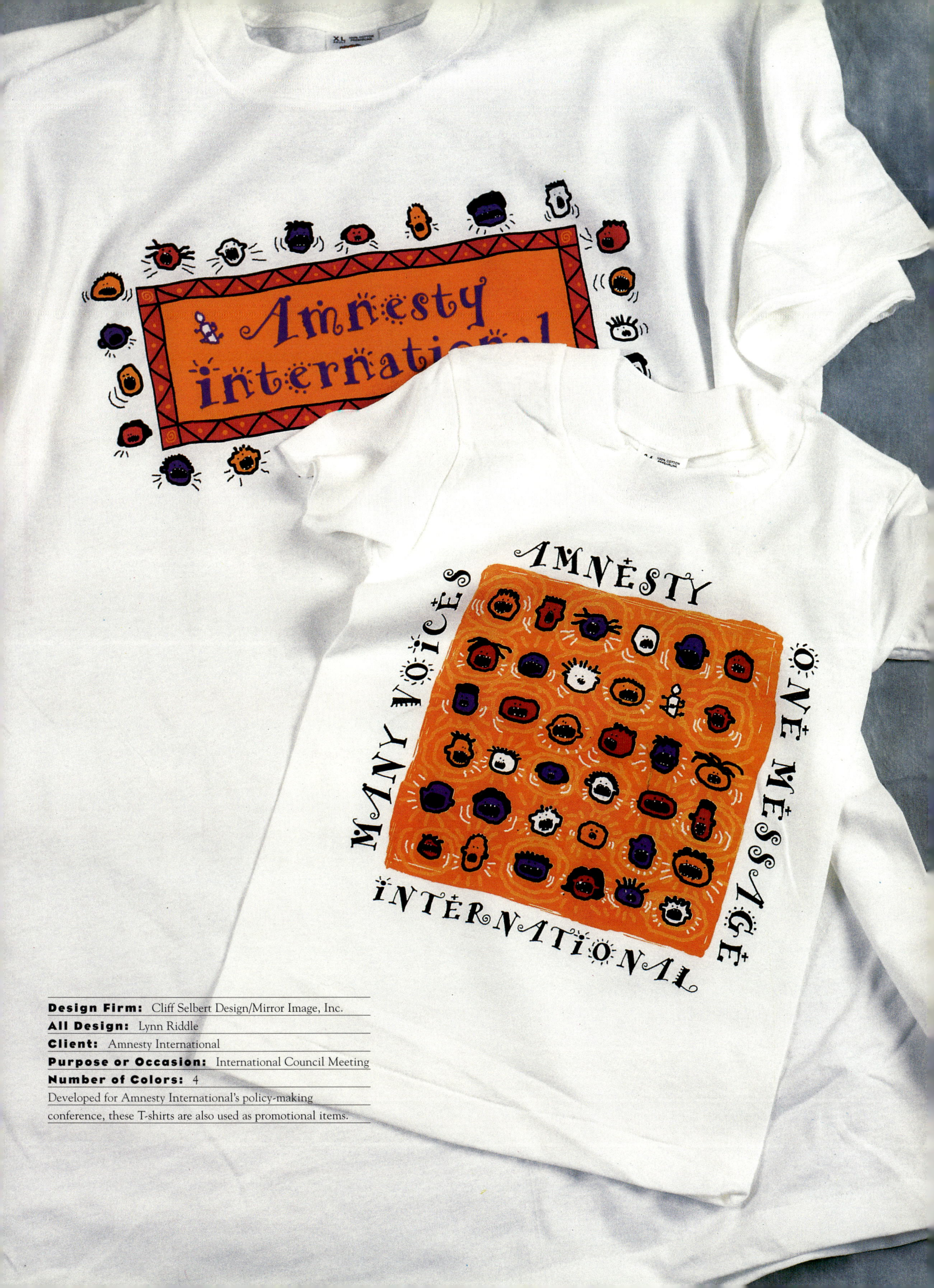

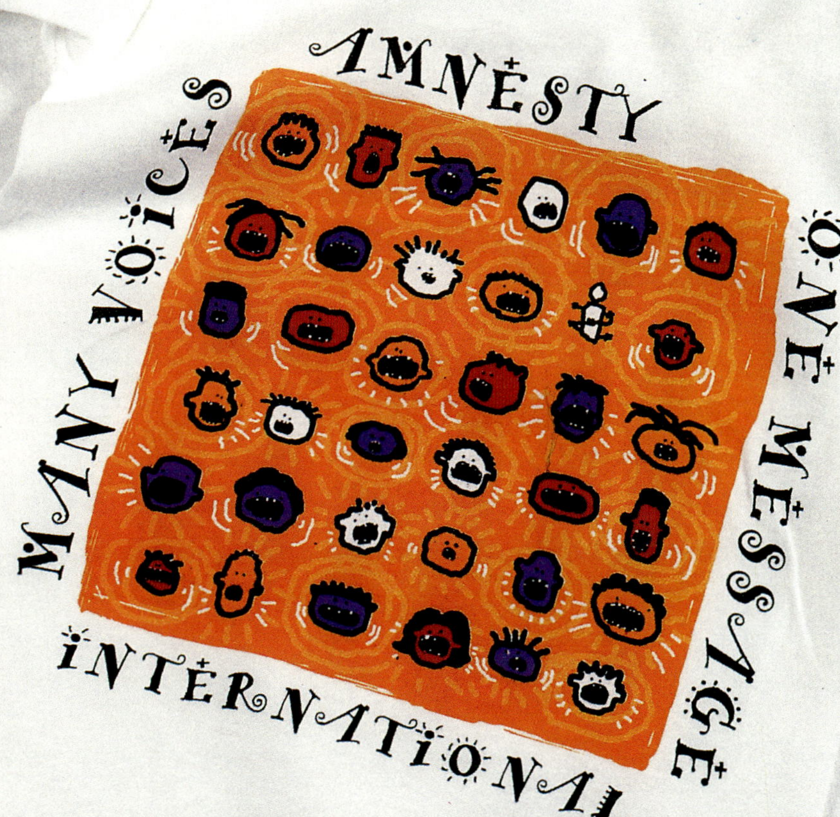

Design Firm: Cliff Selbert Design/Mirror Image, Inc.
All Design: Lynn Riddle
Client: Amnesty International
Purpose or Occasion: International Council Meeting
Number of Colors: 4

Developed for Amnesty International's policy-making
conference, these T-shirts are also used as promotional items.

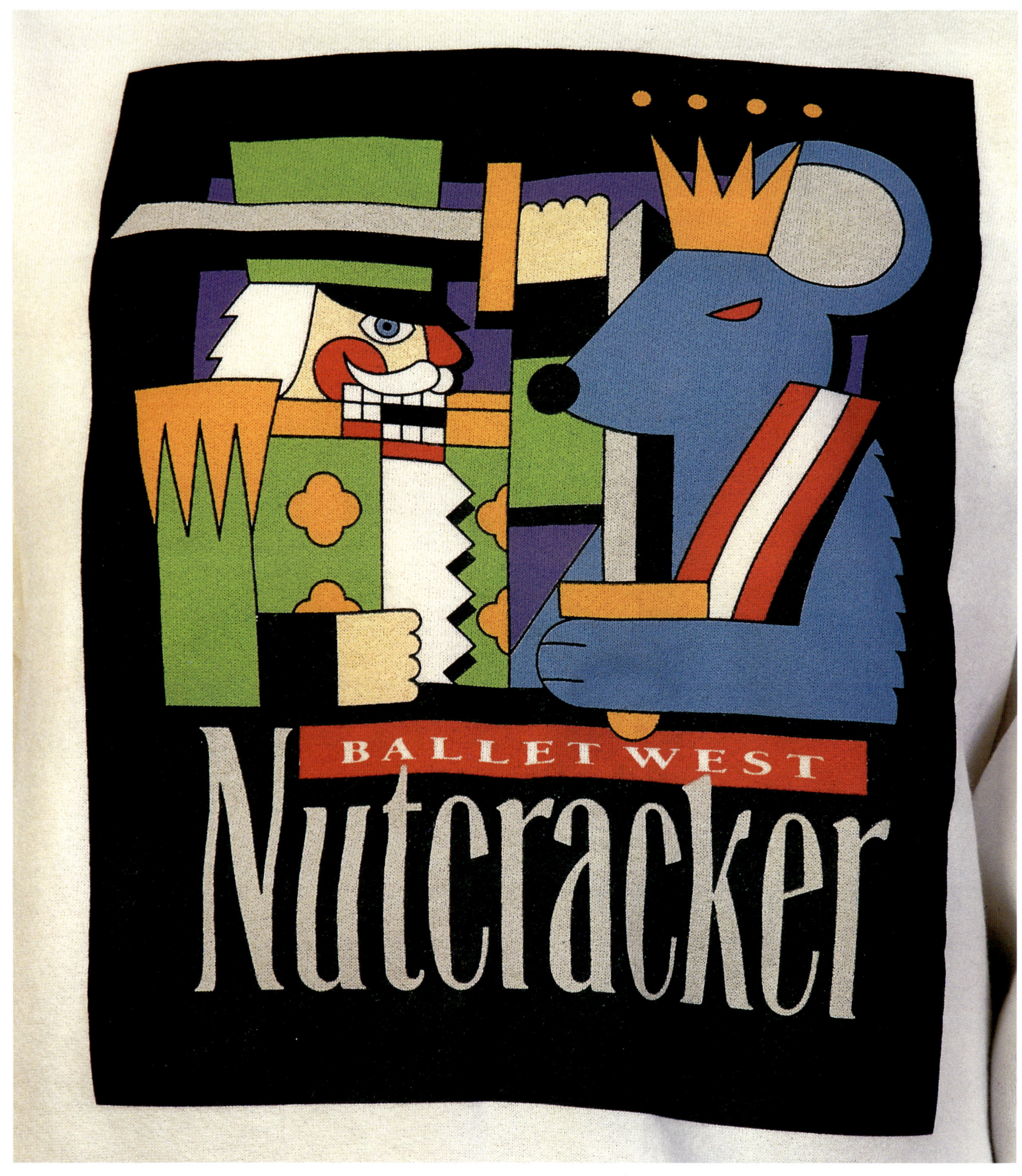

Design Firm: Richards and Swensen, Inc.
All Design: William Swensen
Client: Ballet West
Purpose or Occasion: Retail
Number of Colors: 6
Sweatshirt designed in conjunction with the
yearly performance of *The Nutcracker*.

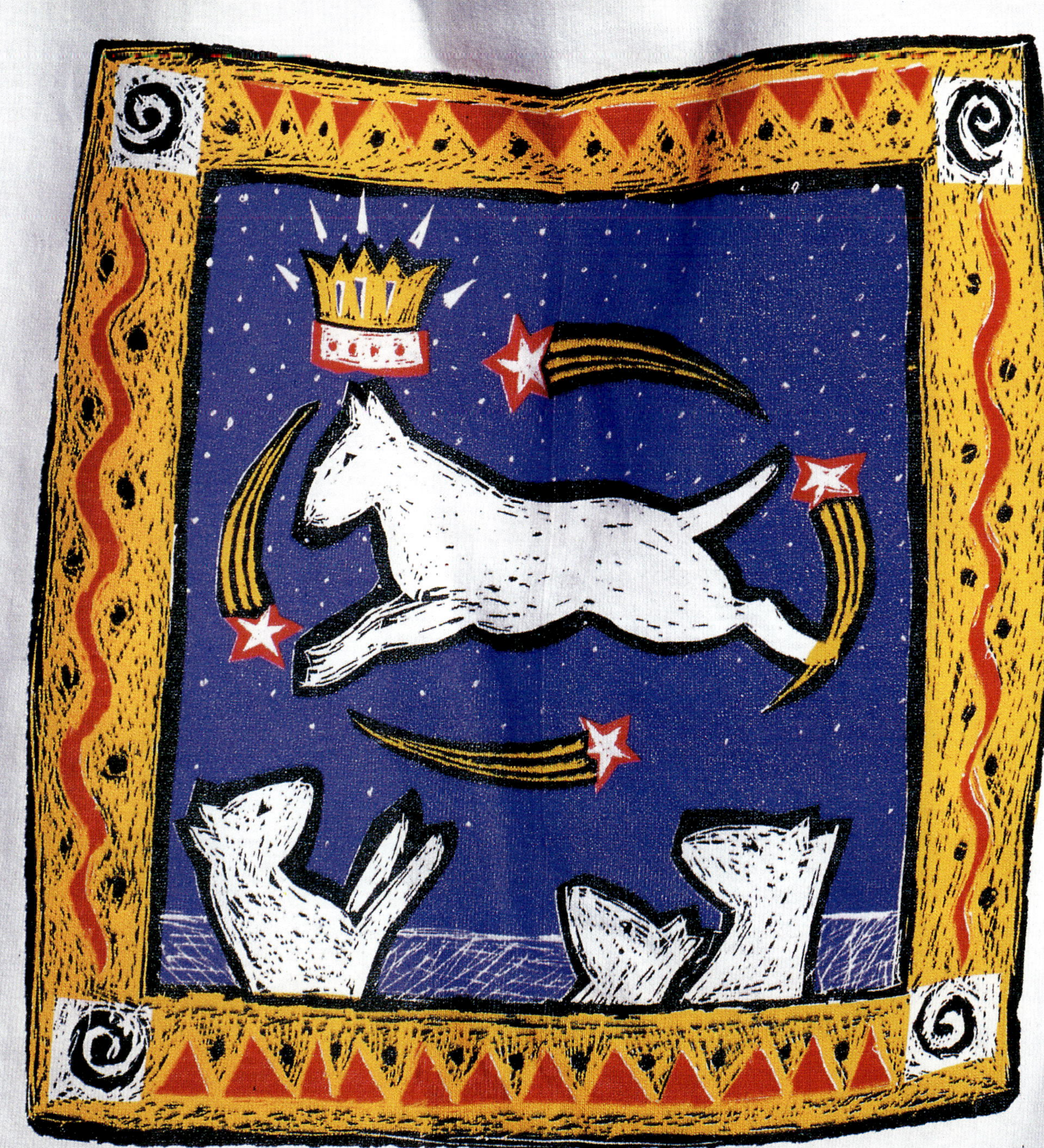

Design Firm: Sibley Peteet Design
Art Directors: John Evans, Don Sibley
Designer: John Evans
Illustrator: John Evans
Client: Bull Terrier Club of Dallas
Purpose or Occasion: Dog Show Award
Number of Colors: 4

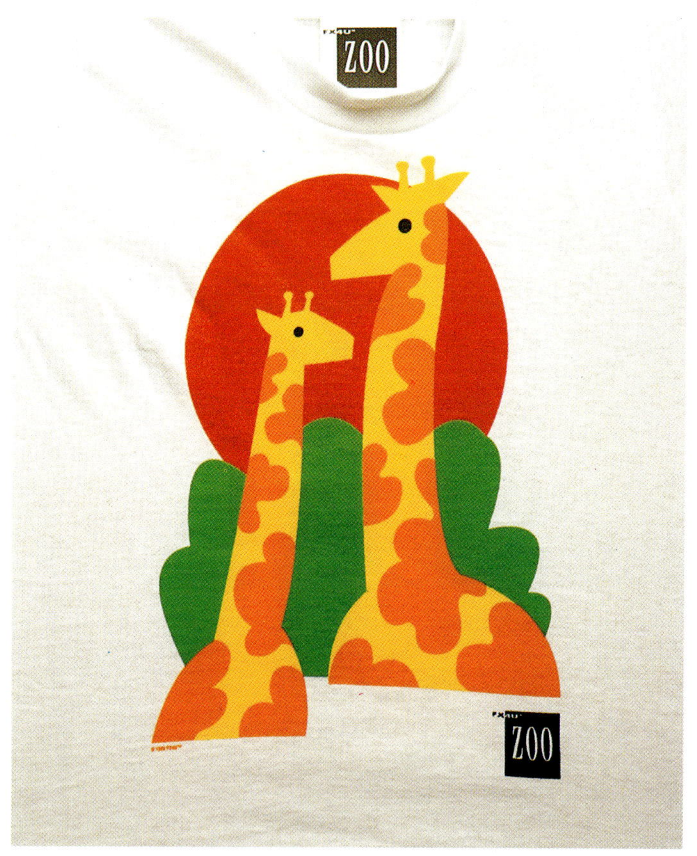

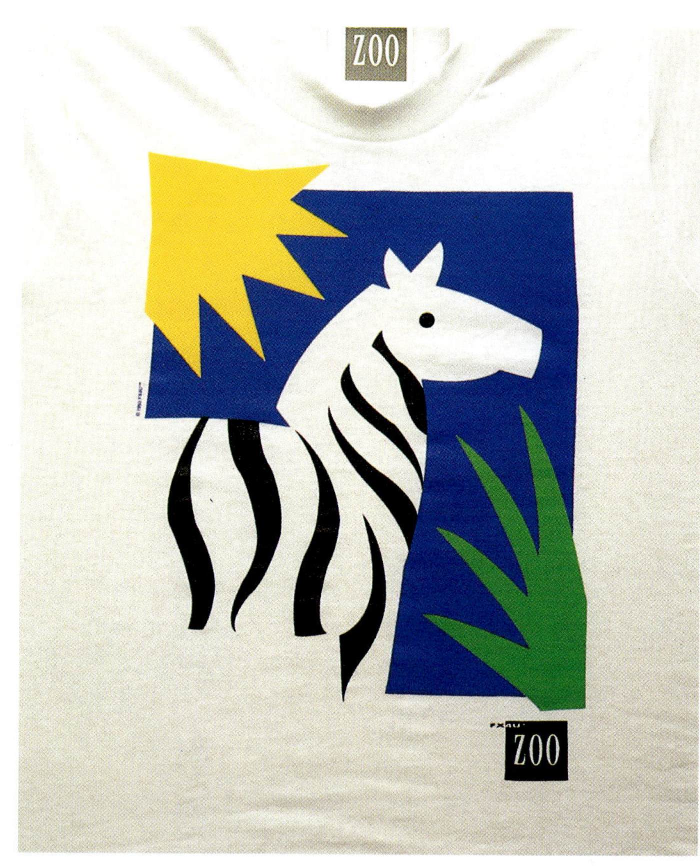

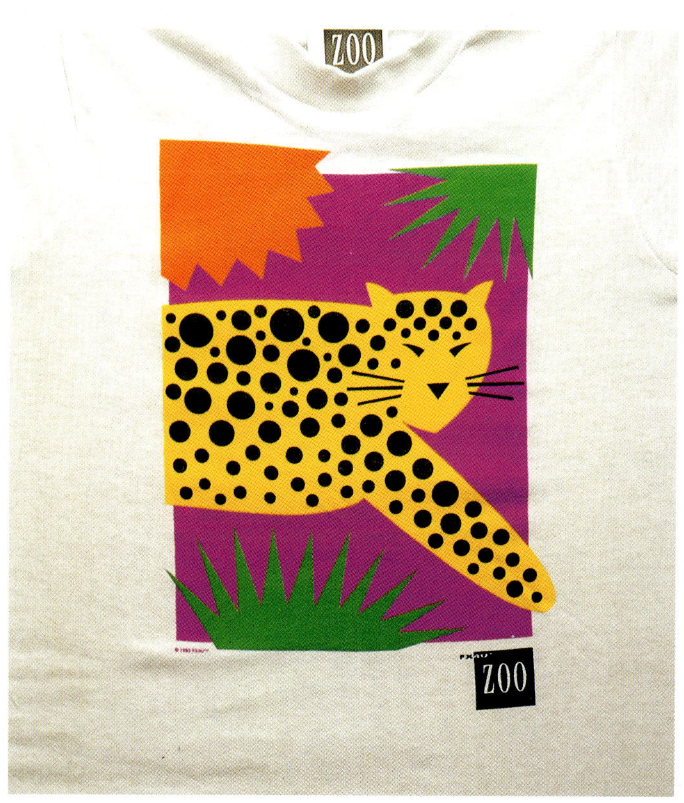

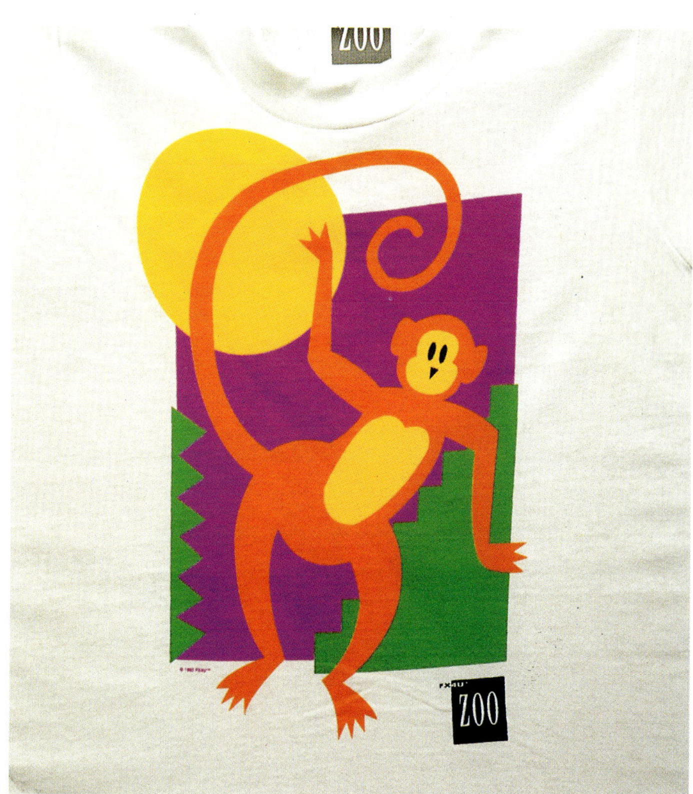

Design Firm: Lehner & Whyte
Art Directors: Donna Lehner, Hugh Whyte
Designers: Hugh Whyte, Donna Lehner
Illustrator: Hugh Whyte
Client: FX4U Zoo
Purpose or Occasion: Retail
Number of Colors: 4

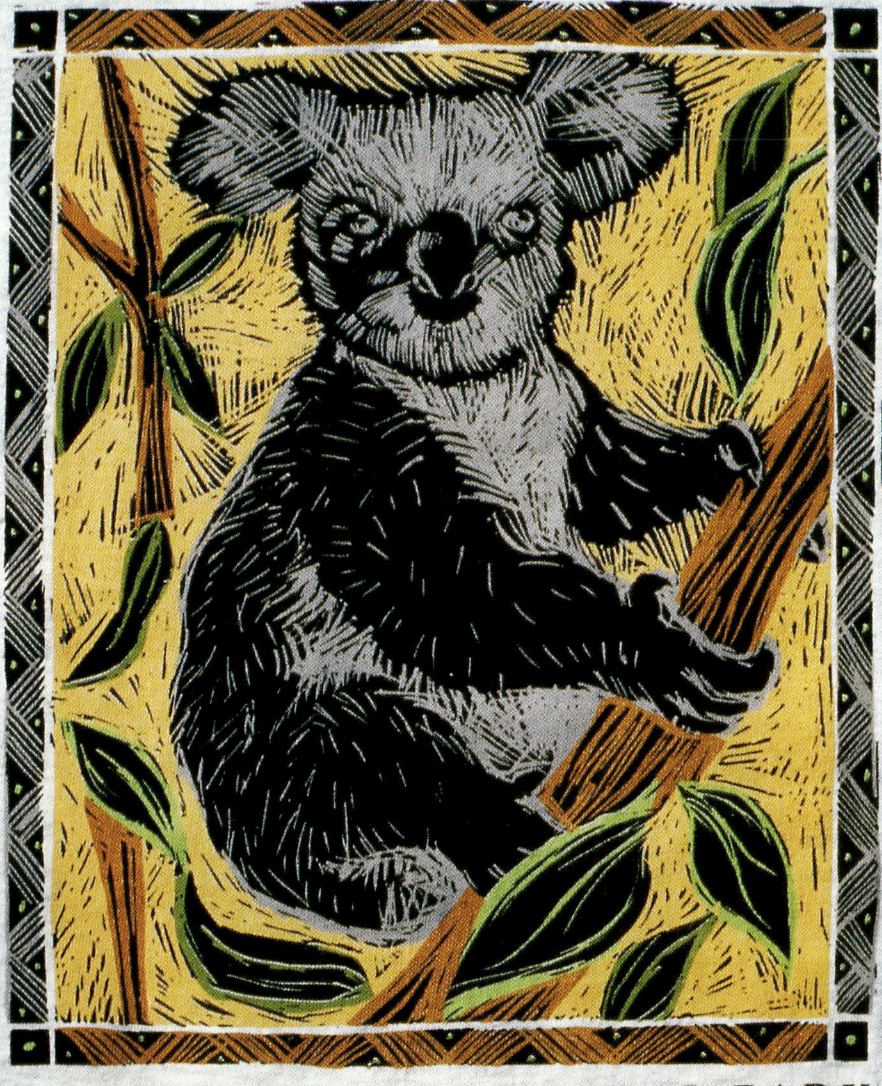

◀

Design Firm: Barbara Ferguson Designs
All Design: Barbara Ferguson
Client: Zoological Society of San Diego
Purpose or Occasion: Merchandising
Number of Colors: 5

▼

Design Firm: High Cotton, Inc.
All Design: Kathryn Glick
Client: High Cotton, Inc.
Purpose or Occasion: Retail
Number of Colors: 5

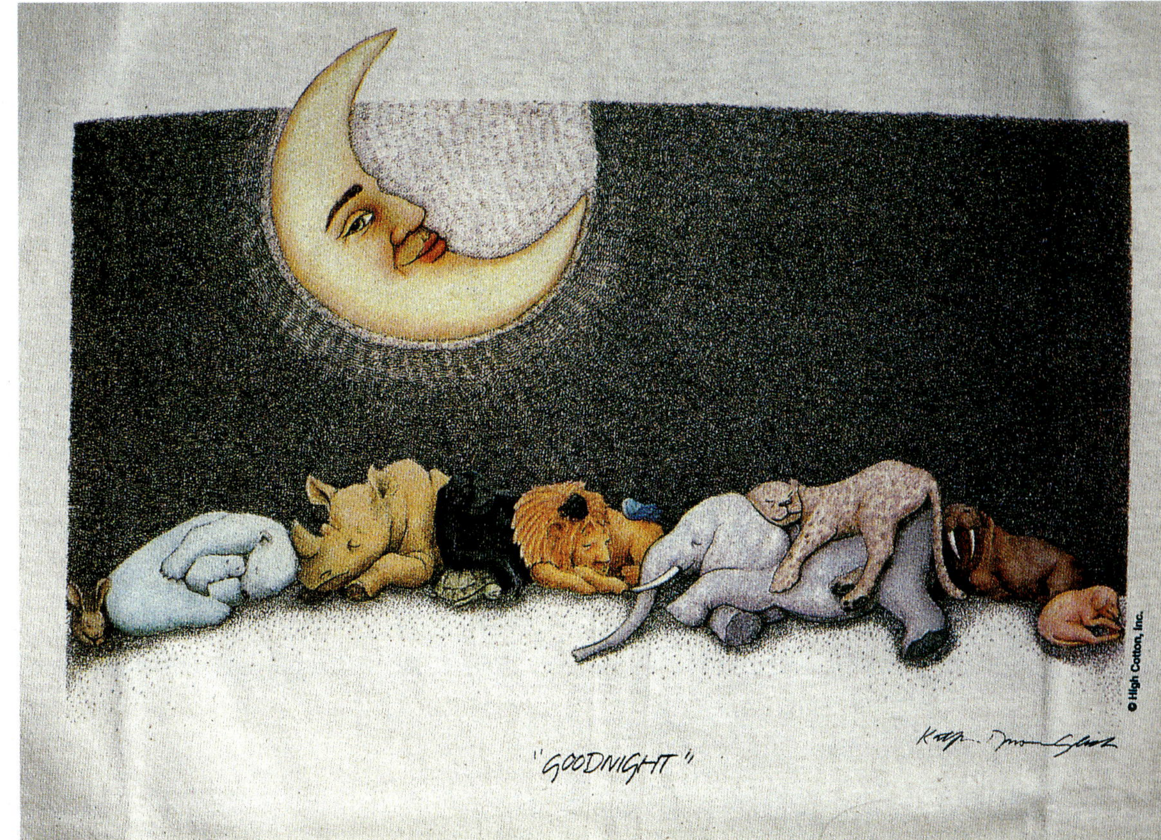

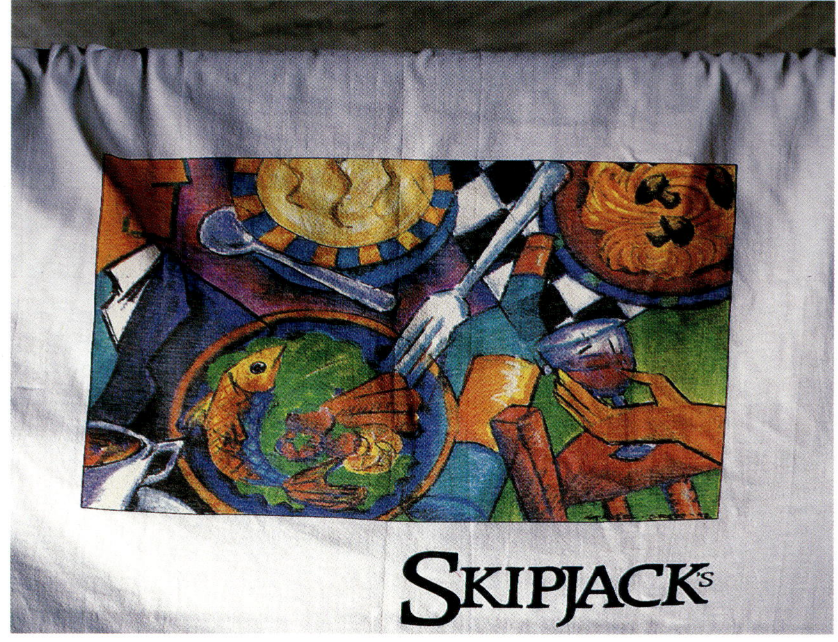

Design Firm: Bi Bi Dee
Client: Basic Publications
Purpose or Occasion: Custom orders
Number of Colors: 4

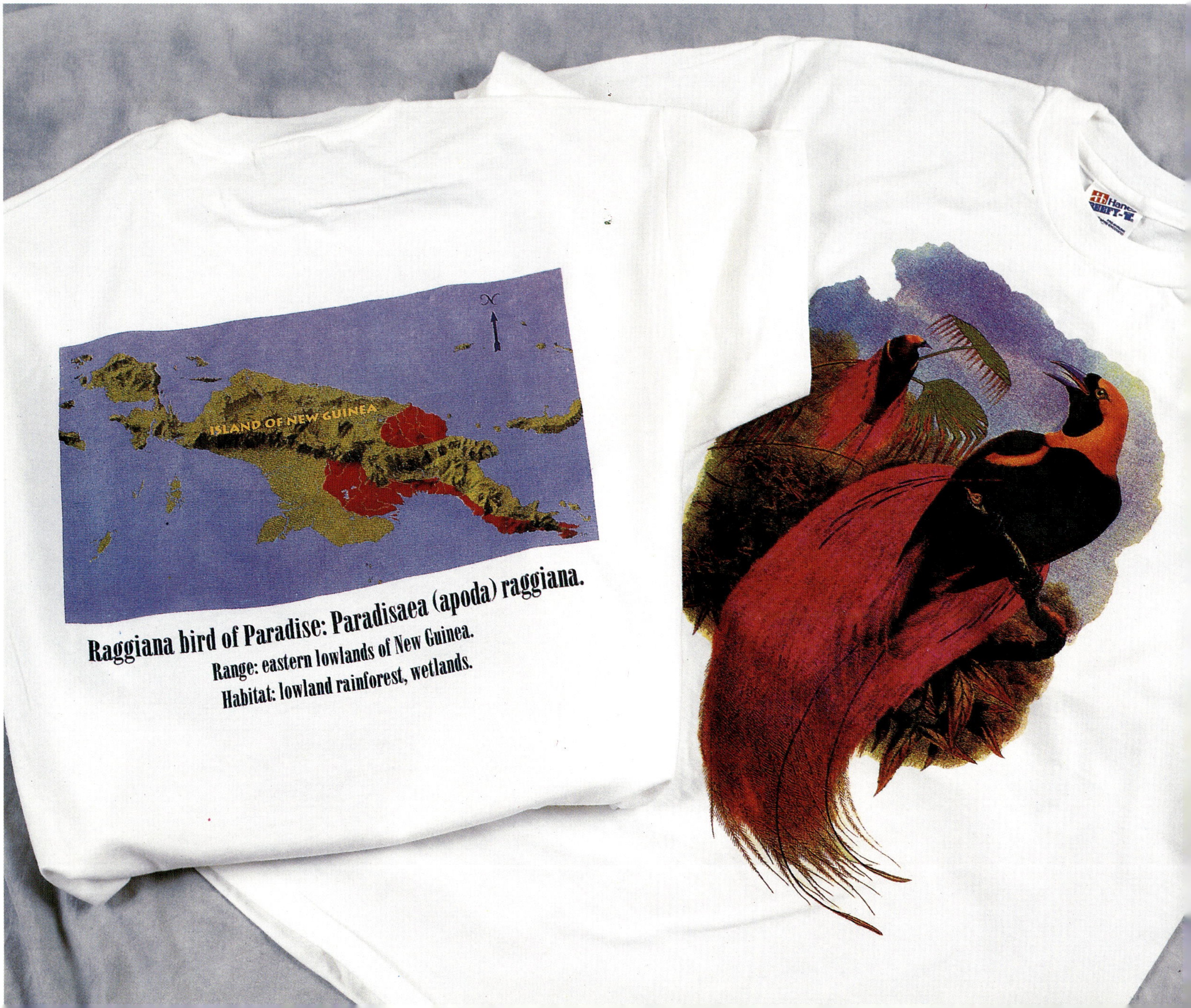

▼

Design Firm: Mike Salisbury Communications
All Design: Mike Salisbury
Client: GOTCHA
Purpose or Occasion: Retail
Number of Colors: 5

▼

Design Firm: Mike Salisbury Communications
Art Director: Mike Salisbury
Designer: Terry Lamb
Illustrator: Terry Lamb
Client: GOTCHA
Purpose or Occasion: Retail
Number of Colors: 4

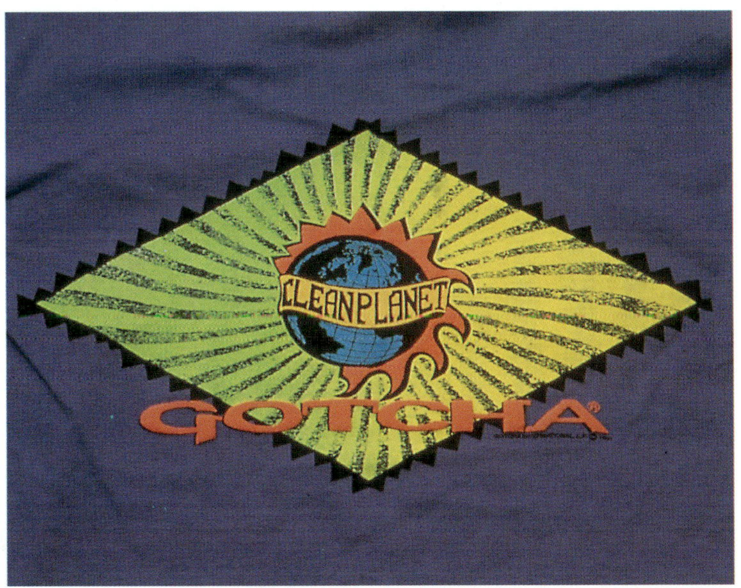

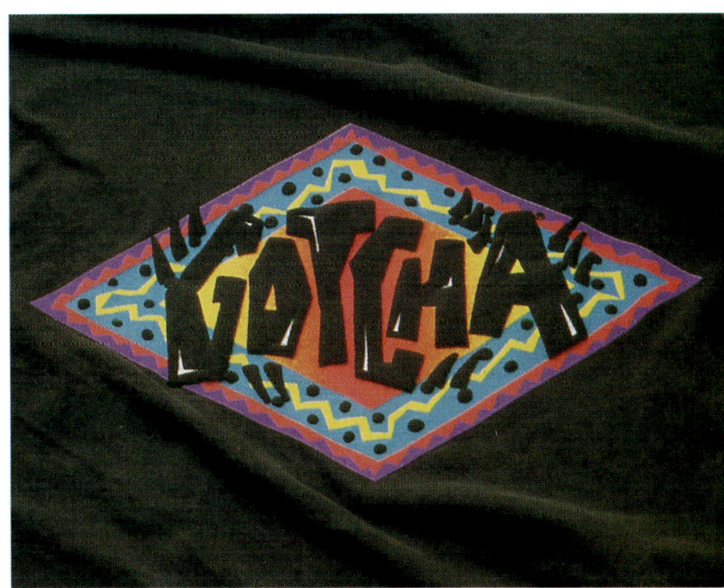

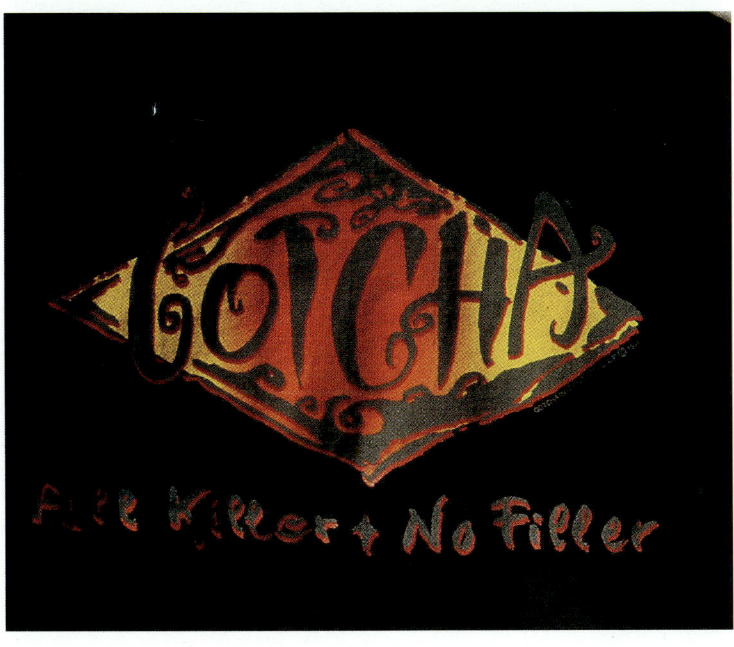

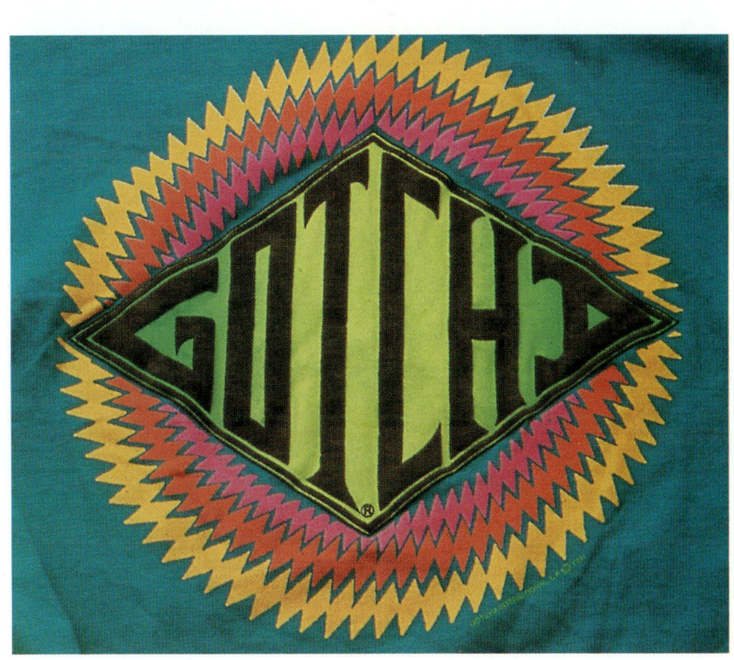

▲

Design Firm: Mike Salisbury Communications
Art Director: Mike Salisbury
Designer: Damion Gallay
Illustrator: Damion Gallay
Client: GOTCHA
Purpose or Occasion: Retail
Number of Colors: 4

▲

Design Firm: Mike Salisbury Communications
Art Director: Mike Salisbury
Designers: Terry Lamb, Mike Salisbury
Illustrators: Terry Lamb, Mike Salisbury
Client: GOTCHA
Purpose or Occasion: Retail
Number of Colors: 7

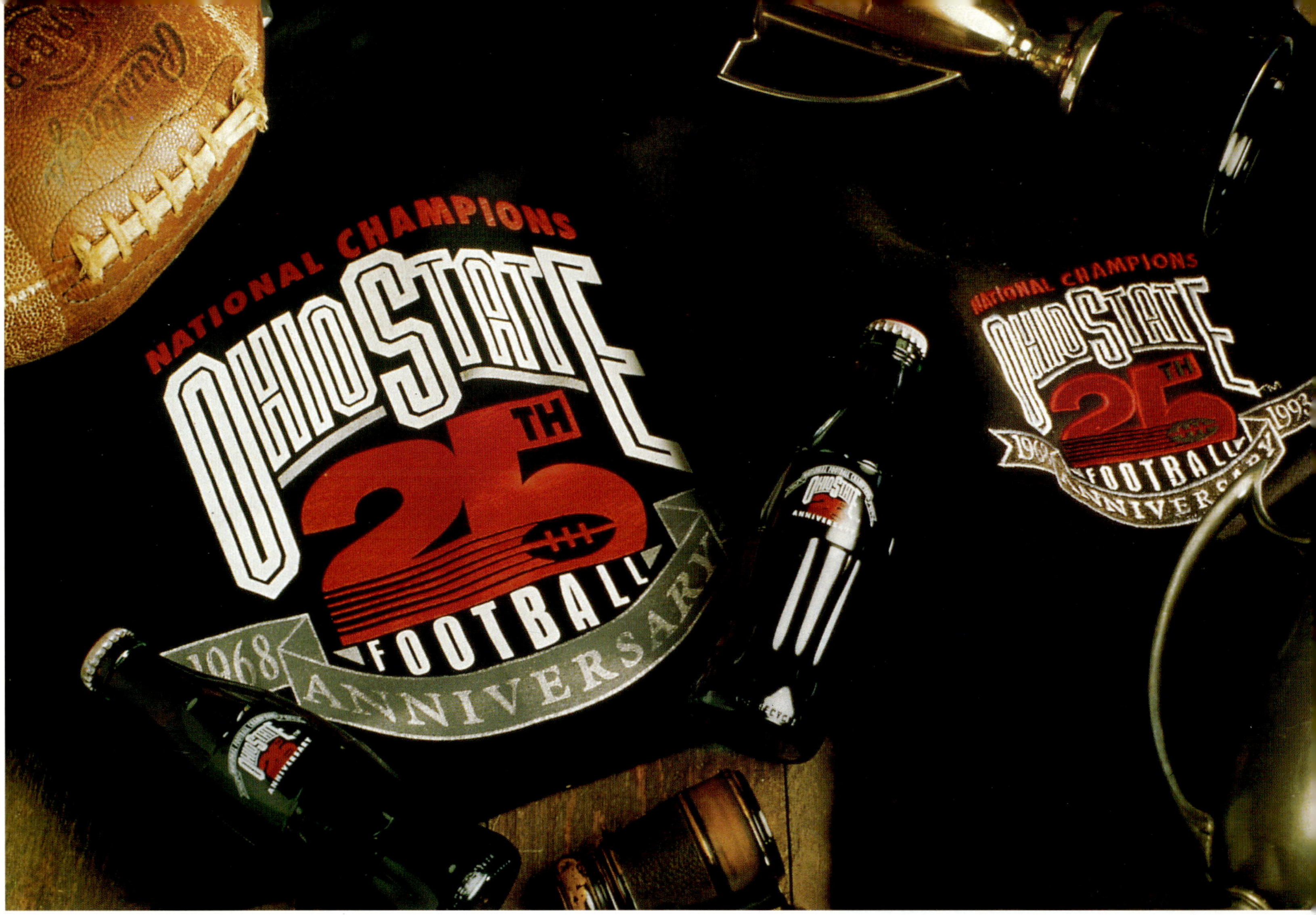

▲

Design Firm: Rickabaugh Graphics

All Design: Eric Rickabaugh

Client: Ohio State University Athletics Dept.

Purpose or Occasion: Twenty-fifth anniversary of Ohio State University football National Championship

Number of Colors: 4

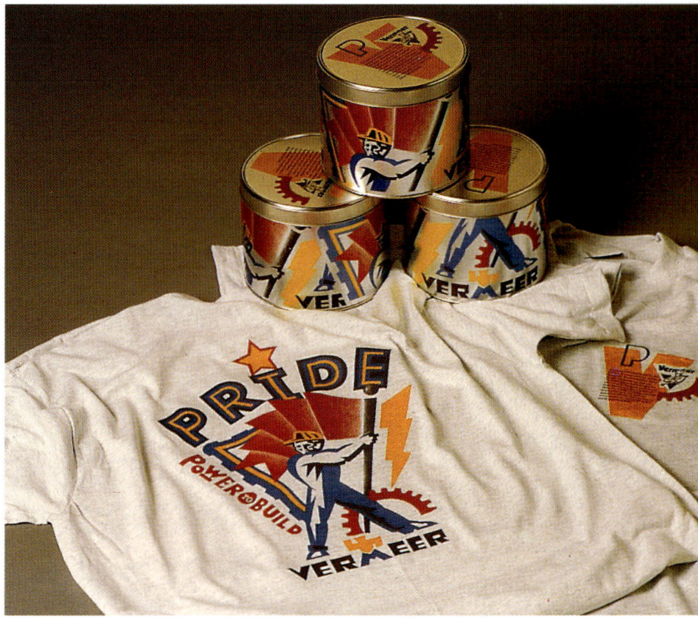

▲

Design Firm: Sayles Graphic Design

All Design: John Sayles

Client: Vermeet Manufacturing

Purpose or Occasion: Employee incentive

Number of Colors: 4

Presented in a custom-designed can, this shirt was given to Vermeet Manufacturing employees at an annual event.

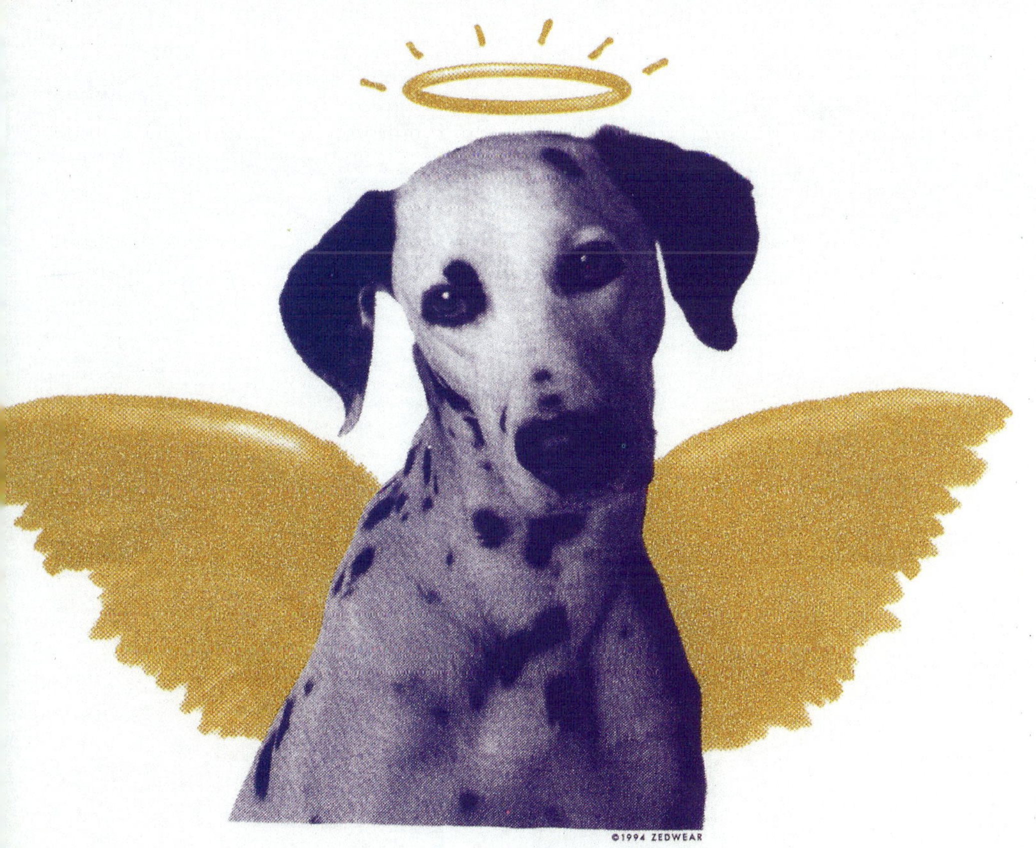

Design Firm: ZEDWEAR
Art Director: John Klaja
Designer: John Klaja
Illustrator: John Klaja
Client: ZEDWEAR
Purpose or Occasion: Retail
Number of Colors: 2
Printer: Tasty Shirt Company
This *Good Dog* design expands the ZEDWEAR line with a series of T-shirts featuring images inspired by "Zed", the owner's dalmatian.

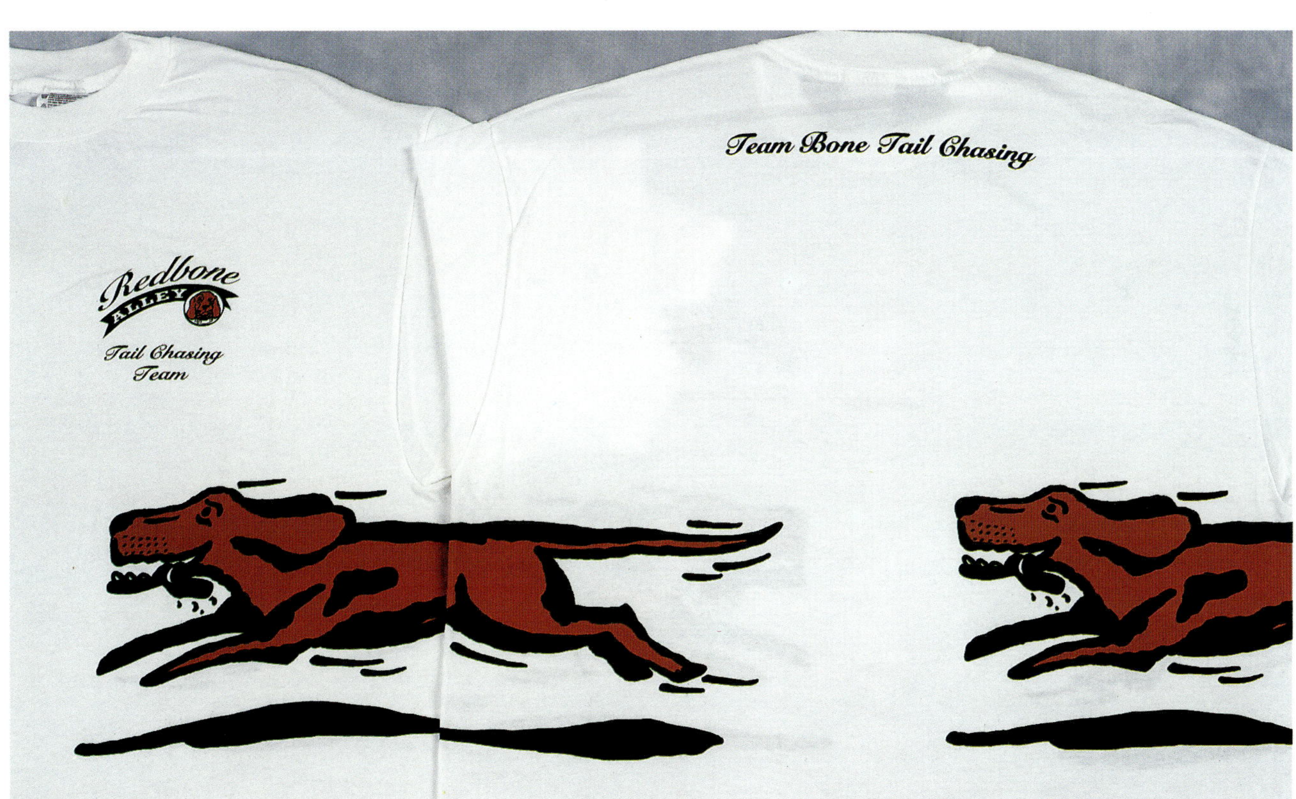

Design Firm: Gil Shuler Graphic Design, Inc.
Art Director: Gil Shuler
Designers: Gil Shuler, Steve Lepre
Illustrator: Gil Shuler
Client: Redbone Alley Restaurant
Purpose or Occasion: Merchandising
Number of Colors: 2

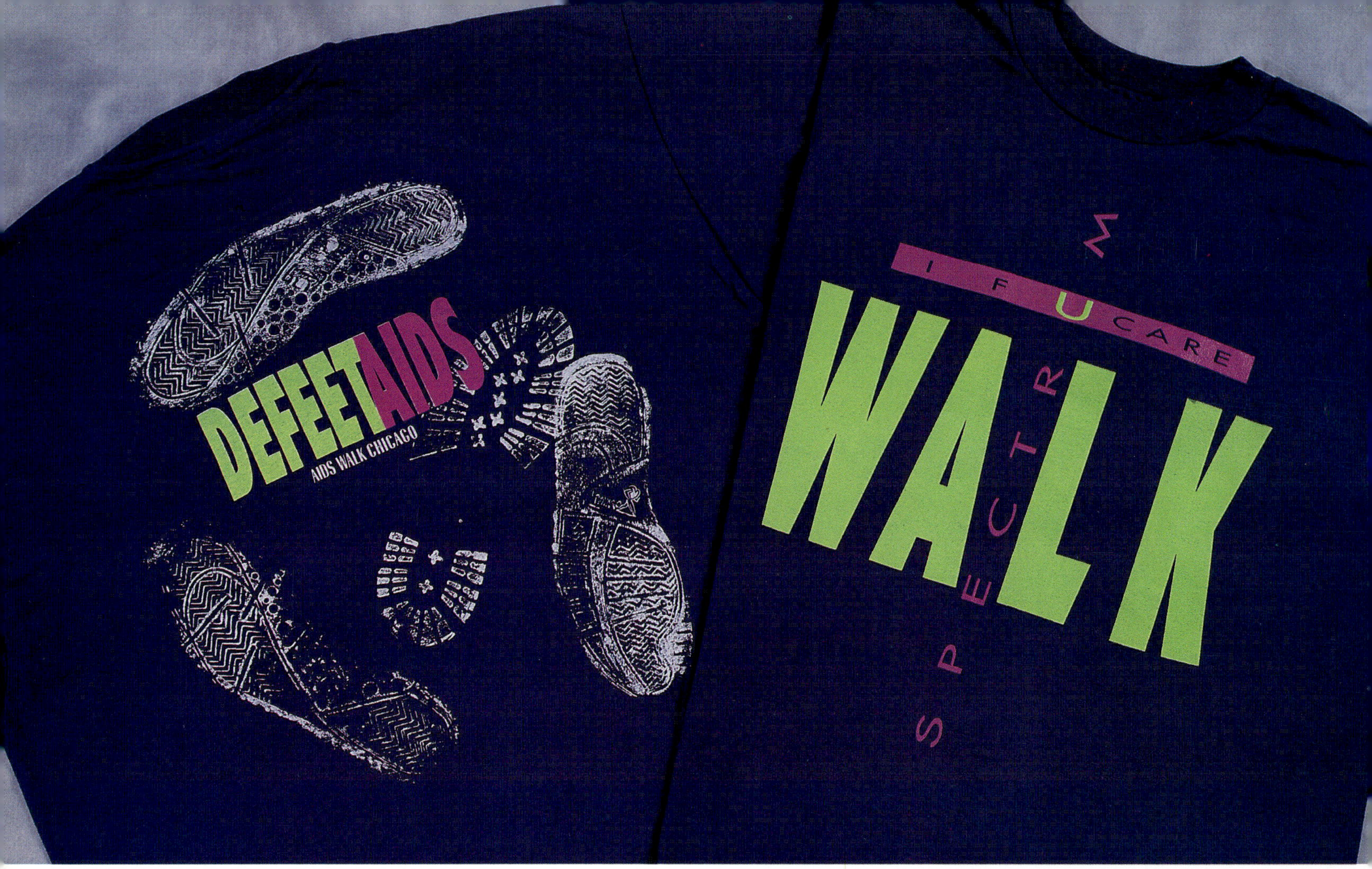

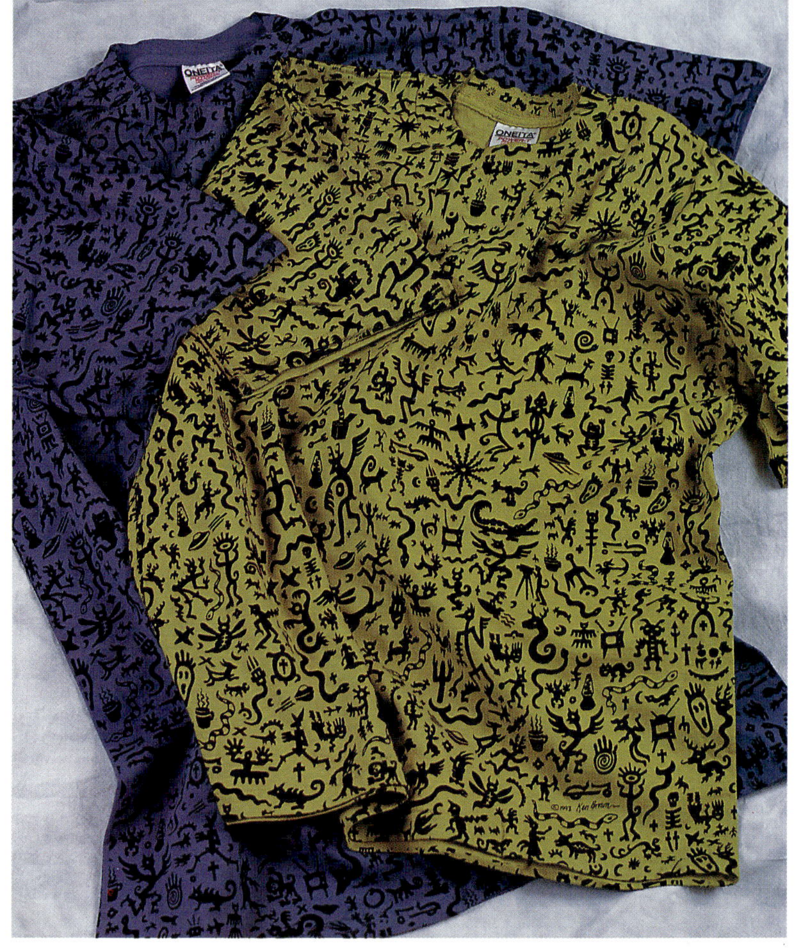

Design Firm: Scoville Creative
All Design: Laura Scoville
Client: Spectrum Center for Integrated Care
Purpose or Occasion: Aids Walk Chicago
Number of Colors: 3
Printer: Propaganda

This T-shirt won the "impact" prize out of more than 30 entries from all the corporate sponsors and teams. Its indigo color made the team stand out, while its printed message inspired dialogue.

Design Firm: Ken Brown
Designer: Ken Brown
Purpose or Occasion: Retail
Number of Colors: 1

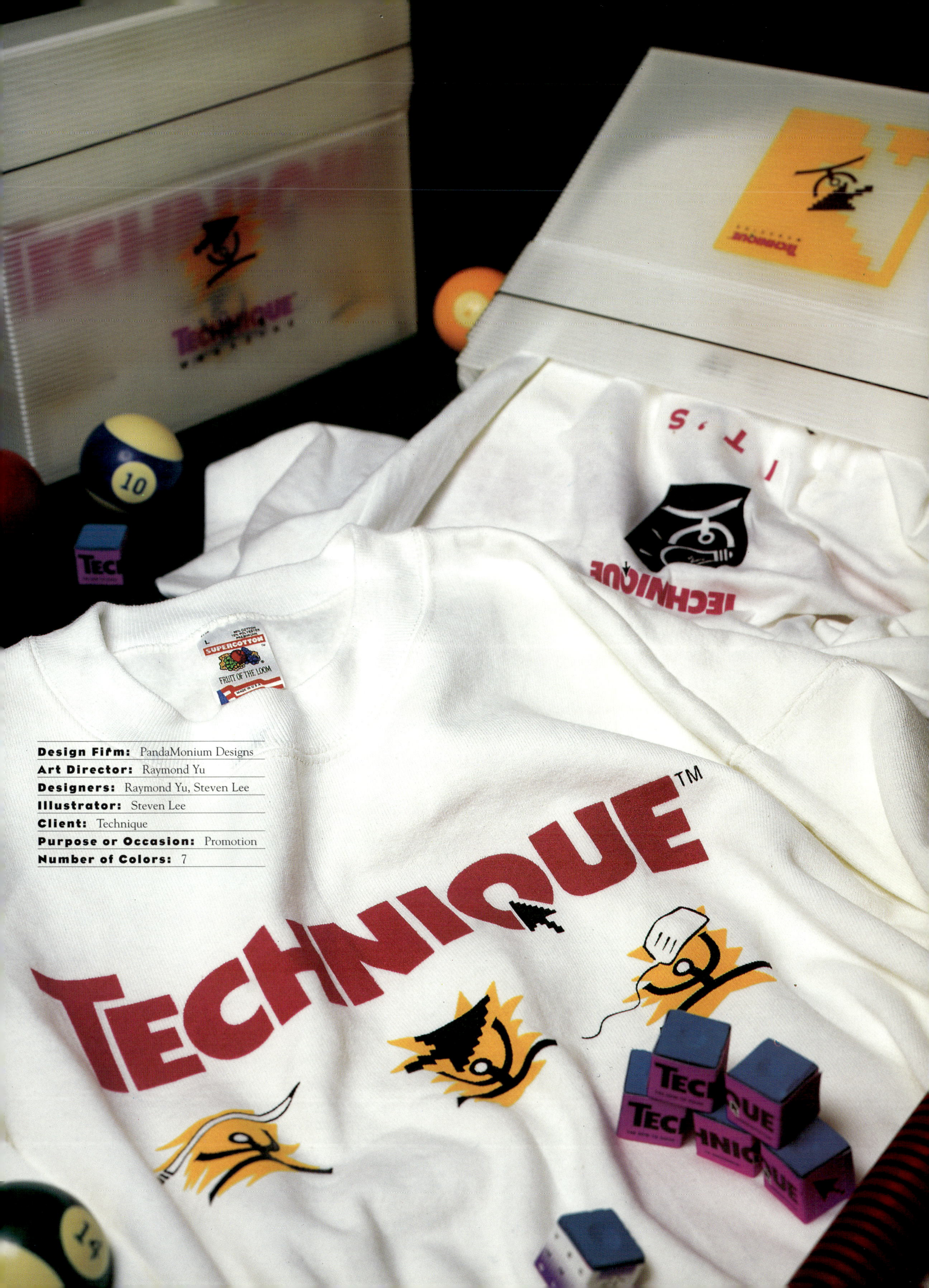

Design Firm: PandaMonium Designs
Art Director: Raymond Yu
Designers: Raymond Yu, Steven Lee
Illustrator: Steven Lee
Client: Technique
Purpose or Occasion: Promotion
Number of Colors: 7

▼

Design Firm: Garrabrandt Enterprises, Inc.
All Design: Bruce S. Garrabrandt
Purpose or Occasion: Retail
Number of Colors: 5
An original colored pencil drawing painted on a T-shirt depicts the artist's theory that ʊws are notoriously bad drivers.

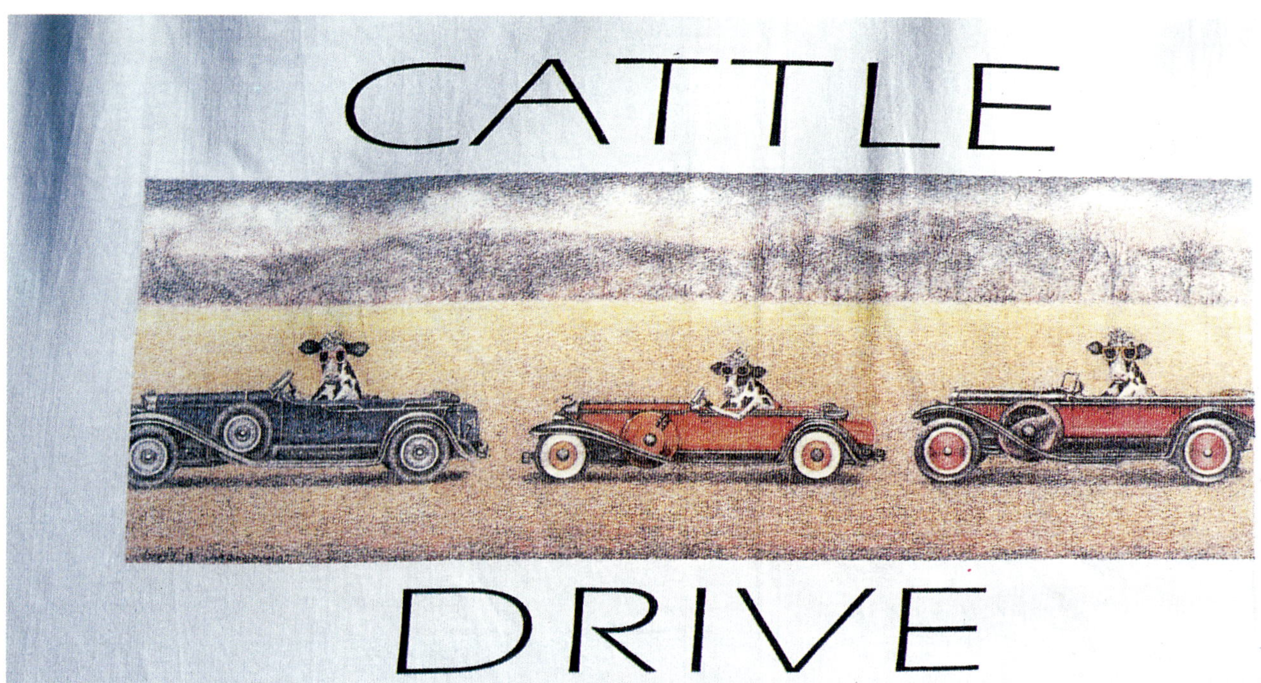

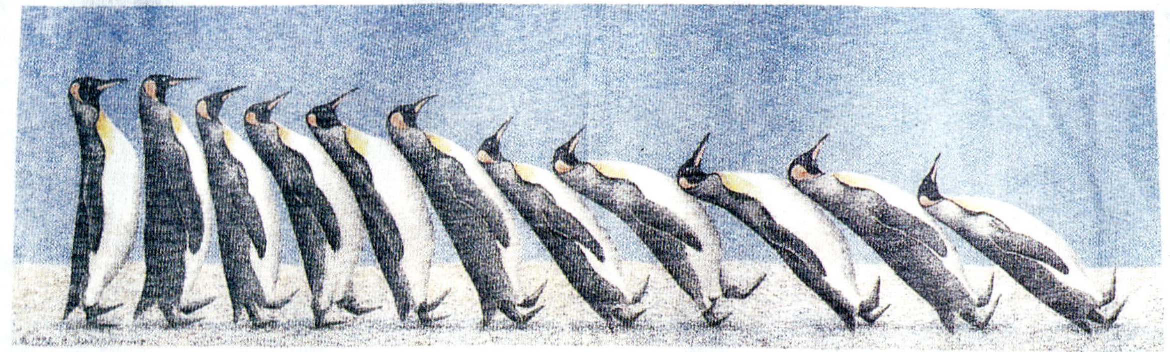

▲

Design Firm: Garrabrandt Enterprises, Inc.
All Design: Bruce S. Garrabrandt
Purpose or Occasion: Retail
Number of Colors: 5
This original colored pencil drawing painted on a T-shirt proposes that penguins are proof that God has a sense of humor.

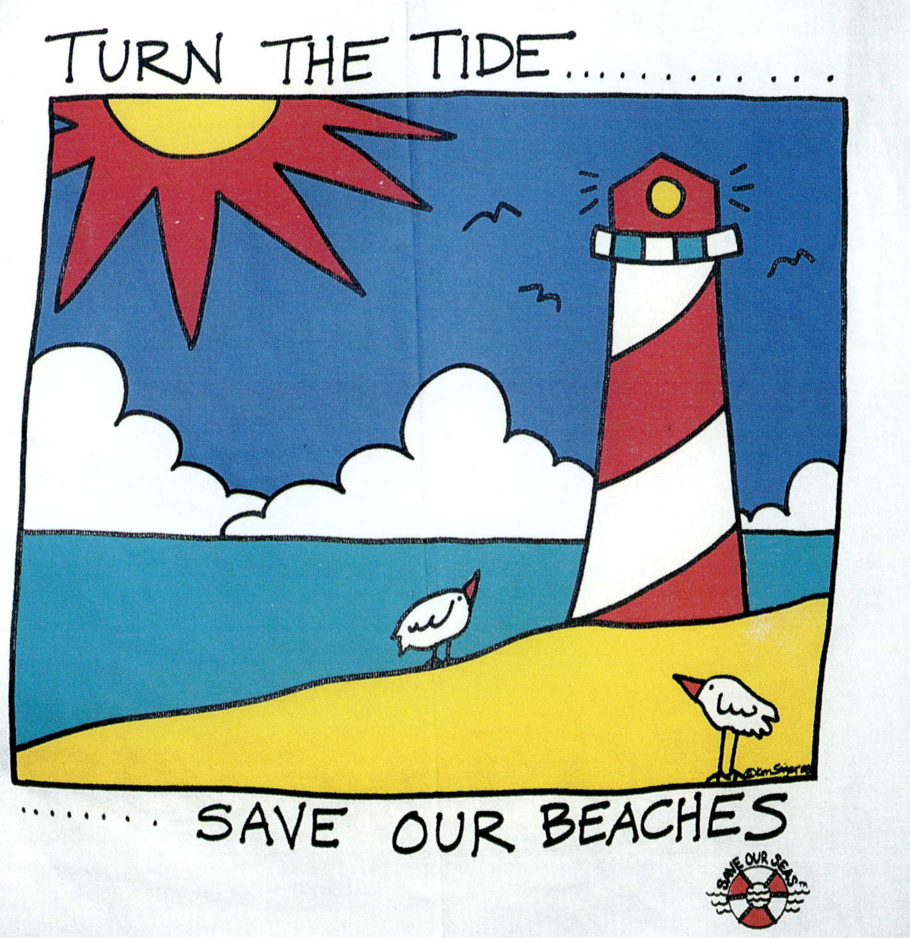

Design Firm: Ricardo Beron Castro
All Design: Ricardo Beron Castro
Purpose or Occasion: Retail
Number of Colors: 5

Design Firm: 90° Angle
All Design: Kim Sager
Client: Prelude Design
Purpose or Occasion: Summer retail
Number of Colors: 5
This T-shirt is designed to bring attention to pollution problems.

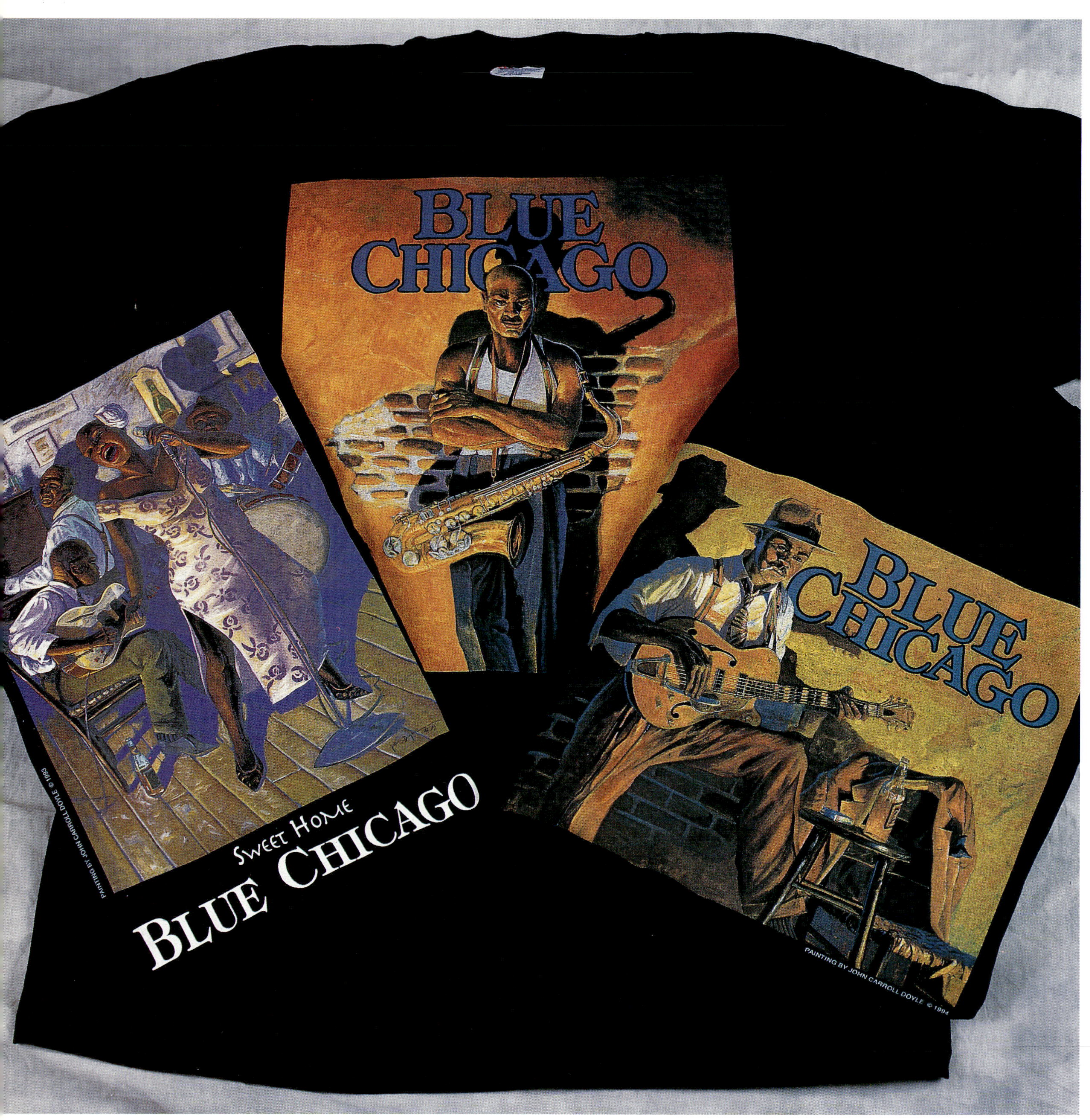

Design Firm: Blue Chicago
Art Director: Gino Battagia
Designer: Gino Battagia
Illustrator: John C. Doyle
Client: Blue Chicago
Purpose or Occasion: Retail
Number of Colors: 10

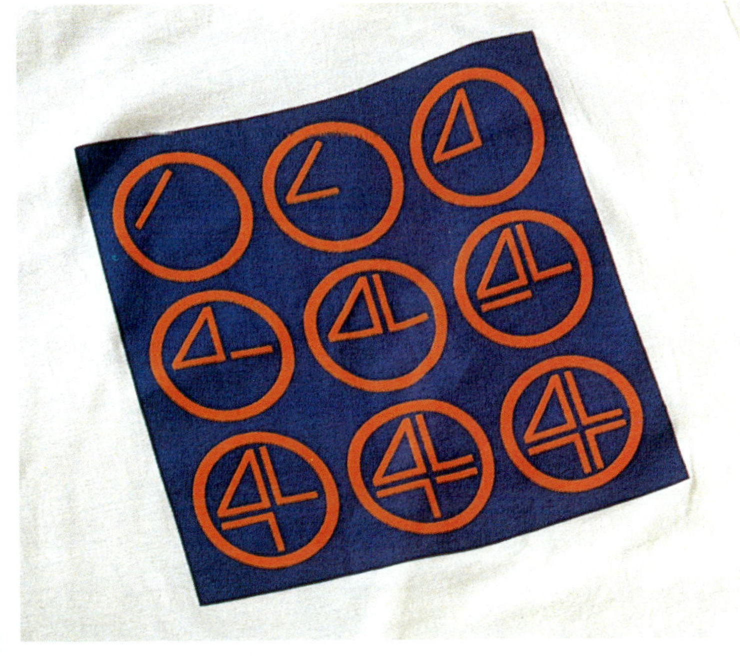

Design Firm:	Lee & Yin
Art Director:	Maria Lee
Designer:	Chris Yin
Illustrator:	Chris Yin
Client:	Semay, Inc.
Purpose or Occasion:	Promotion
Number of Colors:	2

Design Firm:	Russell Leong Design
All Design:	Russell K. Leong
Client:	Intempo Toys
Purpose or Occasion:	Celebrate the Arts
Number of Colors:	4

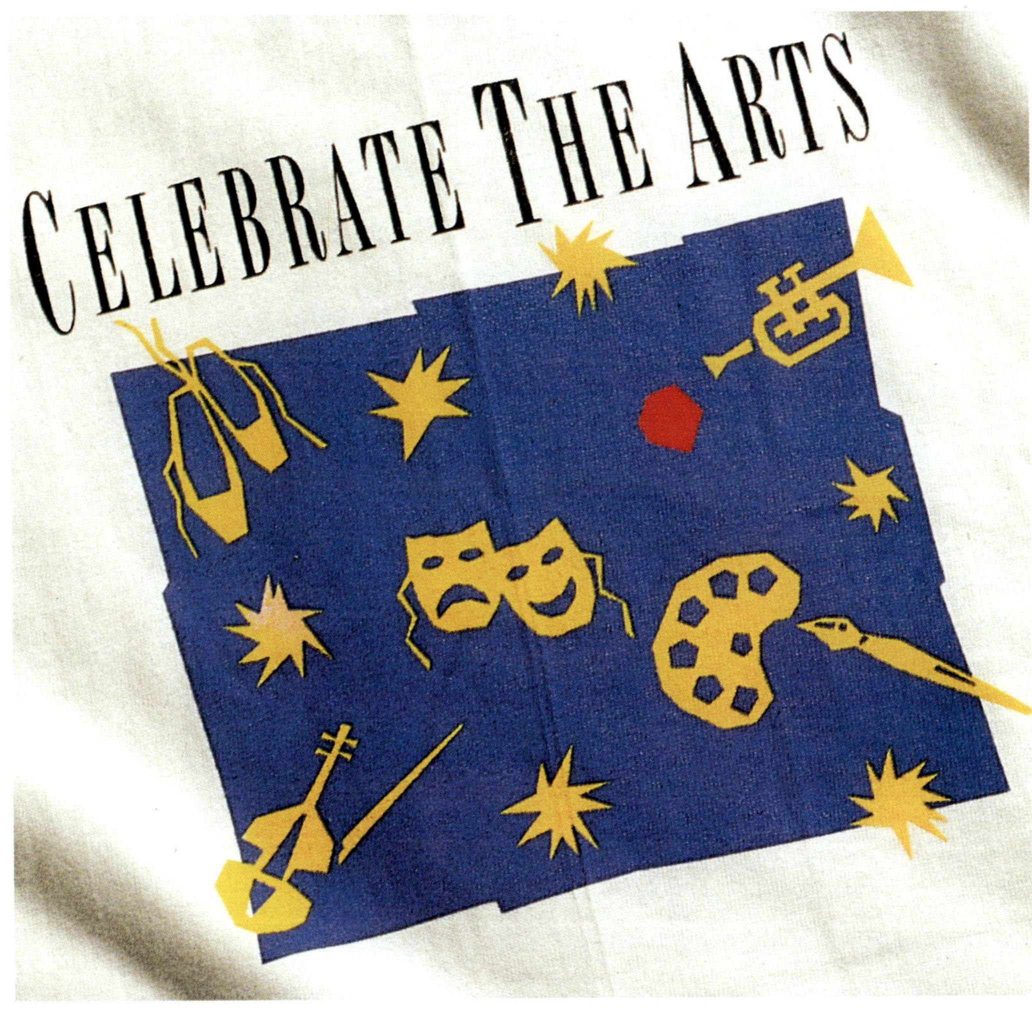

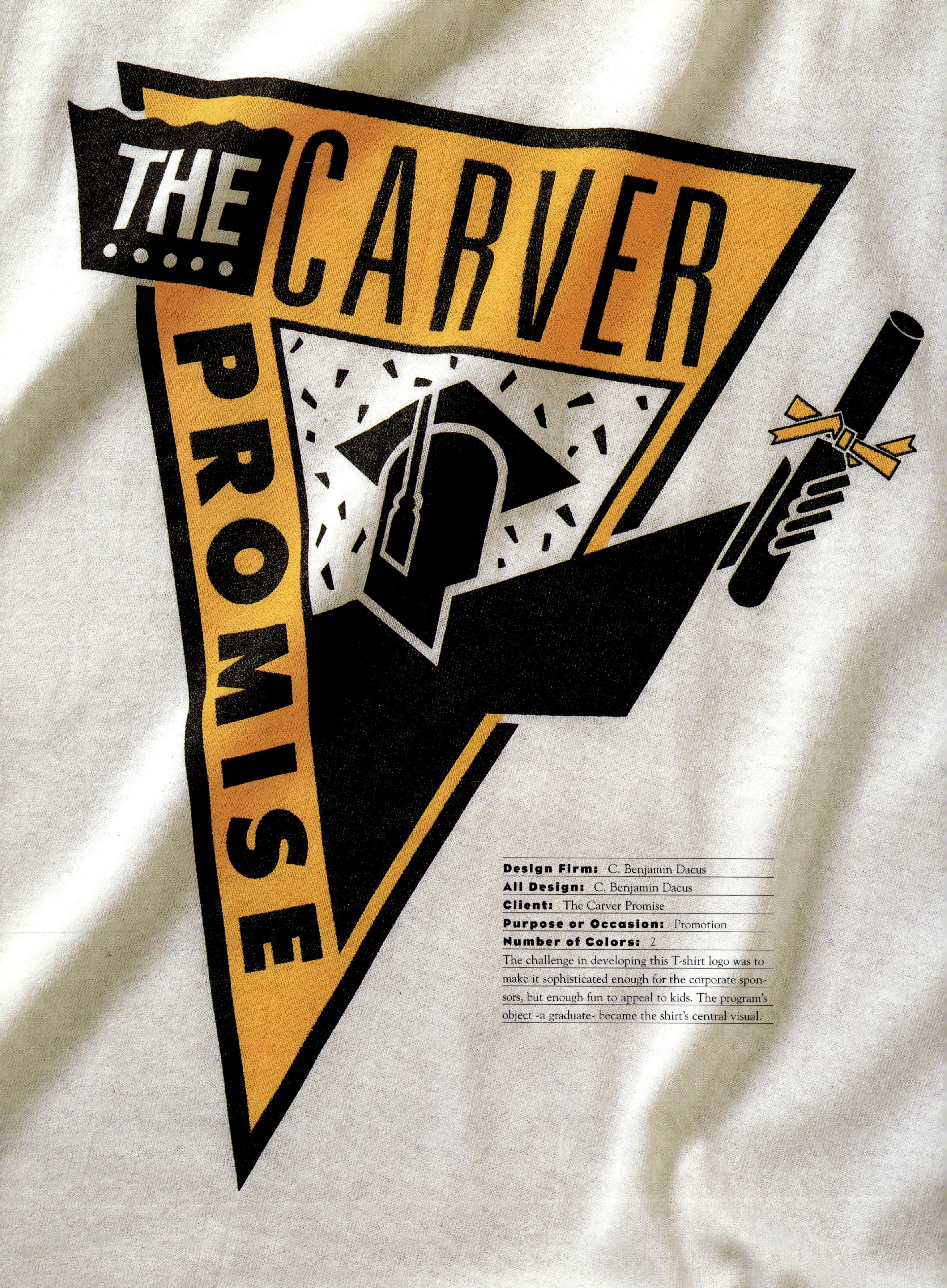

Design Firm: C. Benjamin Dacus
All Design: C. Benjamin Dacus
Client: The Carver Promise
Purpose or Occasion: Promotion
Number of Colors: 2

The challenge in developing this T-shirt logo was to make it sophisticated enough for the corporate sponsors, but enough fun to appeal to kids. The program's object -a graduate- became the shirt's central visual.

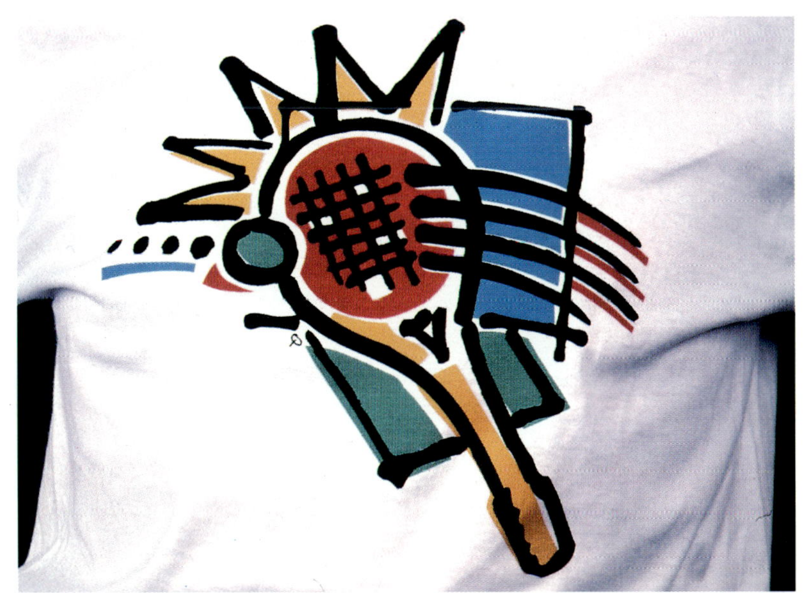

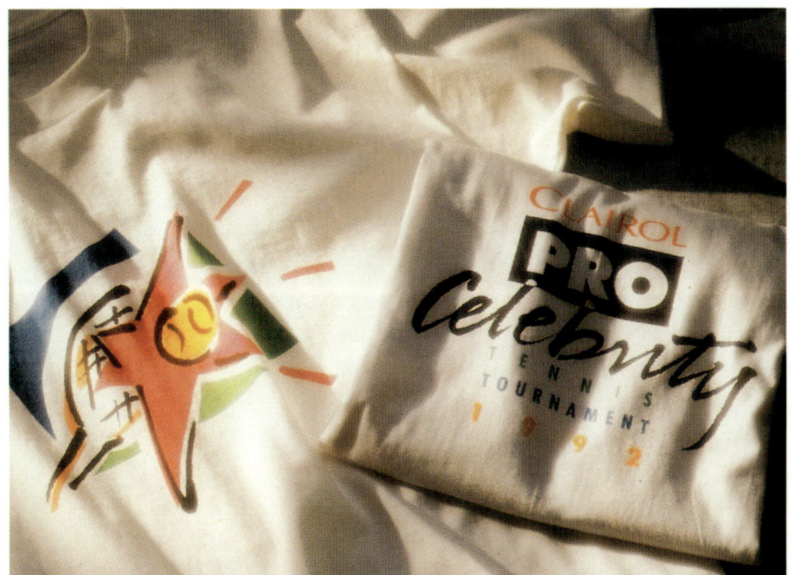

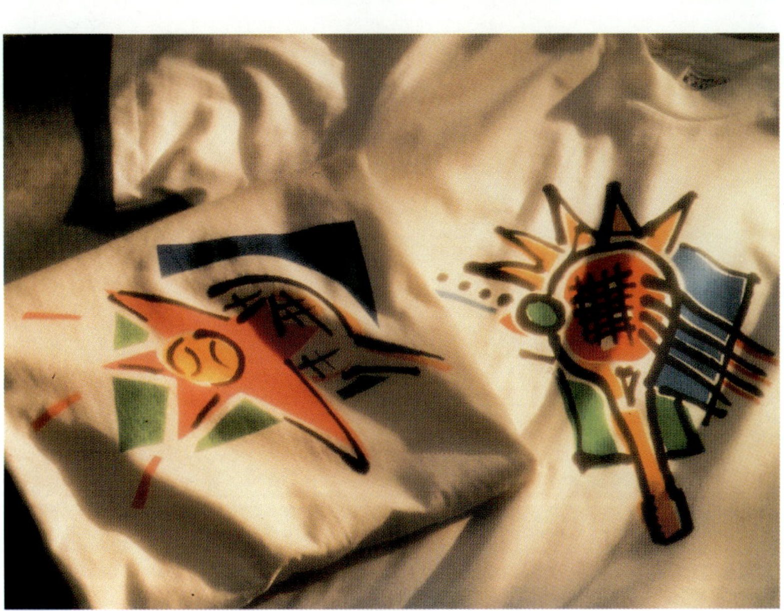

Design Firm:
Mike Quon Design Office
Art Director:
Mike Quon, Scott Fishoff
All Design: Mike Quon
Client: Clairol
Product/Purpose:
Tennis tournament promotional
T-shirt
Illustration done by hand, scanned
into the computer, and colored in
Adobe Illustrator 5.5. Design was
printed on products with a silk
screen process.

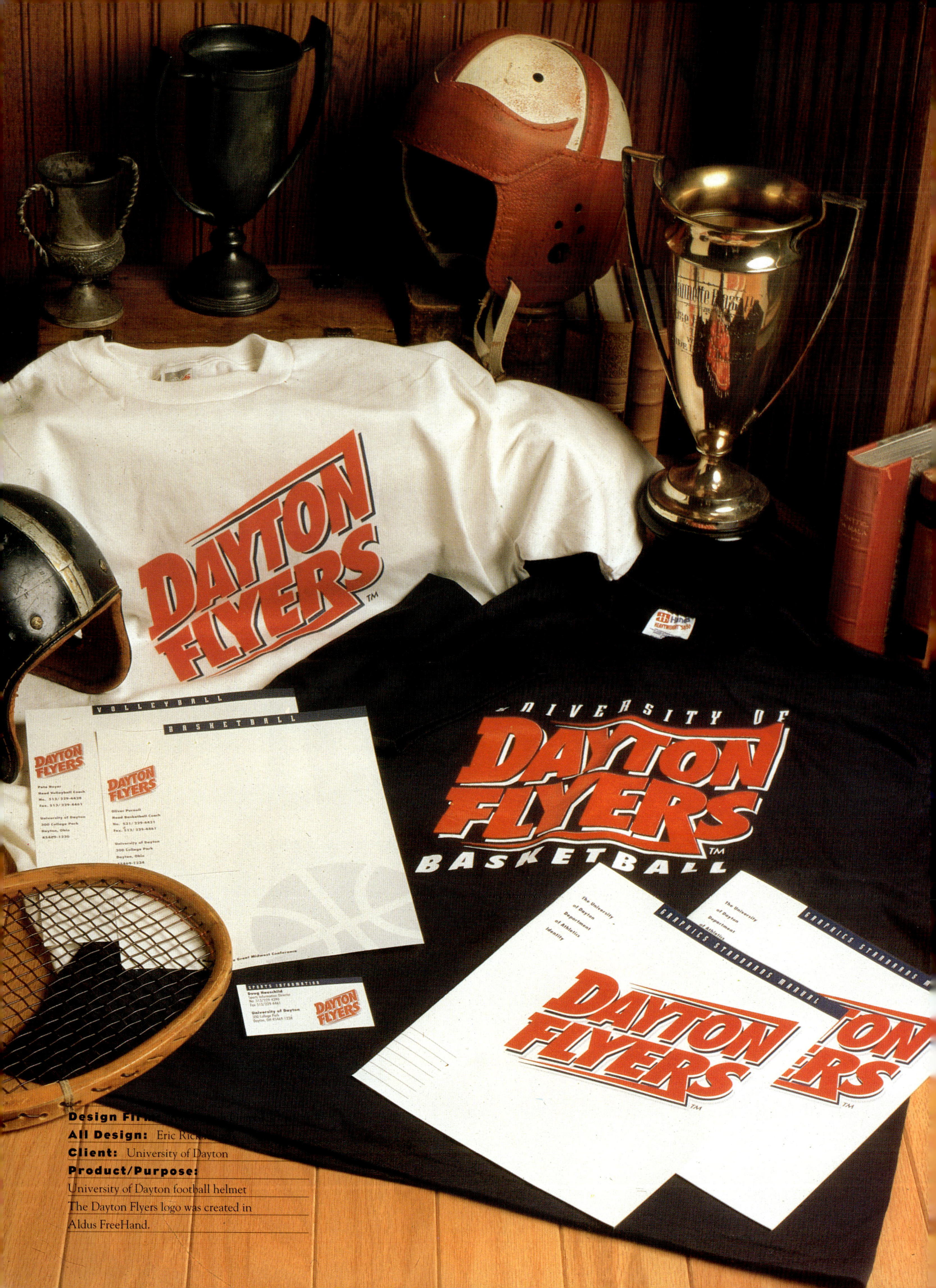

Design Firm:
All Design: Eric Rick
Client: University of Dayton
Product/Purpose:
University of Dayton football helmet
The Dayton Flyers logo was created in
Aldus FreeHand.

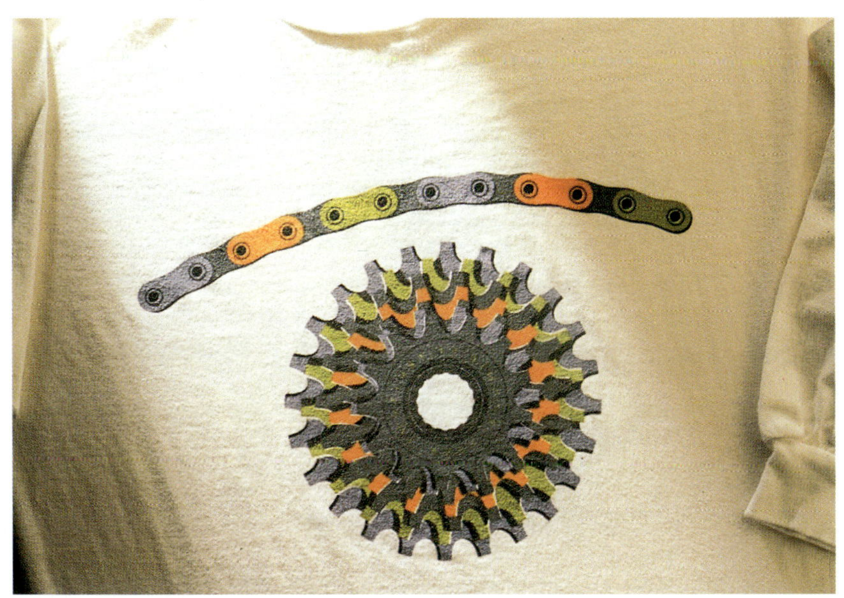

Design Firm:
Hornall Anderson Design Works
Art Director: Jack Anderson
Designer: Julie Keenan
Illustrator: Julie Keenan, John Anicker
Product/Purpose: T-Shirt

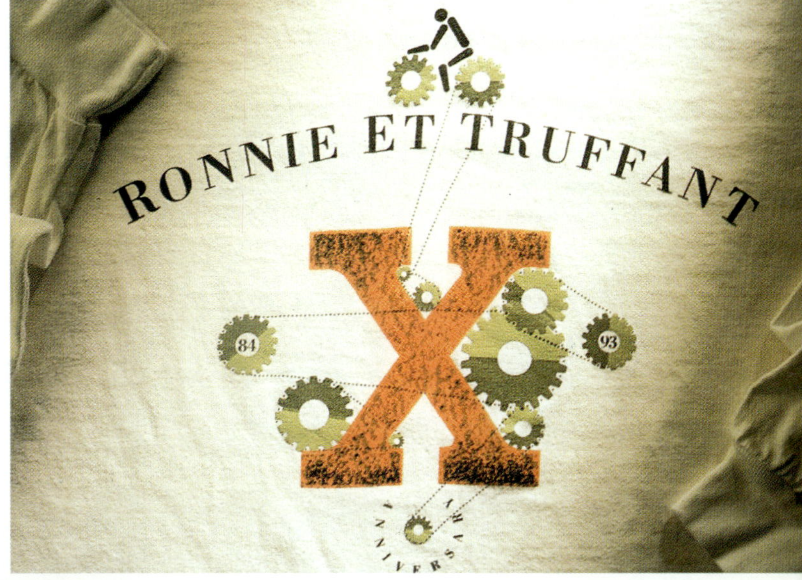

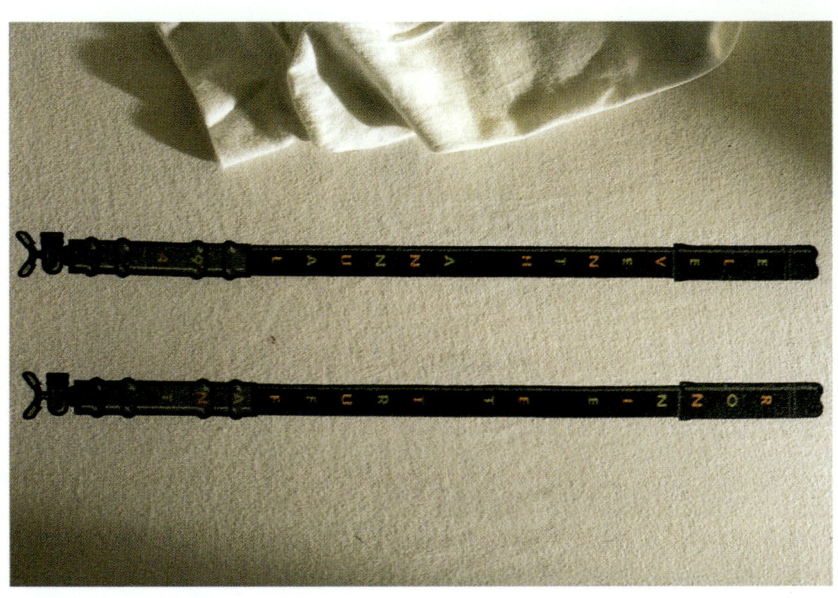

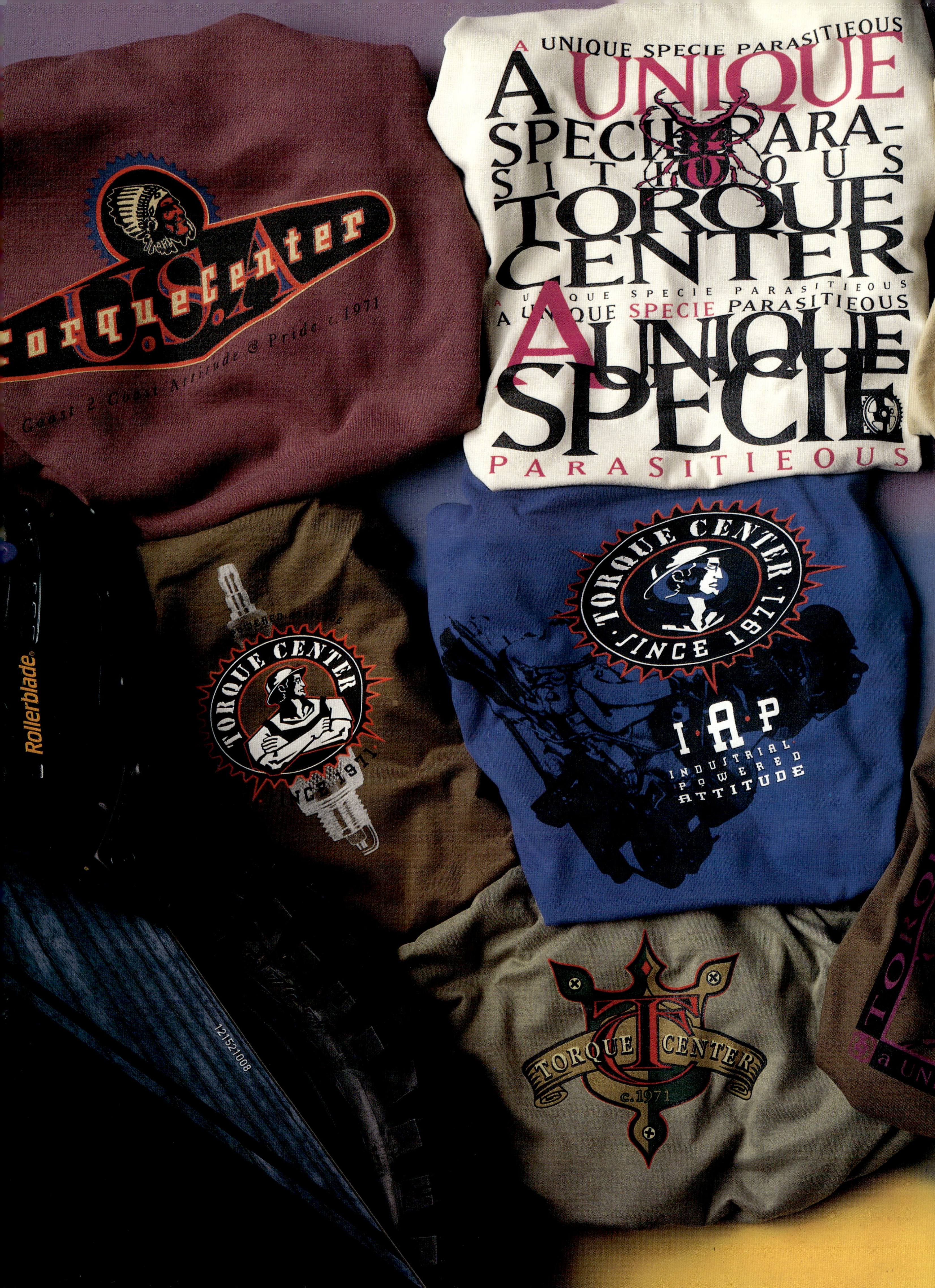
Torque Center U.S.A.
Coast 2 Coast Attitude & Pride c.1971
A UNIQUE SPECIE PARASITIEOUS
A UNIQUE
SPECIE PARA-
SITIEOUS
TORQUE
CENTER
A UNIQUE SPECIE PARASITIEOUS
A UNIQUE SPECIE PARASITIEOUS
A UNIQUE
SPECIE
PARASITIEOUS
TORQUE CENTER
SINCE 1971
I·A·P
INDUSTRIAL
POWERED
ATTITUDE
TORQUE CENTER
c.1971
Rollerblade
121521008

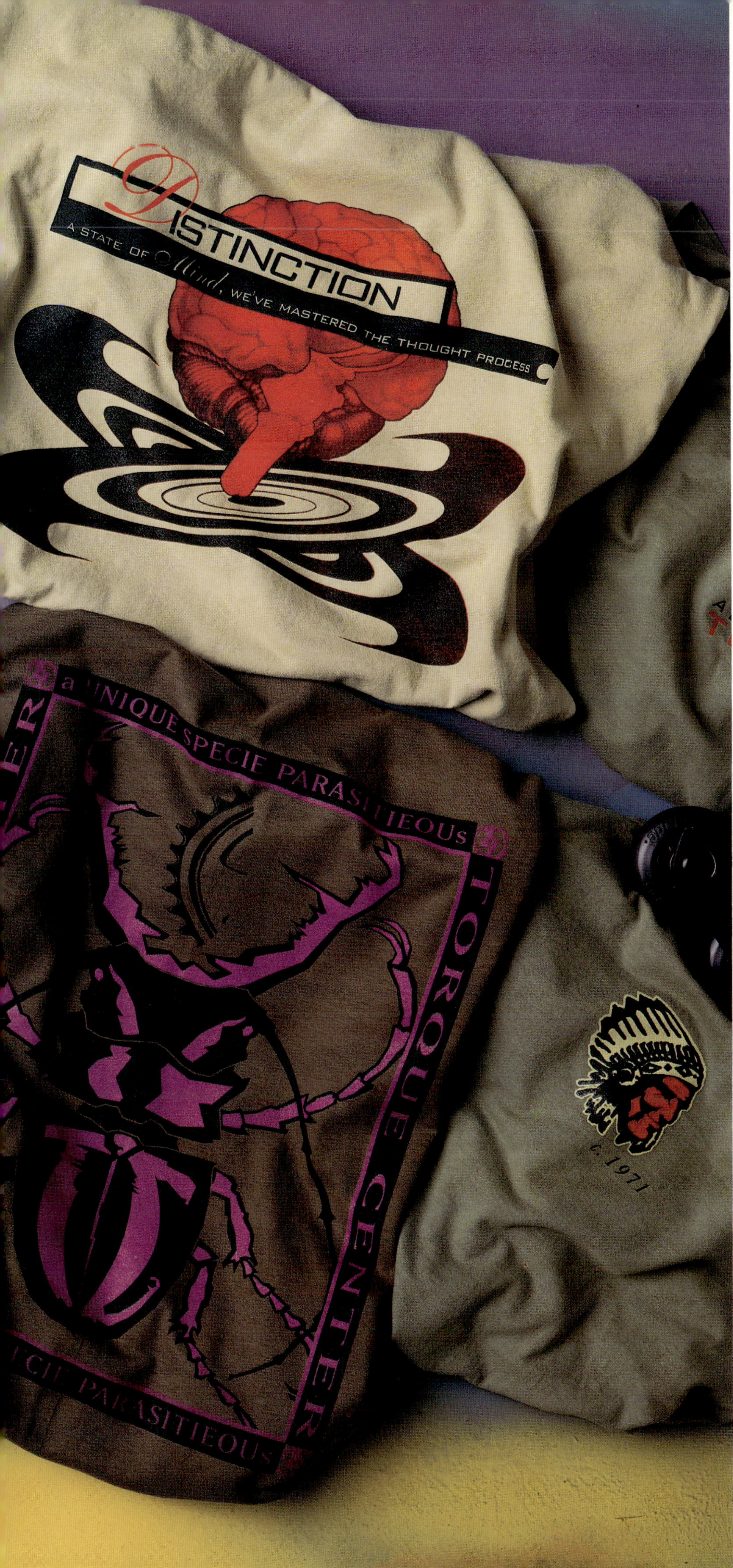

Design Firm:	Rocket Advertising Design
All Design:	Eric Timm
Client:	Torque Center USA
Product/Purpose:	Apparel

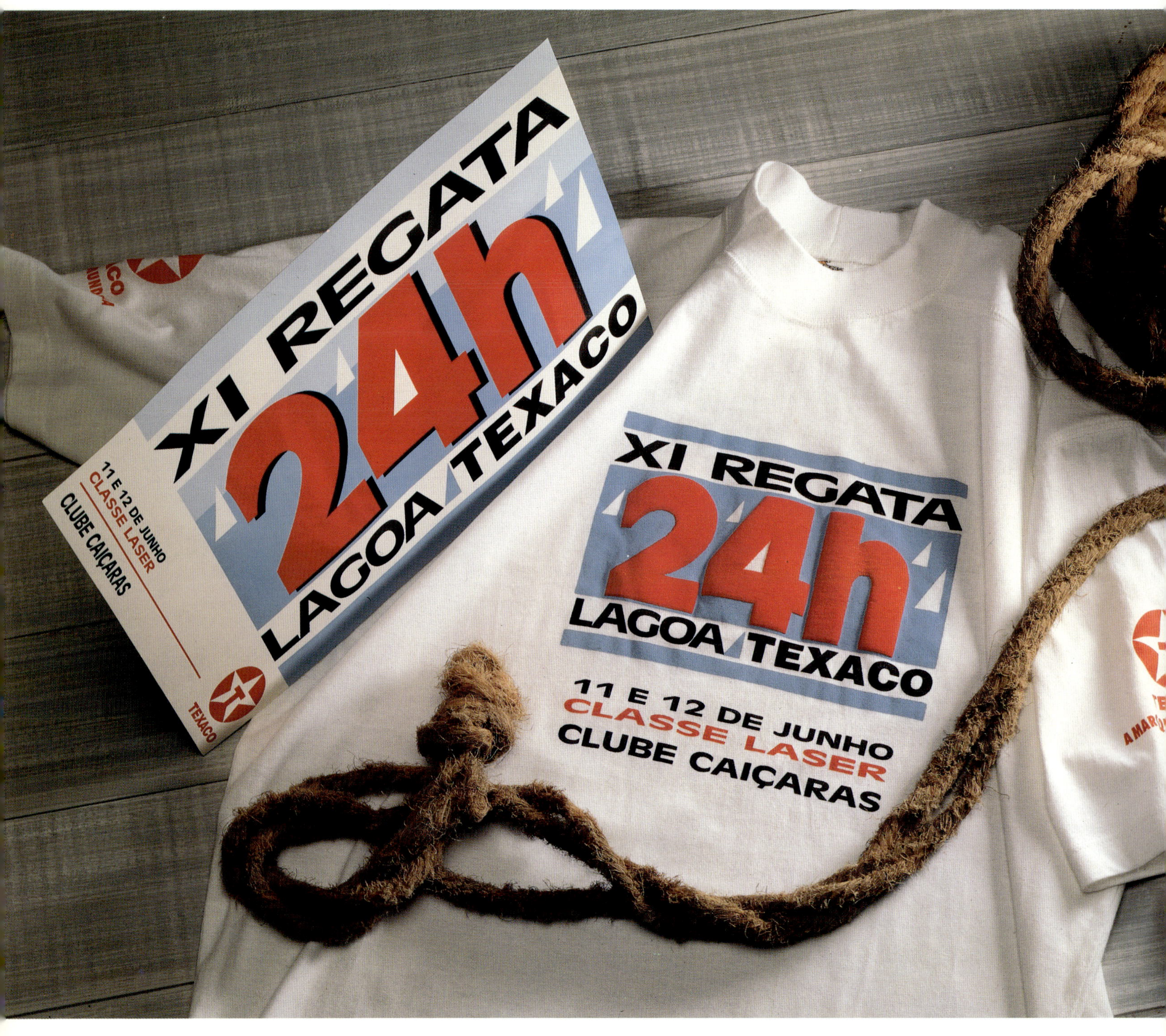

Design Firm: Animus Comunicação
Art Director: Rique Nitzsche
Designer: Felício Torres
Illustrator: Felício Torres
Client: Texaco Do Brazil S/A
Product/Purpose:
Sailboat race merchandising items
CorelDraw 4.0 software was used to create the
design, which was then silk-screened. The
material was created for a 24-hour sailboat
race on Lagoa Rodrigo de Freitas in Rio De
Janiero, sponsored by Texaco Do Brazil S/A.

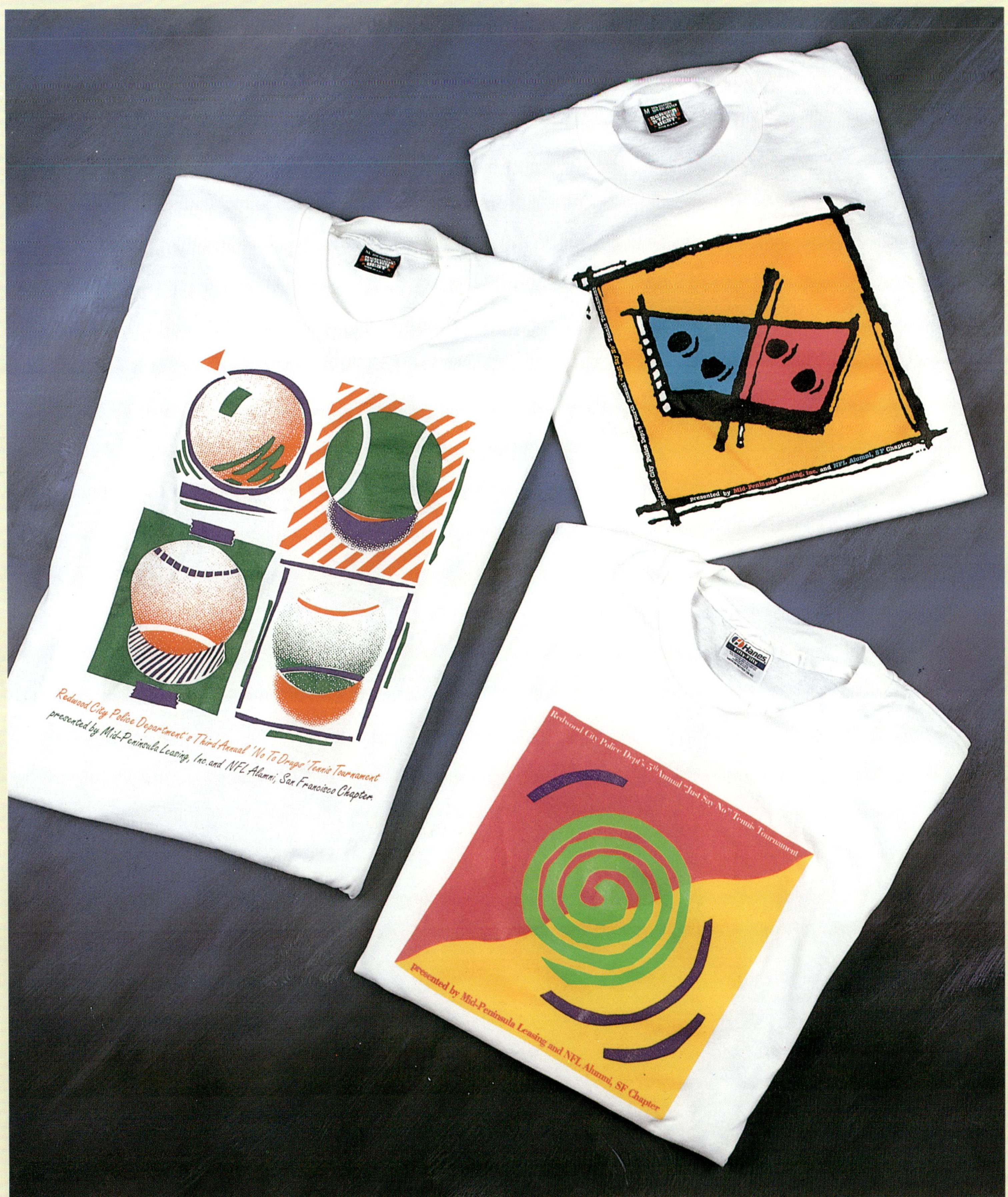

Design Firm: Dan Frazier Design
Art Director: Dan Frazier
Designer: Dan Frazier
Illustrator: Dan Frazier
Event: Just Say "No" Tennis Tournament
Description of Piece(s):

T-shirt series